"I gobbled up these essays. Michelle Tea is riotously, wickedly funny, with an uncommon knack for naming the more hideous and complex parts of being human. Her particular genius makes the hardest truths and sorrows an irresistible joy to read."

—MELISSA FEBOS, author of *Abandon Me*

ALSO BY MICHELLE TEA

*The Passionate Mistakes and Intricate
Corruption of One Girl in America*

Valencia

The Chelsea Whistle

The Beautiful

Rent Girl

Rose of No Man's Land

Coal to Diamonds

Mermaid in Chelsea Creek

How to Grow Up: A Memoir

Girl at the Bottom of the Sea

Black Wave

*Modern Tarot: Connecting with Your Higher Self
Through the Wisdom of the Cards*

*Pills, Thrills, Chills, and Heartache: Adventures
in the First Person* (coedited with Clint Catalyst)

*Without a Net: The Female Experience
of Growing Up Working Class*

*It's So You: 35 Women Write About
Personal Expression Through Fashion and Style*

*Sister Spit: Writing, Rants &
Reminiscence from the Road*

AGAINST MEMOIR

COMPLAINTS, CONFESSIONS & CRITICISMS

MICHELLE TEA

FEMINIST PRESS
AT THE CITY UNIVERSITY
OF NEW YORK
NEW YORK CITY

Published in 2018 by the Feminist Press
at the City University of New York
The Graduate Center
365 Fifth Avenue, Suite 5406
New York, NY 10016

feministpress.org

First Feminist Press edition 2018

This book was made possible thanks to a grant from New York State Council on the Arts with the support of Governor Andrew M. Cuomo and the New York State Legislature.

First printing May 2018

Cover and text design by Suki Boynton

Library of Congress Cataloging-in-Publication Data
Names: Tea, Michelle, author.
Title: Against memoir : complaints confessions + criticism / Michelle Tea.
Description: First Feminist Press edition. | New York, NY : The Feminist
Press at the City University of New York, 2018.
Identifiers: LCCN 2017049287 (print) | LCCN 2017054713 (ebook) | ISBN
9781936932191 (E-book) | ISBN 9781936932184 (trade pbk.)
Subjects: LCSH: Tea, Michelle. | Authors, American--20th century--Biography.
| Lesbian authors--United States--Biography.
Classification: LCC PS3570.E15 (ebook) | LCC PS3570.E15 Z46 2018 (print) |
DDC 813/.54 [B] --dc23
LC record available at https://lccn.loc.gov/2017049287

For Dashiell, for everything, forever.

CONTENTS

WRITING & LIFE

ART
&
MUSIC

ON VALERIE SOLANAS

It's hypothetical. No, hypothetical is the wrong word. It's just a literary device. There's no organization called SCUM . . . It's not even me . . . I mean, I thought of it as a state of mind. In other words, women who think a certain way are SCUM. Men who think a certain way are in the men's auxiliary of SCUM.

—*Valerie Solanas,* Village Voice, *1977*

I was thinking a certain way when I first came across the *SCUM Manifesto.* I had retreated into the desert of Tucson, Arizona, in the midst of what I now refer to as my Radical Lesbian Feminist Nervous Breakdown. I make light of it, but it was a dark and dangerous moment in my life. I only just learned that my stepfather had been spying on my sister and me through holes he'd stealthily carved in the walls of our home—the bathroom walls, the bedroom walls. Throughout my teenage years I'd lived with the suspicion that this was happening, a state of mind that had me tipping on a chasm of anxiety and denial I feared could end with me going totally insane.

The thing was, my stepfather was *cool.* The dad he replaced had *not* been cool, he'd been a moody alcoholic who'd fight with my mom till she cried. When he came home from work adulterously late and fucked up on booze or pills, we didn't know what we'd be getting. But this new dad was a *cheerful* alcoholic. He'd played drums in bands and had a pierced ear and a homemade tattoo on his finger. He was always nice to my mom and to the rest of us. He took delight in cooking extravagant family dinners—three-alarm chili washed down with pint glasses of lime rickeys, gutted limes scattered across the kitchen table filling the house with the sharply optimistic smell of summer. How could he be spying on us?

For years, I lived with the understanding that there was something wrong with me. Something dark and perverse. To see such a nice man, a man who finally loved me and my mom the way a father-person should, a man who went to the courts to adopt me, who bar-brawled with my birth father at the local Moose Club over his love for us, his family—to know all this and then think that he's *watching* me? Sexually, I guess? What a creep. What a creep I was.

What a fishbowl my teenage bedroom was. I loved to be inside it, reading books and magazines, listening to records, sneaking cigarettes out the window. Painting band names on the linoleum with nail polish, playing with makeup, lip-synching in the mirror. I'd be wrapping my blackened mouth around the voice of Siouxsie Sioux and would suddenly freeze—*What if he was watching me right now?* My room suddenly turned eerie, spooky, I was a girl in a horror movie. There was a terrible stillness, I felt like I'd been caught. To break the spell, I'd do something bizarre, or lewd—grab my crotch, squeeze my breasts, squish my face into the mirror, my tongue lolling out. I'd look like a madwoman. I wouldn't have done *that*, touched myself *there*, if I *really* thought my stepfather was watching. So I didn't *really* believe it, and so it wasn't happening.

Later, before sleep, I'd burrow under my neon-striped comforter to touch myself. I tried to make my face look really, really still in case he was watching. I didn't want him to know what I was doing. I tried to put my face under the covers, but felt smothered. I popped my face back out into the cool air. He couldn't be watching. He couldn't be watching because if he was then I couldn't masturbate and I *really* wanted to masturbate. What a creep. What a creep I was.

This was a long-term, low-grade crazy, a steady hum I could live with. When I found out it was all true—that there were holes in the bathroom door that fit perfectly with a hole in the jamb, creating a tunnel that aimed your eye right at the toilet, where I would sit and pee or poop or smoke a stolen cigarette or masturbate. That there were holes carved into my bedroom wall, holes a person could access by walking into the back hallway, nudging over a stray piece of paneling, peeling off the electrical tape (dry and curled from being pulled so many times), and looking through the hole in that wall right into the hole in my own. I looked through that hole myself and saw it all—my bed, my posters on the wall, my clothes strewn on the linoleum, the mirror I kneeled before, lip-synching. When it all came down I got a new, sharper crazy. I couldn't hide it like I'd hidden the schizoid feelings of being watched and being creepy. I was filled with an electric hurt, a frenzied rage. I was sick, sickened.

My mother rushed to take his side, to protect him. It shouldn't have been a surprise, we had spent the past three or four years fighting weekly, if not daily, about the way I looked, my white face makeup and dyed-black hair, my torn clothes. People would beat me up for looking the way

I did, men and boys. I got into fistfights or they just threw things at me from car windows, they just spit at me in the street, they just called me a freak and a slut as they sped by in their cars. That was how it went outside. Inside, it was a war with my mother, who thought I'd brought it on myself. I didn't have to look that way. And then I went queer and that was a problem. And then the insanity I'd been staving off, *I think my dad is watching me*, erupted into reality and I sort of lost my mind.

Having to leave my house, I moved in with my girlfriend, a prostitute. Needing more than the minimum wage I was making at a Greek deli, I became one too. Notice I didn't say I "got work as a prostitute," "found a job as a prostitute," "was hired to do prostitution." Prostitute is not a job, it's something a woman *becomes.* Me and my girlfriend would keep the phone numbers of the men we saw and crank call them after. We'd tell their wives. Make fun of what they'd wanted, make sure they understood we had not enjoyed it. Ask them to please stop calling prostitutes. I stole things from their homes, little things—a candle, a photograph, a toothbrush. I wanted them to feel unsafe, to become vulnerable. I felt so unsafe—every call I went on I gathered in my mind my exit plan, what I would do if something went wrong. Would I know if a man was planning to kill me? I feared my intuition was destroyed from all those years of doubting what I'd known and turning it back on myself. I scanned penises for anything that looked unhealthy, trying to keep myself safe in that way too. None of these men would ever know anything about a life like this, a girl's life.

It was clear to me now that men could do anything they wanted. A man could move into a family and secretly get off on the daughters for years, and when the truth came out, nothing really happened. He would have to deal with the shame of being caught, but he kept the house, the daughters had to flee. He kept the wife the daughters would never again be able to trust as a mother. He came into the family like an invasive parasite, killed it, and inhabited its dead body.

I ran away to Tucson. No reason, it was just where my girlfriend wanted to go and she was all I had now. She was my housing and she shared my rage. In Tucson, I was a prostitute and read books, feminist books. I read *The Courage to Heal*, the sexual-abuse survivor's bible. I read Mary Daly and learned about the murdered witches, about widowed Indian women forced to fling themselves on the funeral pyre. I was learning about the global history of male violence against women and how all social systems accommodated it, from the government to my family. I started seeing so much it hurt. I started thinking that if I pushed my brain a little harder I could see into a person's mind. It scared me too much to do it, but I knew that I could. It's easy to lose your grip on reality when your entire world is suddenly laid bare as a surreal conspiracy horror show.

I read Andrea Dworkin's *Mercy*, and the concept of killing men as a feminist action was introduced to me. A lighter read, *Lesbian Land*, enchanted me with the reality that I could live in a world without men, that other women before me had begun to create these places and I could perhaps run to them. I visited one outside of Tucson. The woman who gave us a tour was straight and brought her male lover in at night, which was okay with everyone. She slept on a mattress rigged up on a pallet and concrete blocks right there in the middle of the desert. I saw a naked woman giving another naked woman a massage on a massage table set up in the shade of a mesquite tree. I met the land's owner, a sixty-something-year-old woman high up in some scaffolding, building herself an octagonal house.

I thought I would move to that land someday. Meanwhile I lived in a rented adobe downtown, close enough to the university to stage "tit-ins" on the lawn there, inciting women to take off their shirts to protest the laws that made women keep their shirts on, sexualizing their breasts, allowing them the freedom to be topless only in places like strip clubs, where men could profit and get off on them. My house was close enough to downtown that I could walk to the liquor store for mezcal, pausing to rip the busty St. Pauli Girl posters off the wall and dump the Slurpee I bought on the way at 7-Eleven on the porn rack. Before I left home, I'd stopped by my mom's house and stuck Queer Nation stickers all over my stepdad's porn mags. Especially over the women who looked like me, with their punky hair and ripped fishnets.

My house was close enough to frat row, that line of adobes housing frat boys, that I'd been hollered at by them passing by and learned not to turn down that street. I thought about blowing one up. I was very serious. I thought it would be fairly easy and we could probably get away with it, and if we didn't I was actually prepared to go to prison for my part in this war. Because that's what it was, a war. Men got to do anything to women and women got to walk around scared and traumatized and angry. Men got to do anything, period. Men got to do everything. Something had to take them down. The only reason I didn't blow up the frat house is that, once she learned I was serious, my girlfriend refused to do it with me. I didn't want to do it alone. That would mean I was crazy. If I did it with others

I was part of a movement. Sisterhood Is Powerful. I could be sitting in jail right now. An act of violence and that one moment in my life—traumatized and desperate, unable to cope with what I'd experienced—could have become the rest of my life.

There's no way for me to talk about Valerie Solanas without talking about all this, the trauma I experienced as a female sensitive to misogyny in this world. Valerie suffered sexual abuse from her birth father, then didn't get along with her stepfather and was sent to live with a grandfather, and then her grandfather beat her up. She ran away at fifteen and was impregnated by a married man—I've no understanding of the nature of that relationship, but it's safe to presume it was at a minimum statutory rape. Valerie's kid was taken away from her and she lived on the streets from then on.

"The effect of fathers, in sum, has been to corrode the world with maleness. The male has a negative Midas touch—everything he touches turns to shit," Valerie writes in the *Manifesto*. From where I sat, on my porch in Tucson, Arizona, drinking a glass of mezcal and paging through it, she got everything right on.

From the start, I understood the *Manifesto* to be totally for real and totally not. It was an ideal, a utopic vision too out-there to ever be realized, and its dense, dark humor struck me as exactly correct. It was outlandish. I'd done die-ins with ACT UP and kiss-ins with Queer Nation, I'd waved coat hangers at Christians trying to block clinic doors, so I had a deep appreciation for the way Valerie used humor as a device to hit the truth like a piñata, again and again, throughout the tome. To see the *SCUM Manifesto*'s humor, to let it crack you up page after page, is not to read it as a joke. It's not. Valerie's use of humor is not unlike any novelist's use of fiction to hit at the truth. The truth of the world as seen through Valerie's eyes is patently absurd, a cosmic joke. The hilarity in the *Manifesto* is fighting fire with fire. Humor such as this is a muscle, a weapon. It was the truth, and the truth is so absurd it's painful.

Valerie did her work in the sixties, when it was legal for men to rape their wives, when girls who bled to death from back-alley abortions deserved it. In 1969, a year after Valerie's famed shooting of Andy Warhol, feminists, like Shulamith Firestone, who rose to speak at the New Left's counterinaugural to Nixon's inauguration in Washington, were greeted by audience cheers of "Take her off the stage and fuck her!" and "Fuck her down a dark alley!" And these were the progressive men.

I'm thinking that going totally fucking insane is a completely rational outcome for an intelligent woman in this society, and I think this idea only becomes more solid the farther back in history you go. The writer Roxanne Dunbar-Ortiz, a supporter of Valerie during her dark days, says,

> I look at someone like Dorothy Allison, who was a teenager when we started rabble-rousing, and how she testifies that it was women's liberation that saved her life. Here's a person that was routinely raped by her stepfather for her entire childhood, and from the time she was about eight years old, lived in the most horrible conditions. She was the very kind of person who could have ended up like Valerie Solanas had women's liberation not been there.

I live in a large community of would-be Valeries—queer people, formerly or presently female, many of whom have survived the violence of their heterosexual families. Writers with sharp intellects and incredible talent whose stories are routinely rejected from the still male-dominated literary worlds, both mainstream and underground, independent and corporate. Author Red Jordan Arobateau, in a review of the San Francisco production of Valerie's contested play, *Up Your Ass*, writes, "The reason I'd like to get on my knees to give Valerie a blowjob is because I identify with her and know she needed more joy. So much of my own life was hell, being a butch dike (now Transman) typing manuscripts in a hotel room, lonely, unpublished, not a dime to my name, not a friend in sight, and finding johns a lot easier to get then the love of a woman."

To be living so low yet so close to the largest artist of your time. To have caught his interest and been put in his films. All around you ideas are flying, becoming real. To be so near to power, to hand him your work, to know how he could help you, to hope that he would.

"Did you type this yourself? I'm so impressed. You should come type for us, Valerie." This is what Andy reportedly said as he received it. That he never returned the play, the sole copy in a time before computers and Kinko's (never mind producing it), is history. The existence of *Up Your Ass* in Warhol's archives at his namesake museum in Pittsburgh suggests the artist did indeed have the work the whole time. Why didn't he just give it back to her? She probably wasn't worth his time.

Genderqueer Valerie, a big dyke. On top of everything, she walked around in her newsie hat, her scruffy hair, baggy men's clothes, cursing and smoking. It's irresistible to think of Valerie in 2013, when templates exist for so many genders. Would she be a butch dyke? A genderqueer in-betweener, bashing the gender binary? Would she transition, after all that, to male? She certainly wouldn't be the first trans man with some rabid man hating in her past.

Brilliantly minded, bold enough to present herself honestly—she took the *Village Voice* to task in 1977 for writing that she wasn't a lesbian, "I consider the part where you said, 'She's not a lesbian' to be serious libel," during a time when writing about someone actually *being* a lesbian was grounds for a very profitable libel case. "The way it was worded gave the impression that I'm a heterosexual, you know?"—Valerie's understanding of gender was limited by her place and time. The *Manifesto*'s fatal flaw is also the very thing it requires to exist: strict adherence to a binary gender system and its attendant biological determinism, all in spite of Valerie routinely being in the company of trans women such as Jackie Curtis, Holly Woodlawn, and Candy Darling, who lived in the same SRO hotel. Perhaps it is the influence of these women that inspired Valerie to allow for the survival of "faggots who, by their shimmering, flaming example, encourage other men to de-man themselves and thereby make themselves relatively inoffensive." I read *faggots*, in this entry, to include queens and transgender women, as there was scant consciousness about trans lives and *faggot* existed as a catchall slur for anyone presenting as queer or genderqueer.

Again and again as one reads the *Manifesto*, one asks, *What the hell is this?* It is so, so funny that it's hard for me not to condemn anyone bothered by it as painfully lacking a sense of humor. Check this out: "SCUM will conduct Turd Sessions, at which every male present will give a speech beginning with the sentence: 'I am a turd, a lowly, abject turd,' then proceed to list all the ways in which he is. His reward for doing so will be the opportunity to fraternize after the session for a whole, solid hour with the SCUM

who will be present." Hilarious and begging for a perfor-
mance-art enactment, SCUM is also a very unfunny critique of American culture, then and now, delivered with
the fearlessness of someone so thoroughly rejected by the
system that she has nothing left to lose. Many of Valerie's
notions are excellent and plausible, such as, "SCUM will
forcibly relieve bus drivers, cab drivers, and subway-token
sellers of their jobs and run buses and cabs and dispense
free tokens to the public." (Clearly the vision of a broke
New Yorker.) The *Manifesto* is as much a call for a class
war as a gender apocalypse, with "eliminating the money
system" coming in behind overthrowing the government
and before destroying the male sex in the opening mission
statement. Indeed, the hysteria at a woman threatening to
kill men within a culture where men kill women regularly
has been so great as to even now distract from the class
rage inherent in the book. Is that why Valerie never found a
home among her feminist peers? Although Valerie worked
and wrote alongside the tremendous second wave feminist
revolution of the sixties and seventies, Alice Echols writes
in her history *Daring to Be Bad: Radical Feminism in America, 1967–1975*, "Radical feminists in New York Radical
Women knew next to nothing about Solanas until she shot
and nearly killed pop artist Andy Warhol in June 1968."
Valerie had been to college, but every academic line she
writes is followed by something completely potty-mouthed
or shocking. Her writing has less stylistically in common
with feminist writings of the time and more in common
with the absurdist manifestos of art movements, or with
punk rock, which hadn't even happened yet. According
to filmmaker Mary Harron, who went on to memorialize
Valerie with the wonderful film *I Shot Andy Warhol*, the

SCUM Manifesto is "deadpan, icily logical, elegantly comical: a strange juxtaposition, as if Oscar Wilde had decided to become a terrorist." Declares the Special Collections Library of Duke University, "Solanas is not generally considered to be a part of the Women's Liberation Movement." Who will claim her?

Though she does employ the adjective *groovy* in reference to the ideal SCUM woman, Valerie was certainly not a member of the moment's male-dominated anti-establishment proto-hippie counterculture. "Dropping out is not the answer; fucking-up is," she wrote, calling bullshit on what looked like a culture of narcissistic male navel-gazing, but also she's really not a joiner: "SCUM will not picket, demonstrate, march or strike to attempt to achieve its ends. . . . SCUM will always operate on a criminal as opposed to a civil disobedience basis." *SCUM* is a manifesto written by a criminal—a queer when queer was illegal, a prostitute, woman who looked like a man living by her wits, an artist.

In the end, it may be the criminals, the prostitutes, and the artists who claim her. In the 1990s when I was prostituting and writing my own manifesto in a café, I was approached by a queer woman who looked like a man and wanted to bum a piece of paper off me. I vaguely knew this person, her name was Fiver and she was part of a San Francisco dyke street gang called HAGS. She was sitting at a table with a few other HAGS, all butch dykes and all, for the record, hot. Valerie would not have looked out of place among them.

"We're making stencils," she explained. "About Valerie Solanas. You know, she wrote the *SCUM Manifesto*? We're going to tag them around the Tenderloin, she died in a hotel there." That's how I found out that Valerie had lived and died in my own city, from drug addiction and the poor health that comes with it, that comes with street prostitution, shitty housing, mental illness, and lack of community. I wanted to join the HAGS in their Valerie crafting, but I was scared of them. They were a real gang and pulled crimes and did harder drugs than I did then. They loved Valerie, and they lived and died like her. In a few years, Fiver and another dyke would be killed by a batch of heroin tainted with flesh-eating bacteria. Another, Johanna, her mental illness would flare up severely, keeping her homeless until she died of cancer, struggling with her addiction right until the end. Most surviving members of the gang got sober and/or transitioned to male, saving their lives.

This is who Valerie stood for, and these are the people who will not just remember her but cultivate a remembrance of her. April 2013 marked the twenty-fifth anniversary of her death, and a performance I had curated to explore her complicated legacy was canceled when an unexpected controversy grew large enough to make me concerned about the safety of such an event (plus sucked the fun out of it). Gay men accused me of giving voice to a person they likened to Hitler, Jim Jones, and Harvey Milk's assassin, Dan White (all men who I believe would have fallen first to Valerie's sword). Trans women, understandably traumatized by the trans hatred in so much second wave feminist rhetoric, sparked intense internet debate. As time wore on, response to the event grew to a stressful clamor. A trans female performer who previously had no conflict with performing (and from whom a trans critique of the *Manifesto* would have been hugely welcome) considered withdrawing and instead enacting her performance outside of the venue in support of a transfeminine protest. The surviving ex-HAG who had planned to talk about what Valerie meant for that gang of queer bandits was frightened of taking the stage and thought about canceling; another writer I'd invited to read from the *Manifesto* did cancel. The woman working the door feared for her safety and asked if I could find someone to work alongside her. Possibly Valerie—loyal to no demographic but her own constructed, imaginary SCUM woman—would have appreciated the hoopla, but I was frankly too exhausted and bummed out to carry on and pulled the plug on the event, which was meant to benefit the St. James Infirmary, a free clinic in Valerie's old neighborhood that serves sex workers and trans people and could have, had it existed earlier, prevented Valerie's death at age fifty-two. Inspired by the "dialogue" (a generous word for an emotionally heated Facebook fight), one writer held a response event, inviting everyone who had weighed in on the internet to show up and have a conversation about Valerie's legacy and the problematic legacy of second wave feminism. Nobody came.

Instead of hosting the event, I spent the evening of the twenty-fifth anniversary of Valerie's death at an artist's talk by the photographer Catherine Opie, a butch dyke whose early work documented the sexual and gender outlaws of San Francisco. In another time she could have been Valerie, a disadvantaged genderqueer artist panhandling at the edges of the art world. Today she's an art star, giving a lecture at the Museum of Modern Art. It seemed the perfect start to a night that ended outside the Bristol Hotel in the Tenderloin, on the street where Valerie made her money. We drew a chalk circle on the sidewalk and stood around it with candles, each reading a piece from the *Manifesto*. All around us the drug-addled swayed, curious, then darted away, perhaps mistaking us for Christians or something. A woman exited the bar behind us and fell onto the ground, too drunk to walk. We posted Valerie's picture on the hotel door, and someone handed out tiny women's symbol earrings. We all put them on, all of us SCUM members whatever our gender, because as she said to the *Village Voice* in 1977, back in New York after her stint in jail and follow-up incarcerations in mental hospitals, SCUM is a state of mind. And to those of us who "think a certain way," the *SCUM Manifesto* will always be a fascinating, confusing document: a product of a place and time that remains sadly relevant, a piece of political literature, pre–riot grrrl riot grrrl, pre-punk punk, prescient and perturbing and revelatory. For all of its enduring controversy, or perhaps because of it, this work will be with us for the ages, to be wrestled with and fought over and never quite figured out. Congratulations, Valerie, you made a work that sticks. May you rest in peace.

First published in AK Press's 2013 edition of *SCUM Manifesto* by Valerie Solanas.

ANDY WARHOL'S *SELF-PORTRAIT*

In my home there was no art and in my schooling there was no art, but Andy Warhol was so big that even my family knew about his Campbell's soup cans. Is that art? My family didn't think so. My family were the sort of people who believed art was a scam pulled by high-class grifters. *I could do that* was a frequent and appropriate response. My family was insulted that an artist, a rich person, would try to pass off shit from our pantry—dented cans of soup, a box of Brillo pads for scrubbing the Hamburger Helper from the frying pan—as art. It was like he was making a joke of them, and they weren't going to help him out by going along with it and calling it art. *That's not art.* But Andy was from Pittsburgh. He loved Coca-Cola because everyone drank it, the rich and the poor. Andy's American supermarket was a sort of kingdom of heaven, its narrow automatic glass doors a bit tough for the rich to slide through.

Andy said, "Art is what you can get away with," and Andy got away with it, laughing all the way to the bank, as my mother would say. He started painting money because it was his most favorite thing and, really, isn't money everyone's most favorite thing? I woke up thinking about money this morning, like a lover who haunted my sleep. Lying in my bed, I wondered where my money was. Would

my money run out on me? What could I do to make my
money stick around? Andy kept it real about the fake, sort
of humbly authentic within the land of total artifice he both
observed and cultivated. He wanted to be plastic, he wanted
everything to be identical; when not saying "um," he said
the most marvelous, honest things, like a crazy, bewigged
oracle, his tone total Quaalude. "An artist is someone who
produces things people don't need to have." Now that
sounds like my family talking. Chelsea, Massachusetts, is a
lot like Pittsburgh.

I act like I got Andy, but really I didn't know anything.
And there was art in my house. It came from these parties my mother hosted, Home Interior. Like a Tupper-
ware party. A bunch of women came over and my mother
baked brownies from a box and the Home Interior woman
brought all these little suitcases. When she opened them
up the inside was wallpapered and hung with a sconce
and a bronze butterfly. You purchased the whole set, and
your house could look like the inside of the suitcase. My
stepfather, a nurse, was an artist in the tradition of Bob
Ross, whose kit he purchased and whose televised direction he would come to follow. He also would trace Disney
characters in Magic Marker to woo my mother. This is all
very Warholian, is it not? What is the difference between
my stepfather tracing a drawing of Mickey and Minnie
outside Cinderella's castle, and Andy's soup can? Is it the
difference between Carnegie Mellon and the free nursing school at the VA hospital? Or is the difference that
Warhol may have loved the soup can, really loved it, but
he didn't believe in it. Or he believed in it but he could
see himself believing in it, which broke a certain spell. My
family totally believes in Disney. They went bankrupt

taking so many vacations to Disney World, going on Disney cruises where sculptures of Donald Duck, carved from butter, adorn the buffet table. They have no distance from Disney and no distance from their belief in Disney. In their world, Campbell's soup cans contain soup, and soup contains warmth and nutrition and maybe even love. My stepfather believes in the Eeyore he is tracing with his Sharpie, which totally ruins it.

Sometime during the eighties, in my parents' home in Massachusetts, I woke up to the world around me. I started to see the produced world—the world of soup cans and cartoon mice and Home Interior butterfly wall sconces—and got that taking this world seriously was the wrong way to live. But raging against it wouldn't work either, what a drag that would be, to fight the landscape all day every day. Like a maddening Zen parable, Andy's way was the proper way: gleefully embracing the produced world while seeing through its bullshit, and all the while observing yourself in the midst of it, for you are part of the produced world, and so there must be a way to embrace yourself as well while not taking yourself too seriously. This is Andy Warhol's middle path. Touring with the *Sex Workers' Art Show* I tried to convince the performers to all get matching dollar-sign tattoos. "It's the sex workers' *art* show not the sex workers' *money* show," snapped one hooker. If I believed in that hooker's dollar I wouldn't want it on my body either. But there is a dollar behind the dollar, winking at you like a Warhol soup can, and I watch myself loving it. I am so going to get that tattoo.

I couldn't believe it when I learned Andy Warhol died. I heard it from a radio DJ, in my bedroom, when I was sixteen. From his gallbladder! Gallbladder seemed like something poor, old people died from, wasn't he rich? His work sold for the most a work has ever sold for, and still he died the death of an immigrant from Pittsburgh. I was sad. Knowing little about his art, I loved Andy the *artist*: that you the person can be the art, because your hair is so big and your suits so stiffly wonderful and you say weird and witty things and hang out with colorful people and most of all, most importantly, you see the world in this very special way, and what you see is true. Fearing I had no talent but yearning deeply for the excitement of a creative person's life, I clung to Andy Warhol. Plus, I too had big hair, and an unpopular way of seeing the world, and so far, this had not been celebrated. How could I market my point of view and become so exceptional, so famous, like Andy Warhol? I wanted to run away from home, to New York City where everyone spectacular lived, away from teenagers who would laugh at your exquisite hairdo, away from crabby, Disney-loving parents who always said what was not art but never, ever said what was. I wanted to find Andy. When I wonder now about which of his pieces I like best, I imagine him lying in his coffin in a cashmere suit and sunglasses, his perfect wig glued to his head. "I never think that people die," Andy Warhol said, "they just go to department stores."

Speech given in 2010 at the San Francisco Museum of Modern Art.

TIMES SQUARE

Times Square was shot on location in Times Square in the year 1980, and in that way it will remain forever a historical document of that place and time. The director, Allan Moyle, whose later film *Pump Up the Volume* may be more familiar to you, cast the neighborhood itself as a main character, with its denizens—street folk, OG hip-hoppers, pillheads, hookers, primarily people of color—as the vital, living, breathing landscape. The flashing neon lights, sex cinemas, and liquor stores aren't sinister, they're the blinking, cheerful midway of the neighborhood's carnival. There is a moment in the movie when the teenage heroines are on the run from the cops and outwit them by dashing through a porn theater. One girl stops briefly to mock the sex on the screen, and all the perverts in the audience cheer, and cheer on our outlaw girls. *Times Square* illuminates Times Square as a sort of community of outsiders—sexual, chemical, economic—who have each other's backs. And, of course, there are other, darker sides to the story, but we know those movies—girls get exploited, raped, hooked on dope, murdered, etc. We don't know this one—the playfulness, freedom, and community that exists on the outskirts of sanctioned culture.

So, what is this movie about? It's about two young

girls looking to find safety in the world, and they access it, briefly, in one another and in this seedy, dismissed neighborhood. Pamela Pearl is privileged, the motherless daughter of a wealthy politician running for mayor of New York City on the platform of cleaning up Times Square. During puberty, some of us acquire an invisible set of antennae that allows us to begin to see the world as it really is. It is a sometimes-cataclysmic revelation, inspiring and clarifying and crazy making and terrible. Our Pammy is waking up to the hypocrisy of her father and, through him, the hypocrisy of the elite world she was born into. When she dares speak out, her father has her tossed into the loony bin, "for testing." Her roommate, whom she is instantly captivated by—to the point of writing poetry—is the flower-eating, cigarette-smoking Nicky Marotta, a butch street punk, the same age as Pammy but a million years older. Nicky seduces Pammy into sneaking out of the psych ward by lingering outside her door blaring "I Wanna Be Sedated" on her busted-up boom box. Together they steal an ambulance and make their way to an abandoned warehouse on the river where they begin to play house.

Times Square is a butch-femme queer-girl love story. There were actual lesbian make-out scenes shot, but they got cut per the order of a producer who had just made a bunch of cash off of *Saturday Night Fever* and didn't want any underage homosexual love mucking up his chances for another box-office smash. He also weaseled some disco into the incredible punk rock/new wave soundtrack, and drove the director off the project—which is why the movie ends in such a disappointing manner, but we'll get to that.

I want to dissect the butch-femme dynamic that exists between these young lovers, because it is very familiar to me. Pammy, who is more functional than Nicky not only due to her upbringing but also because of her gender normativity and lack of PTSD and mental illness, makes their ramshackle squat a home. She nurtures Nicky, listens to her song lyrics, and Nicky listens to Pammy's poetry. It's a freaking punk rock runaway Gertrude Stein and Alice B. Toklas. For Nicky, a nobody, someone who risks falling through the cracks daily, who arguably already has, safety comes from being seen, and fame offers the ultimate protection, artistic fame in particular. She wants to be a rock star—she is one by nature—but like so many cast-off queers of past generations, there is no path for her. Pammy, with her wider, class-based belief in possibility and her understanding of opportunity, nurtures Nicky and pushes her to actualize her dream. With the help of Johnny LaGuardia, a sleazy radio DJ with ulterior motives, Nicky's music creates a movement of young women who also feel both ignored and abused by the culture—Sleez Sisters. As Nicky's anthem goes—trigger warning—"Spic, nigger, faggot, bum / your daughter is one." A sort of sloppy stab at intersectionality; a proclamation of alliance, using the language of the street and the day. A young girl defiant, fumbling the commonality of struggle, the common roots of xenophobia. Knowing it intuitively, via emotion—the young girl's genius—and allying herself with the objects of racism, homophobia, homelessness. *Your daughter is one.* I had that painted on the back of my leather jacket in 1994, in a banner floating above a dumpster-diving dyke in a trash can, eating a piece of secondhand pizza. The name of the song is "Sleeze Sister Voodoo," and another chorus chants, "Stick. / Pins. / Into. / You." Sympathetic magic. All girls are witches.

Although Nicky and Pammy's relationship is one of

the most passionate and romantic I've ever seen on film, their affair is also horrifyingly dysfunctional. Is it because I first viewed this film at the tender age of twelve, my body teeming with hormones, desperate for romance, that their specific dynamic imprinted itself on me, setting me up for decades of valorizing and romanticizing, really worshipping, the gender misfits I nurtured and supported? Is this why it took me into my forties before I finally understood that that certain something, that spark, the *je ne sais quoi* that mysteriously drew me to those I would love, was actually a stormy gray cloud of mental illness? Anxiety, depression, sociopathy, narcissism, borderline personality disorder, Nicky seems to have them all, as have many of my lovers. Unlike those I love, I am traditionally female, gender conforming, and there is no underestimating the way that this has protected me in the world. Though Nicky and Pammy's passionate love checks all the boxes of fantasy love, it is in reality a codependent femme's nightmare—trapped in a relationship with a person so reliant on you, who drains your many resources, who you feel too guilty to leave because you understand all too well the honest way they have come by such damage. Never mind your own female damage acquired from this world, the way you've been molested or date-raped or casually humiliated your entire life. You get a job stripping and support your unemployable butch. Which is what Pammy does, though magically she gets to keep her clothes on. Which probably fucked me up more than anything else in the movie.

But the way Nicky and Pammy's affair unravels is also a butch's nightmare: the straight-passing, normatively gendered female begins an intrigue with a cisgender man, one who possesses all the power and cachet the butch never will, one who wears the same indicators of masculinity and is never punished for it but celebrated, and is ignorant as the dumbest beast of this privilege in the world. The butch sees they were wrong to trust the femme, that her gender privilege will be traded upon, the potential for straight privilege latent in bisexual women actualized while the butch remains cut off from society. Ugh.

I was oblivious to all of this when I first found *Times Square* at the age of twelve thanks to *Night Flight*, a deliberately strange, proudly countercultural punk and new wave TV show that aired on USA Network Friday and Saturday nights from midnight to 6:00 a.m. from 1981 to 1988. I vividly remember lying on my scratchy wool couch printed with autumn-colored flowers, an afghan knitted by some random neighbor draped over my body. The couch and the afghan and the throw pillow I laid my head upon, my hair and my skin and everything around me smelled of cigarette smoke, because I lived in a house of smokers. I gazed out at the television set over a coffee-table landscape of ashtrays, empty plastic cups sticky with soda, and crumpled bags of potato chips. *Saturday Night Live* had just ended, I flipped to MTV to see if anything interesting was on. Nope. I surfed over to *Night Flight*, which screened documentaries about the Clash, a show called *New Wave Theater* featuring Gary Numan and other sexy androids, concert footage of Lou Reed and Fear. Cult-classic films, black-and-white movies like *Reefer Madness* screened ironically alongside ridiculous horror films and newer, cooler productions like *Times Square*. I watched the film and I watched my dreams and fantasies and longings take shape and stream out of me, into the dark colors of the film and back through my unbelieving eyes. Two girls, alone together and free in late-seventies New York City. This was everything I ever wanted. To run away. Always I waited to see if my life would get bad or weird enough to call for it, but never did it. Yes, my mother's boyfriend woke up drunk and pissed in the corner of the bedroom, hallucinating a urinal. Yes, tough kids regularly menaced me in the streets. Tough girls slapped me, tough girls I was too frightened to slap back for fear I'd be slapped even harder, forever. Packs of boys on dirt bikes following me in the street, barking because I was ugly like a dog, but still it never felt like enough to break my mother's heart. Oh, how I longed for Times Square, where I could hook up with girls like Nicky who used her toughness for good, not to bully. I would find clothes on the streets and dress like them, in men's leather and gauzy scarfs. I would no longer suffer through school, so boring and irrelevant, so many nuns, and instead spend days doing what I wanted to do: writing, making music, maybe becoming an artist, maybe I already was an artist, but I would never learn this about myself stuck in smoky, sad, racist Chelsea, Massachusetts. I would have to go to a city to become an artist. I would have to go to a city to become myself.

A major theme of *Times Square* is gentrification. The enemy, Pammy's dad, sees the whole neighborhood as a scab needing to be ripped off in order to allow a healthier neighborhood to heal there, one with Trump towers and fifty-foot LED advertisements crawling with Disney characters. Pammy's stand for truth is a stand against gentrification and the idea that the people who go there are somehow disposable, throwaway people. We queers, artists, activists, intellectuals, misfits, know with the instinct of any migrating animal that we must go to the city to find ourselves, our lives, and our people. *Times Square* shows beautifully what is lost to us when we lose our cities, our scruffy, scuzzy, cheap, and accessible cities; our inspiring, cultured, miraculous, dangerous, spontaneous, surprising cities. A place that's not the suburbs, where everything is already known and experience is as prefabricated as the houses. In the city anything can happen and so everything happens, the kinds of things that happen when so many people from so many backgrounds come together in respect and mutual need. *Times Square* ends before gentrification wins, but we all know what has happened.

Queers have always needed the city. And now the city is a suburb. As Sarah Schulman writes in her brilliant book *The Gentrification of the Mind*, "To me, the literal experience of gentrification is a concrete replacement process. Physically it is an urban phenomena: the removal of communities of diverse classes, ethnicities, races, sexualities, languages, and points of view from the central neighborhoods of cities, and their replacement by more homogenized groups. With this comes the destruction of culture and relationship, and this destruction has profound consequences for the future lives of cities." I watched *Times Square* as a jaded adult, on my thirty-ninth birthday, when I rented out the lovely, dumpy Red Vic Movie House on San Francisco's Haight Street, a co-op theater collective you could join, seeing movies all the time for free in exchange for working the box office or snack bar—a snack bar that had shakers of nutritional yeast for your popcorn, a theater whose seats were couches and that once a year screened *Harold and Maude*, handing you a daisy as you exited the lobby, a theater that buckled under the city's now-famous gentrification, run out of town. I rented the theater for $300 and invited everyone I knew to come watch *Times Square* with me. I wondered, because how could you not, where Nicky and Pammy would run to today. Patti Smith suggests Detroit. "New York has closed itself off to the young and struggling," she has said. "New York has been taken away from you. Find a new city."

I want to return to Nicky and Pammy's relationship dynamics and the way I lived those dynamics in my own life. Coming of queer age in the 1990s, to love queers was to love damage. To love damage was a path to loving yourself. Perhaps this is changing—I believe it is changing, perhaps in some locations the transformation is complete. But in the nineties and in decades earlier and surely so very often today, queers do not come out of the minefield of homophobia without scars. We do not live through our families' rejection of us, our stunted life options, the violence we've faced, the ways in which we've violated ourselves for survival, our harmful coping mechanisms, our lifesaving delusions, the altered brain chemistry we have sustained as a result of this, the low income and survival states we've endured as a result of society's loathing, unharmed. Whatever of these wounds I didn't experience firsthand, my lovers did, and so I say that, for a time, it was not possible to have queer love that was not in some way damaged or defined by damage sustained, even as it desperately fought through that damage to access, hopefully, increasingly frequent moments of sustaining, lifesaving love, true love, and loyalty, and electric sex.

So in this way *Times Square* gave me a real notion of queer romance, the kind that happens between gender-variant and gender-normative females. In this way, it provided me with a Romeo and a Juliet, role models of passion and glory, so that I could know that the difficult relationships that broke and squeezed and fucked my heart were this kind of love, a Nicky-Pammy thing, like when Nicky makes them practice screaming one another's name in the industrial wasteland of their squatted home, NICKY! PAMMY! NICKY! PAMMY! until it is no longer bearable, because she knows that their world is dangerous and that they must have one another's back, they must know with their whole bodies that they are there for one another, that they will answer each other's screams.

But they don't. I hate the end of the movie, hate it worse than people hated *Thelma and Louise* with their fatalistic drive off the cliff. I wish Nicky and Pammy jumped into the East River together, their lungs filling with garbage. No, instead Pammy betrays Nicky, by doing worse than intriguing with Johnny LaGuardia—played by sexy Tim Curry, after all, so who could blame her—by returning to the safety and privilege of her father, her family, and all that it—I was going to say *symbolizes*, but it's not a symbol, it's the real thing. White, heterosexual, moneyed, patriarchal power. After all Pammy has experienced—goofily mugging dudes under Nicky's tutelage, go-go dancing at the Cleo Club, experiencing the nightly bonhomie on the streets of America's most vilified neighborhood, and most of all, loving Nicky Marotta—still, she goes back to her normal, privileged life. She watches Nicky's big show with the girls below, and it's the smile that gets me, this condescending little smile, like she's *proud* of Nicky. Why does this irk me so? I want her to be humbler in the face of Nicky. I don't want to see her proud. There is a sadness in the smile, but a light sadness, sweet, and you can see the hint of nostalgia that will grow, and see how she will come to look back on this moment with a type of gross wistfulness, sharing the stories with future lovers, men and women from her own class background: "Yeah I ran away once and lived with this street girl, she was really a genius but so troubled . . ." At the end of the movie Pammy returns to her life, which makes her a slummer in Nicky's reality. And at the end of the movie there is every reason to presume that Nicky goes to jail.

Oh no, did I just shit-talk my most favorite movie in the whole world? It is only because I love it so and have thought so much about it. *Times Square* is an inspiring document of New York City during possibly its last lively era, its last era of possibility. Nicky is a completely authentic late-seventies teenage butch, played to raspy, passionate perfection by Robin Johnson, a straight woman by the way, who last I knew made her living doing traffic reports for a midwestern radio station. In 2016 there is nary a rough-and-tumble scuffed-up butch who wears her working-class history on her sleeve on the television. There is Bullet from *The Killing*, a Seattle street kid with more emotional stability than Nicky but less physical safety. Can you think of any others? Not a soft butch who blurs into tomboy, something the culture has always made some room for. I mean an "Are you a boy or a girl?" genderqueer, a "You're in the wrong bathroom" type of butch, the type of butch who is *always* working class because you simply cannot get employed when you strike gender panic into the hearts of employers. I'm coming up empty. But we have Nicky. Always and forever, my first queer love.

From a 2016 talk at Butte College in Oroville, California.

ON ERIN MARKEY

Erin Markey lives partly on the internet, which is great because then we can all hang out with her, like in her bedroom. Imagine you're sixteen and you smoked pot for maybe the fourth time and your best friend is Erin Markey and you're super high and she puts on R. Kelly's "Pregnant," which if you don't know is a really creepy and absurd song where R. croons, "Gurl, I wanna get you pregnant," again and again in the melodramatic R & B way, and then Erin is lip-synching to it in black lipstick, and then she pulls her hair out of her ponytail and it's all wild and because she is a legitimate *actress* she can keep a straight face while she does this, make her wide eyes wider, sort of sexy and intense. You don't have to be stoned to enjoy this. It's on YouTube, part of her *Just a Little Something* series. Another episode has her gyrating insanely in a mirror in her pajamas to Jay-Z's "99 Problems." Watching these, I think: This is like harm reduction for Erin Markey, like her brain is so full-up with constant bananas hilarity and weirdness she has to create these quickie videos to let off a little steam. Like the tiny earthquakes that give us a tremble so the Big One doesn't totally destroy us—that's Erin Markey. What is it like inside her brain? Let's talk about it.

I've seen Erin's fast and bizarre internet videos and I've

seen excerpts from some of her one-woman shows. *Puppy Love: A Stripper's Tail* is a sex-work narrative, but in the form of a *musical.* The problem with most sex-work narratives is that they are *not* musicals, and I guess by that I mean they don't innovate a story that we've now heard a lot, a story that doesn't really change up all that much. But Erin brings into it her voices, her singular artistic voice of course but also her singing voice, which is *really good.* Like, she could go on *American Idol* or something. The phrase "She can really belt it out" is sort of disturbing if you think about it, so let's use it. It sounds like something deep inside Markey is being cranked when she sings. She practically unhinges her jaw to let the sound spill out—more on this later. In *Puppy Love* she erects a pole in the middle of the stage, she swirls her body around it, you can see how being a stripper could be fun, like being a fairy, and you would like—I would like—to go to a strip bar and watch girls who look like Erin spin themselves like ribbons round a maypole. Once, in Las Vegas, I took ecstasy and went to a strip club and sat at a platform the size of a dining-room table and watched girl after girl climb the pole with the skin of her thighs and slowly undulate back down. Mesmerized, I watched for hours, drinking water from a giant gallon bottle I managed to smuggle inside. Once a stripper held her arm out to me so that I might peel her long, leopard-spotted gloves from her arms. Her skin smelled like a candied flower and was poreless as a dolphin's. In *Puppy Love*, Erin is a stripper and she falls in love with another stripper. In *Puppy Love*, Erin is female, so she has this body you spin around poles for cash, but she's queer so she sees through it, too. It's like you're god, being queer in such a situation, you're the omniscient narrator. You're the girl who has the body and the lez who wants the other girl's body, and you see how the whole thing is so stupid and cheesy and prefabricated (because you're a feminist, duh), but you see how it works, too, how it's powerful, and it's even more powerful—the allure of it—when you have all that knowledge and *you* are the one you're lusting after, when you can let *all* of it in: the gross and the cute, the hardscrabble realness and the silliness, the artifice. Your intellectual and aesthetic brain is engaged, but so is that lazy part, the lizard brain that's like, I don't *want* to think so much I just want to space out and watch this girl spin around the pole so slow it's like she's turning over in bed, just waking up from a dream.

Erin Markey has a soft spot for preciousness. It's like she wants to cuddle it and destroy it, kill it, eat it, and then, for our pleasure, become it. Families are precious. Babies are precious. We are all precious, our bodies and our longings. It's sort of pathetic, we are, and also poignant, it depends on the angle. Erin Markey hits *all* the angles. Once I watched her walk onto a stage naked and somber. She began to talk about the history of feminist performance art. This is maybe a little dry for Erin but the thing is, you know she is very well versed in the history of performance art. No matter how bonkers her work gets, how off the rails she allows herself to fly, there is always a heavy intellect behind the wheel, and I want to know what she knows, so I'm listening close. She's talking about Carolee Schneemann's *Interior Scroll*, the classic seventies piece where the artist pulls a long scroll of paper from her vagina and reads from it. Performance theorist Jeanie Forte said it was as if Carolee's vag itself was speaking about sexism; it's an amazing piece. The writer Laurie Weeks calls the vagina "nature's little backpack." I mean, it's such a cool contraption, you can smuggle drugs, have a baby, have sex duh, hold on to a tampon, famously there are women who can shoot ping-pong balls from theirs (fun!) and open a bottle of beer, or, sadly, smoke a cigarette. So much activity from a site that the larger world—don't make me say *patriarchy*—sort of thinks of as a *void*, maybe a fanged void, but a void nonetheless.

Did Erin Markey do a cover of *Interior Scroll* that night? She pulled a spiral of paper from her vagina and proceeded to proclaim, in a loud, proud Munchkinland accent, the Munchkins' welcome to Dorothy from *The Wizard of Oz*. A Fluxus happening for our time, when everything is a mash-up, everything is known, all information is available, all references are everyone's references. The shock of it was extreme and extremely funny. Later she came out dressed as a Dickensian orphan and took up a collection by passing around a baby doll and making people place their money in its hollowed-out genitals.

This is queer work. Families and babies and all that are branding materials for the "heterosexuality" ad campaign, and even our wildly capitalist society doesn't want our business. Being dumped outside the common dream shows it to be absurd, a lie, tragicomedy. This is how we get drag queens and the gay male tradition of camp and kitsch. Erin Markey's work is what happens when that queer eye is not male, a queen, but female, a female witch-queen with that same sharp wit and deadpan eye for irony and hypocrisy. Coming through Erin—and I'm going to say that this is because she is female—the work is both bloodier and more compassionate. Life teaches us (the queer us) that all these things that are supposed to be so sacred actually aren't, and with that understanding it is hard to hold even our foremothers as sacred, hence Schneemann's *Interior Scroll* merges with *The Wizard of Oz*—a queer classic—and what you get are these sort of grotesque and snarfling Lollipop Kids coming out of your vagina.

Erin Markey has said in interviews that "our bodies are all we have." A female will always know how quickly she can be reduced to that, but there is an inverse power in this: our bodies *are* all we have, what excellent, beautiful monsters we can be! She has also said, "I've got a soft spot for people with big dreams." It shows. *The Dardy Family Home Movies by Stephen Sondheim by Erin Markey* is loosely based on her own childhood. There is a tenderness in Erin's portrayal of Dardy family matriarch Molly Dardy; her desires are simple enough to be cliché, derided—a family, a happy American family. And they are simple enough to be fair enough—a family, a happy American family, is that really so much to ask for? The sweetness of this plain desire and the darker realness of the compound psyches that build a family—the undercurrents of ignored and denied energies, of the banished negative—this forms the force field Erin steps into, jaw unhinged.

Since we only have our bodies, let's talk about Erin's. She is beautiful, and there is something very terrifying about the way she is beautiful. Her hair is *too* lustrous. Is it a wig? No, that's just her long, incredibly thick hair. Her face is angular; at certain angles her face falls off the edge of her cheekbone like a cliff. Her eyes are huge. She can either look alluring or like she's going to pull open her jaw with both hands and crack her head open to show you the monster beneath. And you'd be like, Yes! I had a feeling that was in there! It is fortunate for Erin, an artist interested in investigating and embodying both the innocence and horror of

being alive, that her visage can flitter so seamlessly between
classic beauty and something more primordial. I was lucky
enough to be in New York during the brief run of *Green
Eyes*, a lost Tennessee Williams play that was staged in a
very small hotel room in the Hudson, an actual hotel. Two
sets of folding chairs, fourteen total, were arranged against
a wall, facing the bed. We were *right there*. The play is about
a couple, just married, on a honeymoon in New Orleans.
The man is an alcoholic soldier, the woman is maybe cheat-
ing on him, maybe fucking with him—well, either way she
is fucking with him—and she is Erin, and in this role as a
cruel, sexed-up, manipulative new bride she is lightning.
The play is violent, the couple is physical, and you're in the
room with them, practically on top of them. Eventually,
Erin will lock eyes with you, and it's like a tiger bounded
into the room and you're in its stare now, will be in its jaws
in moments. I forgot to breathe when Erin looked at me;
she crackles. The play got stupendous reviews, critics called
her scary, observed that she seemingly had no boundaries.
That's part of the high-wire act of watching her: How far
will she take it? She seems capable of taking it awfully far.
And what does that mean for you, in the audience? Who is
the netless one, exactly?

But Erin does have boundaries. She got rid of a dead-dog
storyline embedded in *Puppy Love* because it was "too
weird." I love that. Artists knowing their limitations is
just as exciting as limitations being pushed—it creates this
boundaried chamber where the work can bounce around,
where it can grow to the size of its tank and be done. Once
I saw a performance artist in a Buddhist space enact a performance that involved him jerking off his elbow, lighting

up a cigarette and smoking it with a pair of cooking tongs
while making Holocaust jokes, then using a neti pot and
drinking the neti-pot water. Maybe he gargled with it and
sang; I don't remember, like everyone else in the audience,
I had left my body in horror. The beauty and value of Erin
as a performer is that there are limits on where she will go,
and if they are not visible to us, the audience, how much
more thrilling to remain on that edge in her safe, manipulative hands. It's *not* a free-for-all, there's a point here—art,
thought, hilarity, surprise, something poignant, something
vulnerable, a darkness, and then something ridiculous. Erin
Markey is a carnival ride, one operated by a recent ex-con
whose facial tattoo hasn't fully healed yet.

Erin performs a lot at a regular event at Joe's Pub in New
York City called Our Hit Parade, where performers do covers of that week's top ten songs. You can watch videos of it
on the internet and again get a feeling for what it's like to
be in proximity to Erin Markey in action. She sings Bruno
Mars's codependency ballad "Grenade" in a sports swim-
suit, her hair in a "whatever" ponytail, her neck rippling
with the storm of her voice running through it. The lyrics
are melodramatic, "I'd catch a grenade for ya / Throw my
hand on a blade for ya / I'd jump in front of a train for ya,"
but in Erin's muscular clutch they get real creepy real fast.
That she weaves in a bit of "Wind Beneath My Wings"
makes it even creepier, a stalker torch song. But the real
performance is in Erin's face, the sneer of her lips, the eyes
that grow huger . . . and huger . . . ! She bends over with the
effort of the singing but doesn't break a sweat. She cracks a
joke and leaves the stage. In another act, she sings Shakira's
"Hips Don't Lie" with a fake pregnancy and fake black eye.
She performs Wiz Khalifa's blackout anthem "No Sleep"

as that weirdo little boy orphan with a smudged-up face, suspenders, and all her hair tucked under a scrappy beanie. Her voice takes on a tinny, little-kid timbre: "The bitches, the hotel / the weed is all free!" Then she passes around the baby for people to put money in. "The drinks is on me!" A gang of other disturbing fake little boys with things hanging out of their pants suddenly descend upon the audience grabbing at their money.

Her body, herself! Erin Markey is a maniac who will only keep pushing herself in some sort of breakneck direction, trawling the culture for absurdity and pulling a lot of pathos, sarcasm, sincerity, darkness, and joy into her net along the way. Her range is bonkers, able to take on Tennessee Williams, her mother, her younger self, a Lollipop Kid. I think she is what they call in the biz a "triple threat." The night is young, and she lives in the city that doesn't sleep.

First published in 2011 on the San Francisco Film Society Blog.

ON *CHELSEA GIRLS*

I most remember reading *Chelsea Girls* in the dark, in bars around San Francisco in the nineties—beneath the staircase in the back room at Dalva, in a booth at Blondie's or the Uptown, at little round cocktail tables at the Paradise Lounge or Casanova. I was starting to write stories, but wanted only to write about my life and the girls I was falling in love with, lightly stalking, being dissed by. I wanted to write about being drunk in the daylight and also at night and about having sex in dark, damp rooms, hands smelling like cigarettes and pussy, the beds perpetually grimy, flat on the dusty floor.

Aside from all that, I also wanted to write about New England. I had only recently emigrated from the North Shore of Boston, a grimy, busted city called Chelsea, old-world and hostile. It was a strange, tough place, and I had become preoccupied with it since arriving in San Francisco, partly because people from Chelsea don't move to San Francisco. A person needs money to move, and people in Chelsea do not have any. I myself managed to bundle together a purse by working as a prostitute; had it not been for that wise decision I might still be in Chelsea. Often I meet people from Massachusetts, and they are always from Newton, which has become a bitter joke. Newton is the anti-Chelsea, a place where people have money and go to college and are afforded the privilege of moving around this country.

Of course it struck me that this collection of stories shared a name with my city. Eileen Myles was more than a simple writer; they were bound to their writing in a way that nearly transformed them into a shaman. "At the end / of the world / I am / my poem," so ends the final piece in their poetry collection *Not Me*, "A Poem in Two Homes"; *Chelsea Girls* contains similar proclamations. "I am a significant person," they write in "Light Warrior," an investigation of their name, "maybe a saint, or larger than life. I hear you judge a saint by her whole personality, not just her work."

Of course, the Chelsea in *Chelsea Girls* is not scabby old Chelsea, Massachusetts, but the far more glamorous Chelsea Hotel, where Sid famously killed Nancy and Andy Warhol filmed his *Girls*. It's also where Eileen Myles is fucked for the first time by a woman named Mary, a wholesome-looking lesbian waitress. Mary had "powerful, black Celtic eyelashes," and takes the author to the Chelsea, with its bad art and thin beds. "How do lesbians have sex?" is of course an eternal, offensive question, delivered by leering men and idiots of all genders. However, the secret is that everyone, perhaps especially lesbians, must learn to have sex, must teach themselves and one another, constantly charging up against the limitations of assumptions and convention and imagination, not to mention the body. In the story "Chelsea Girls," the author is delighted to learn they need not give up the vigorous rogering heterosexuality had occasionally provided: "So Mary started fucking me. One finger two fingers three fingers. And her face all that strong part coming out, dissolving her prettiness and pale freckles and Celtic distance into force."

For me, at twenty-three, girls were the mystery, and drinking (being drunk) and writing was the mystery. Eileen Myles was deep in it, solving it, reporting from the inside. These were sacred texts, for sale in the window of a bookstore like no big thing. Look at how they write about their affair with a famous junkie called Robin.

> I must fuck Robin. That was my job. She had the largest ... cunt, vagina I had ever stuck my finger in. It was big red and needy. I stuck two three fingers in and fucked her and fucked her. . . . . She moaned and growled with pleasure. Such a woman, I have never met such a horny animal nor have I ever so distinctly serviced a woman before. Do you want my fist inside you. Anything she shrieked, anything.

Eileen's work suggested this, but my own investigations were likewise proving that females were not particularly fragile. In fact, they had the stamina of professional wrestlers. Queer sex could feel like children's make-believe and a carnival haunted house and a lion devouring an antelope. It could feel like psychic surgery and a new-fangled workout routine and an aggressive cuddle-fest. We were, as Myles reported, "animals." Reading this made me feel happy and alive. I was of this people; I must find my own complicated junkie to have violent sex with. In 1994, nothing seemed like a better idea, save being able to write about it later.

> "I wonder what anybody thinks about using your own life, the actual words people say to you in the secrecy of love, or separation, or the oblivious moments when they've simply torn off an insult and flung it at you and you're the one who remembers every little word, at least the ones

I use and I fling it back in their faces, if not there, then
here, sooner or later and they say, 'Oh, I can't believe I said
that.'"

That's from the beginning of the end of a story called "Jeal-
ousy." It's a big question. Did Eileen feel liberated to spread
their whole personality out onto the page like this? Was it
okay? Could I do it too? These were my questions as I lux-
uriously smoked cigarette after cigarette *inside* various bars,
a pint of amber beer before me, slopping some onto the
pages as I went—my pages and theirs because now I always
brought *Chelsea Girls* with me when I wrote. I would pick
a story and read it before starting into my own notebook.
It was like a prayer before beginning: Dear subconscious
spooky hidden writing place, please hear the glory of this
story, "Bread and Water," one of my favorites ever. A broke
lesbian who has her period and cannot even afford tampons
is sort of bleeding around her East Village apartment hoping for a grant that will never come, tallying the petty but
significant amounts she owes the bakery and her neighbor,
not getting a piddly ten-dollar deposit back from the television repairman. Dear everything that understands how
much ten dollars really is, let this truth and the deceptively
simple, plainspoken way in which it is delivered, a voice just
so cool, please let it trigger in me my own whatever it is, my
own voice, my own cool, let like recognize like and release
something, okay? Gulp, gulp, smoke, begin.

Beyond the seductive enchantment of the voice—blunt,
almost arrogant with authority, tangential, intensely con-
versational, personal, *real*—the deeper zing of *Chelsea Girls*
was the stories about growing up in Arlington, Massachusetts, a city not at all far from Chelsea, and the class bracket

such a place sets you in. *Chelsea Girls* is a significant lesbian book but it is also a significant *working-class* text. Check out this summer job, from "Bath, Maine," "At work we dipped these small—or sometimes fairly large—wooden frames into vats of stain. Their destination was the cheap carnivals, and beach towns of America. Those mirrors that say Grateful Dead, or NY Yankees." Over and over the work reveals itself to be a history of what it meant to be working class in America before globalization, before technology transformed the workspace. How an illicitly sourced diet pill turned the monotony of xeroxing into a light show. The clamor backstage at Filene's Basement (RIP), the infamous Boston designer discount market in the belly of the defunct Filene's department store downtown. There was an underground entrance accessible from the subway, and women would line up outside the glass doors, ready to stampede their way in. My sister worked at Filene's Basement, and, coincidentally, my alcoholic father worked at the post office, just as Eileen's alcoholic father had. This was my occupational landscape, and to find it in this document of serious lesbian cool flipped me out. Eileen worked as a cab driver, a waitress, behind the register slinging tobacco at the Harvard Coop. They worked as a chambermaid at a Holiday Inn, where they were shocked to encounter a disgraced family friend, a woman doomed to die an ugly, alcoholic death in the not too distant future.

Chelsea Girls revisits the death of Myles's own alcoholic father. In "The Kid," a chillingly sad piece, the child Eileen is instructed to "watch" their father and they watch him die, savoring the terrible moment and the proximity to death, that mystery, and the strange bond it strings between them forever. "I would be a beatnik," they declare at the end of the story, as they recount the ways her father's death has altered the family, attempting to control how it would alter them, "I would make everyone so sad and be so cool." Sadness and cool are the twin pillars of Myles's voice, mixed with the detached, dark humor born of the two.

There is also sexual violence, and the casualness of the reportage is deliberate. This is the female day-to-day, is it not? Myles falls in love with an office coworker, who turns out to be a girl famously gang raped at a New England dance in the sixties. "Nothing should take that long she said." The author's own similar assault, at a summer house on the Cape, is detailed in unsentimental, spare language. The effect is wrenching, infuriating. In the morning, sick, hurt, and hungover they walk to the beach and write their name in the sand, EILEEN MYLES, wondering, "I had been raped, right?" That the culture of acceptance and denial is strong enough to blot out the unequivocal horror is a horror of its own.

"Fear of not being understood is the greatest fear I thought lying on the bathroom floor at 11 P.M. worse than not pleasing people, worse than anything else I can think of. Worse than being cold or alone. Worse than getting old." So begins "Robert Mapplethorpe Picture," which explains the cover photo of the 2015 edition, a portrait of the author snapped by Mapplethorpe in 1980. The joke of the story is that Myles offered the image to their mother back in Arlington for her "photo wall," which her lesbian poet daughter was conspicuously absent from. A piece of "real" art smuggled into the regular working-class decor. To be an artist and a queer is to be an outsider in your family as much as in the culture at large, especially in the 1970s or 1980s. The secret Mapplethorpe is a metaphor for the daughter herself—a lesbian icon, an influential poet, "a significant person, maybe a saint," sitting there in their body in the family and culture that neither sees nor understands them. With *Chelsea Girls*, Myles forces a cultural and a literary reckoning with their life on their own terms, demanding understanding, the text held to the reader's throat. What it was like to be female, with that permeable body, to be a lesbian, to be working class or flat broke, to be a poet, a drunk, a speedy pill-popper, to be heartbroken and heartbreaker, to be half an orphan, to have so much to say yet forced to claw out a place to say it with your own ragged, dirty fingernails—this is *Chelsea Girls*.

That it was allowed to go out of print at all is, in the parlance of the North Shore of New England, *a sin*. That it is back in print, able to be placed in bookshop windows, to grab the eyes of a person whose life it may profoundly alter, is not a miracle—it's justice. "I would like to tell everything once," the author writes, "just my part, because this is my life, not yours."

A version of this piece was first published in the *Los Angeles Review of Books* in 2015.

GENE LOVES JEZEBEL

I bought my girlfriend a record player for her birthday. We'd just moved in together and I had this romantic vision of us spending lazy weekends reading the *New York Times* and playing jazz records, so I went down to Urban Outfitters and grabbed one of those Crosley record players that looks like the handsome suitcases of yore, and I mailed in a weekender subscription to the *New York Times*. But why did I think I would want to listen to jazz? I guess because, as I've gotten older, all sorts of things I once thought were really boring have become sort of exciting—monogamy, early bedtimes, decaf, babies, neutrals, preppie clothing. Why not jazz? But it only took me a couple of episodes of *Homeland* to realize it still sounds like what happens inside your head before the voices come and you go insane. What's the word for pre-schizophrenia? *Jazz.*

I used to have a huge record collection, and I left it all in the basement of a brownstone in Jamaica Plain, Massachusetts, when I moved to California. I was in the throes of my Radical Lesbian Feminist Nervous Breakdown and thought I probably wouldn't have any use for my impressive collection of goth, death-rock, glam-punk, and 1980s alternative music in my new life, which would consist of living off the grid on a women's commune and reading tarot cards, perhaps changing my name to Amethyst (still not a bad idea). My recent decade or so of violently ratting my hair, wearing clown makeup as foundation, and spending all my money on European imports and rare remixes of bands like Christian Death, the Sisters of Mercy, and Lords of the New Church made no sense with this new me who had chopped off her hair, gone vegan, sold all of her "objectifying" clothing, and was busy purging all male-created culture from her life. I left a chunk of amazing vinyl in the basement of a building owned by a scrappy Vietnam vet who got by selling shit he found at the dump. He certainly made a bundle on my records.

Now that I have this new record player in my life, I am finding myself flipping through stacks of records, that same familiar stance, the albums falling into my chest, the motion sending dust off of the dust jackets and into my nose. Am I having body memories of the last time I regularly went record shopping, is that why I find myself looking for all the bands I looked for in high school? Music I haven't heard since I was obsessed with it, music that was the soundtrack to everything from my hormonal crying jags to fights with my mom to my teenage alcoholism to the loss of my actual virginity. I want to hear it again. Would I still like it? Would it stand the test of time? Some bands, like the Cure or Siouxsie and the Banshees, are recognized classics and live on in my iTunes. Others, like Alien Sex Fiend, Kommunity FK, or Love and Rockets, I haven't heard in forever.

As much as it drives me crazy to spend money on something I already once spent money on, I decided to recreate my 1980s record collection, one slab of vinyl at a time. First up is Gene Loves Jezebel.

I loved Gene Loves Jezebel SO MUCH that I would shred my clothes into tiny rags and tie them to my hair, down at the root, trying to approximate Jay Aston's hairdo, which had lots of little crimps and rags and wraps and braids and whatnot. This is *not* a hair wrap as we have come to know it today, hippie style. This was something else, something more tangled and creative. Gene Loves Jezebel was (is?) the doomed music project of Michael and Jay Aston, fraternal twins from Wales. Their image was, like, androgynous incestuous brothers. They draped themselves seductively on one another. Jay was more androgynous, with all that ribboned hair and a full face of makeup; Michael was a tad more manly. His hair was short and choppy blond and he wore lighter makeup than his brother.

I once tagged GENE LOVES JEZEBEL on the side of a Cumberland Farms while waiting for the bus into Boston. The next day, someone had taped a photo of the band on the newsstand at the bus stop. I freaked out and daringly left my phone number there in a note, even though Chelsea was crawling with hoodlums and thugs and junkies and murderers. The next day I got a phone call from a girl named Sarra who loved Gene Loves Jezebel *almost* as much as me and who, incredibly, lived around the corner and who wound pipe cleaners into the curls of her hair as a way to approximate Jay's ragged-head look. We were friends for many years, and when my mother would get pissed at me for dyeing my hair pink and blue and then getting beat up on the street for it, she would beg, "Can't you just put pipe cleaners in your hair like Sarra?"

In a subculture of black clothes, Gene Loves Jezebel was a relief of satiny pastels and jewel tones. I was able to wear color because of Gene Loves Jezebel. Also vintage velvets and ruffled shirts and colorful beads and scarves. They were a romantic band and they made romantic music that made me feel very romantic. When they played a show with the Cult at the Orpheum Theatre, I waited outside the doors at sound check, listening to the familiar thumps and fuzzy guitar. I was filled with something rising and manic—my *favorite band ever* was right inside there! I had stopped at one of the little carts that sell things on Washington Street and bought a scarf shot through with golden threads that I thought Jay Aston would love, and I was determined to get it to him. And I did! I waited until someone left the building and dashed inside, chased by a security guard.

"Please, I love them, I just have to give this to themmmmmmmmmm!" I screamed behind my shoulder as I ran down the carpeted aisle to where the band was noodling on the stage. They stopped and looked at me— *Jay Aston stopped and looked at me.*

"I brought this for you," I said breathlessly at the foot of the stage. "You're my favorite band. I love you." Jay Aston bent at the waist so I could drape the scarf around his neck. It was such a humble movement, as if I, a peasant, were bestowing knighthood upon royalty!

"I'll wear it tonight," he said, which kept me high for hours, until the actual show when he, in fact, did not wear it.

"Okay, out of here," the security guard grabbed my arm and hustled me out.

The next day I left school early and took the Peter Pan bus to Providence, Rhode Island, to catch Gene Loves Jezebel's all-ages show at the Living Room with my friend Katie. We got there hours before the show started and froze outside until they opened the doors, and then twitched nervously waiting for the band to show up. This was normal, it was how my friends and I saw bands when they came to town. We constructed elaborate ways to meet them, staged endurance performances of standing for hours or sleeping outside, and it often worked. And it was usually a disappointment. When Jay and Michael strode in, our breaths got tangled in our throats. I grabbed Katie. We watched as the twins decamped to and returned from the greenroom, and then set about trying to become their new best friends.

"Hi," I said to Jay like we knew each other. "I gave you a scarf during sound check yesterday."

"Oh yeah, right," Jay nodded.

"Your show was so great last night!"

I didn't mention the scarf promise, but I hoped the words *scarf* and *show* and *last night* would trigger something in him, and he would be all, "Oh yeah, that beautiful scarf, it was too precious to wear on stage, I slept with it wrapped around my slender naked body instead." Jay Aston was very slender; he sang about it in his songs. His hair was the actual color of rubies, not that I'd ever seen one in real life.

What he said was, "Someone stole Mike's coat from backstage."

"Oh no!" I cried. "How horrible! Who would do something like that?"

"A fan," he shrugged, and gave me a wary look. I wanted to exclaim right then that I would never steal Michael's coat, or steal any of their possessions, but of course that was not true at all, and I was actually sickened with the terrible possibility that there was a Gene Loves Jezebel fan even more rabid and wily than I, and that she had absconded with Michael's coat and was probably sleeping naked in it, because that's what I would do. What Michael didn't understand was that however much he might have loved his coat, that fan loved it more, in a holy way that he never could. She deserved it. Plus, they were rock stars. Couldn't they buy all the coats they wanted?

"It sucks. It's bloody cold." Jay and Michael said things like *bloody* because they were from Wales, which is sort of like England but gloomier and more mysterious, hence even more obscure and gothic.

Then Jay and Michael went to the pinball machine and played a few rounds. Whenever Jay lost a ball he would hip chuck the machine and say "Kuh!" or "Ku-kuh!" They made these noises in their songs. Oh my god! It was like we were *inside* a Gene Loves Jezebel song! Amazing.

After the show, we went and stayed overnight at a hotel, something I do not understand how I pulled off except I must have massively lied to my mother. I remember I was wearing a black skirt with pink tulle lining, and I wore it inside out so it was all tulle. I wore a purple velvet vest and coral Mardi Gras beads—I had tons of Mardi Gras beads from my aunt in Louisiana who always sent us boxes of them. I had a fringed scarf tied into my hair so the fringe dipped down my forehead into my face. There is a picture somewhere of me sitting cross-legged on the hotel bed, the room a haze of pot smoke.

Of all the Gene Loves Jezebel albums available at the Beat, a really great, now closed record store in Sacramento, I chose *Immigrant*. It's their second album so it feels like a middle ground for a band that began strange and moody and became increasingly pop, thus causing a rift between Michael and Jay that continues to this day. Now there are *two* Gene Loves Jezebels (and you didn't even know there was one!), one belonging to Jay and one to Michael, and the only reason Jay hasn't brought a lawsuit is because their mom was dying and begged him not to on her deathbed.

On *Immigrant* Jay does most of the singing but Michael chimes in, and often speaks too. Their Welsh accents make their singing voices strange, like cats or fairy men. And speaking of fairy men, I can't *believe* I didn't understand how gay Jay and Michael Aston were. The wistfulness in their love songs, the longing and impossibility of happiness really sounds like "the love that dare not speak its name." The best song on *Immigrant* is a soothing dirge called "Stephen," a really beautiful love song that goes "When Stephen smiles my heart just seems to grow / if only I could let that poor boy go." With the opening line "We're southern boys with western / smiles," it seems to prophesize the coming of *Brokeback Mountain*'s "I wish I could quit you." It's such a pretty song, and in fact it's the moodier, prettier songs that best stand the test of time. In my youth, I loved the bouncy poppiness of ones like "Worth Waiting For" and "Always a Flame"—which are still good, in spite of the 1980s guitar that nearly ruins it—but now I prefer the dense, plodding ones like "Coal Porter"—another song of unredeemable romance.

The odd, seemingly coded songs "Cow" and "The Rhino Plasty" endure the way art and culture that seem to be created outside of time do. Stay avant-garde and you'll never get old. "Cow" begins with a brag about Jay's muscles while he's baling hay, and then asks, "Did you see the cow with the furrowed brow?" The chorus goes "Weep for her / did you see the cow?"—which made me think it was an animal rights anthem, but there is so much longing in the song and repetition of "don't talk about it" and "don't think on it," there's something else going on. In "The Rhino Plasty" he's all, "you love this boy," and chants "take off your clothes" and "look at our nose." They were weird songs in the 1980s and they're weird now too, and interesting. And *gay*! Bonus.

First published on *xoJane* in 2012.

PURPLE RAIN

I was about thirteen years old, lying on my couch, sulking, when I had a major epiphany: all of my purple life I had been waiting for a boyfriend like Prince. He was *small*, he was *sensitive*, he was *sexy*. He clearly didn't care what anyone else thought of him or else he wouldn't be parading around in majorly ruffled clothing and, like, *heels*. He wouldn't be wearing eyeliner. All of my purple life I had been waiting for a boyfriend who wore *eyeliner*. If anybody in Chelsea looked like this I would know about it, because they would have been murdered and it would have been in the paper. I despaired of ever getting close enough to Prince to let him know how perfect we could be together. And I knew I was no match for Sheila E. It was impossible. I didn't cry. I just sort of exuded trapped melancholia into my environment, like a plant.

I'd met Prince years earlier, in a magazine. He'd been wearing a thong. I think he was in a shower? Maybe I put him in a shower in my mind, because he was, like, pretty much naked, and I had never seen a pretty much naked man before and it seemed like if he was in a shower it could be okay. The article made a big deal about how wild Prince was, and how he had a song called "Controversy" and said things like "Am I black or white? / Am I straight or gay?"

Prince *really* didn't live in Chelsea, because in Chelsea you better fucking *know* if you are black or white or straight or gay and not be sort of musing on it coquettishly in a thong. Because someone in the street was bound to ask you about it in a nonfriendly way and you better have your answer handy and, as he sang in "1999," "Prepare to fight!"

By the time *Purple Rain* came out, I wasn't scared of Prince anymore. According to a really great essay by Hilton Als, "I Am Your Conscious, I Am Love," published in *Harper's* in December 2012, that's because he wasn't scary anymore. He got less gay and more fully clothed, and the black queens were over him and the white girls in places like Chelsea were lying on their couches mooning over him. But let's get serious: *Purple Rain* is one of the best albums ever made. It does not have a bad song on it. Not a single clunker, each one epic and gorgeous and integral to the holistic perfection of the entirety.

I know that the songs from *Purple Rain* continue to get a lot of play in the world, so acquiring it as part of the rebuilding of my teenage record collection may seem unnecessary, but that's not so. This is an album to be listened to in its entirety, not a little "Let's Go Crazy" caught on the radio. It is like an opera. And its non–Top 40 offerings are every bit as wonderful as "When Doves Cry."

"Take Me with U" is super dreamy, and so is "The Beautiful Ones," though it's all dark and sort of cool-synth stormy. I loved when he sang, "If we got married . . ." and then, all tough, asks, "Would that be cool?" "Computer Blue" is kinetic and sort of crazed, and "Darling Nikki" was like every single YA or even adult book being passed around a classroom with the sex parts marked in a *song*. This girl Nikki was a "sex fiend" and it didn't seem to be a bad thing! It took me so long to comprehend "masturbating with a magazine." I had only just understood what masturbating was. I encountered the word in Judy Blume's *Deenie* a while back, where it is explained as "stimulating your genitals." Guess what? I didn't know what genitals were. I knew pussy, twat, cunt, snatch, dick, prick, cock. I knew vagina and penis. I also knew jerking off and playing with yourself. But I didn't know genitals or masturbate. So, when in *Deenie* the girl thinks about how she touches herself and it feels good and that it is "stimulating your genitals," I thought about how sometimes in my bed I liked to run my fingers down the side of my ribs and give myself a little tickle. I figured I was stimulating my genitals. I'd like to take a moment right now to salute my education. All of it.

Anyway, I eventually came to understand masturbating as having sex with yourself, but I still didn't know there was such a thing as a clitoris. I knew that women had sex by putting a penis up in there somewhere, so I figured that's what Nikki was doing with the magazine—she'd rolled it up and was, like, doing herself with it. This didn't seem sexy to me, but I understood that Prince was occupying a separate reality from mine and I trusted him.

The sex laced throughout *Purple Rain* really appealed to me in my beyond-naive—let's just call it ignorant—state. The sex was in the synths, it was in the way the guitar seemed to shimmer. It was in Wendy and Lisa's drugged-out voices as they climbed into a bath to "begin." Animals struck curious poses in "When Doves Cry." It was a landscape as completely shaped by sex as a valley is shaped by wind and rivers. I believed Prince when he pledged he would die for whoever he was pledging death for in "I Would Die 4 U," and I believed he both was and was not all the many things he claimed and disclaimed, once again shrugging off his masculinity, his androgyny too. In "1999" he vowed "If I gotta die I'm gonna listen to my body tonight," and in "Let's Go Crazy" he asserted that "we're all gonna die." And when it comes down to it, Prince's body, and maybe mine and maybe yours, contains multitudes. I wanted to live in Prince's purple world, where you could just be a *dove*. Where, in "Baby I'm a Star," you can proudly claim you got "no money" but that you're "rich on personality." Me too, Prince!

When the *Purple Rain* tour came to Boston, the disco station Kiss 108 had a contest. DJs were going to drive through Boston "hot spots" in a purple Cadillac and give away tickets to people who were wearing purple. I was seized with desperate industry—this was my one and only way to see Prince! The show was already sold out and I couldn't have gotten tickets anyway, being rich only in personality. My mother probably didn't have the money and I doubt she would have let me go to a concert where a black man rose from the stage naked in a bathtub and eventually had simulated sex with the stage.

I cobbled together an outfit. I'd already outgrown my ultimate purple outfit—a striped miniskirt set I'd worn to my Catholic school's Christmas party the year before, causing a scandal wherein my mother was called and ordered to bring me something dull and soul killing to change into.

All I had to work with was a pair of purple shorts with white piping down the side. They weren't particularly cool. All they had going for them was that they were purple. I paired them with a pair of white lace tights and a white lace shirt. I dug from my closet a gauzy white hat, an old Easter bonnet that I hoped maybe looked cool, like a fedora. I had a pair of vintage gloves my antique-hoarder aunt had given me. I'd cut the fingers off them, so they wouldn't prevent frostbite but they really helped my outfit.

When I put on my winter coat it ruined everything. If I wanted the tickets, I was going to have to not wear my winter coat. It was March in Boston. That means freezing. But I loved Prince enough to do it. Inspiration struck: I dug a plain white sheet out of the linen cabinet and found the can of colored hairspray I'd gotten at Halloween. I spread the sheet across the floor and sprayed I WOULD FREEZE 4 PRINCE across it. Then I folded it up and hopped on a bus *to sneak* into Boston because I was totally not allowed to go there alone ever lest I be raped and mugged and raped again.

What did I know about Boston "hot spots"? The only area I knew at all, from very rare trips into the city with family, was Downtown Crossing, the shopping district anchored by the big fancy department stores Jordan Marsh and Filene's. But there was also a Strawberries record store there that was cool. And a really punk store called Stairway to Heaven that sold concert T-shirts and jewelry made of chains. It was the one place in Boston I knew how to get to, so it was where I went. Other Prince people were there, too, so I knew I was on to something. There was a male-female couple who totally looked like Prince and Apollonia, it was crazy. They had serious Prince clothing on, purple makeup, lace veils, they looked amazing. They glared at me. I figured they would easily win the tickets, they were so incredible, but they probably figured that me, a shabby kid with a homemade sign shivering like a Dickensian orphan, would win the hearts of the radio DJs.

A blond guy was there in tight white spandex pants and a purple fedora. I blinked when I saw him, I recognized him. He was my eighth-grade teacher's *roommate*, whom I had glimpsed when my teacher, Mr. Ruggles, had had the class over to his house to watch *To Kill a Mockingbird* and eat brownies. If it wasn't totally clear to everyone that Mr. Ruggles was a big gay (even after his thwarted attempt to cancel math and instead stage a production of *A Midsummer Night's Dream* with choreography lifted from *Cats*), it was pretty obvious that his roommate was, which did the trick of lodging a deep suspicion in everyone's mind. I couldn't believe my teacher's roommate was my competition for the Prince tickets! Would he tell Mr. Ruggles he saw his student dressed like a child hooker in Boston, and would Mr. Ruggles tell my mother, and would I be grounded?

It didn't matter. I stood on that corner catching pneumonia for the Purple One until my curfew approached. It was a pretty early curfew, like five, and I still had to make my way back to Chelsea. And sneak inside in my outfit. I threw my sheet in a trashcan and headed home. Kiss 108 never did stop by Downtown Crossing. Apparently, it wasn't "hot" enough, and everyone who had stood there with me was also too clueless to know that. I never got to see the *Purple Rain* tour and now I will never ever get to see Prince, but possessing an album that surpasses the passing of both time and its author, never losing its mystery no matter how much play it gets, is a gift for the ages.

First published on *xoJane* in 2013.

MINOR THREAT

Once during the eighties this punk girl told me about a party. It was a Friday night and I was hanging out on the steps of the Boston Public Library with twenty or thirty other kids, a mixture of goths, skaters, art fags, punks, and misfit-alternatives.

"It's a straight-edge party," the girl explained. "No drinking."

"And you're *going*?" I asked, incredulous. Whereas I had only just been speaking to a peer, I suddenly felt like I was plunged into dialogue with one of those Bible kids who came round every now and then trying to lure us to something churchy because we were all wearing crosses and rosaries. The whole *point* of finally being a teenager was getting to run around Boston drunk: buying a shit-ton of liquor with a phony ID I'd found in the Commons during a Siouxsie show (the girl in the photo had caked-on makeup and bangs obscuring most of her face, that could totally be me!), making out with drunk skaters, getting in crying fights with friends, getting thrown out of the mall for stealing money from the wishing fountain, getting thrown out of the fancy hotels for trying to pee in their bathrooms, running from cops and skinheads—none of these things could happen sober!

"If you're not going to drink, what are you going to do?" I asked the sober girl, and I think she replied, "You know, hang out, listen to records, eat peanuts." Did she really say "eat peanuts" or was that something snarky I tossed in while telling my drunken goth friends about the absurd invitation? "Oh, you know, they're going to hang out and eat peanuts or something." Straight-edge kids didn't drink (ridiculous), didn't smoke (boring), and didn't have sex. I didn't have sex either, so the boys of the subculture felt safer for that, though there was something creepily puritanical about them *swearing off* sex. Having just been ejected from my final Catholic school, ending nine years of continuous Christian education, the straight-edge kids sounded too much like the nuns I was so recently oppressed by, and that was not cool. I liked the big black *X*'s they drew on the back of their hands with markers, but some straight-edge kids took it to a more disturbing level, carving their identifying insignia into their skin with glass. *What's the point in living so pure if you're so fucked in the head anyway?* I remember thinking. The straight-edge kids were mysteries.

I didn't have Minor Threat's titular album on vinyl, I had it on a cassette, and I listened to it when I was in the bathroom, on the boom box that lived on the back of the toilet. It was a dubbed cassette with *Minor Threat* scrawled on the label, and I don't remember who made it for me. I often wanted to like punk, because I wanted to be harder than I was, tougher. I liked the rage and strength in some punk music, but ultimately the abrasive discord and the wild machismo of most of it made it feel like the audio equivalent of watching a war movie with no female actresses. I just couldn't connect. What about Minor Threat made them different?

Honestly, I think their straight-edged-ness had something to do with it. Guys got scary when they were drunk, so knowing they weren't egging their macho audience on with cries of "Let's drink some beer!" like local hardcore band Gang Green made them feel safer. When other hardcore bands seemed to be all about smashing your face in with what major/giant/terrifying date-raping menaces they were, there was something humble, almost nerdy, about being a *Minor* Threat, knowing your limits.

I didn't know that lead singer Ian MacKaye was a feminist—I didn't know that I was a feminist—but as I listened to the tape in the bathroom I picked up on the subtle harmonies buried in the chaos, I picked out the political messages in the lyrics, and maybe I picked up something of an ally. In "Filler," MacKaye rages against a friend who got religion and turned stupid, and guess what? That had happened to my old best friend Anne Marie, who had been a righteous speed-metal girl turning me on to anti-racist Anthrax songs and cynical Megadeth anthems, and had Voivod's skull logo painted on the back of her motorcycle jacket. Now she was hitchhiking to Amy Grant concerts and holding totally weird, even hurtful beliefs. "You picked up a Bible," MacKaye accused, "And now you're gone / You call it religion / You're full of shit." I wasn't capable of telling my old friend exactly what I thought of her switch, which felt like a betrayal, but Ian was.

Many years later, as I recreated my record collection, I found the green album cover silk-screened with the image of a white skinhead guy with his head in his arms, squatting on a stoop. A drunken idiot who can't get up, on the verge of puking? Or a straight-edge kid overwhelmed by society's idiocy? I put the record on the turntable, impressed by the weight of the vinyl. It was heavier and thicker than other records, not at all flimsy. The roll of drums that opens "Filler" gave me a shiver.

I love an anthem, I can't help it. And this album is full of them. "I Don't Wanna Hear It," with its chorus of "I don't want to hear it / Know you're full of shit" is a great all-purpose fuck-you song, able to be applied to anyone from the Man to your dad to the Pigs to politicians, teachers, or your boyfriend. "Seeing Red" is all about getting fucked with for looking different: "My looks must threaten you / To make you act the way you do." "Small Man Big Mouth" makes fun of violent short dudes, and "Bottled Violence" makes fun of violent drunk dudes. I think about how sort of radical it was for punk dudes to be calling out violent dudes at all, in the 1980s or even now. I really think my burgeoning feminist consciousness—lots of feelings, not a lot of articulation—felt vindicated by Minor Threat's lyrics. Ian MacKaye was like a big brother who had my back, something I really could have used back then.

On to the straight-edge anthems. A treatise, "Straight Edge" details all the shit MacKaye is not going to do— including hang out with zombies, pass out at shows, snort coke or speed, smoke pot, pop pills, and sniff glue. "Always gonna keep in touch / Never want to use a crutch / I've got the straight edge."

As a teenage alcoholic, I would cringe when my mother would say things like, "What, you can't have fun without alcohol?" Because, no, I couldn't—especially not in my teens, when I found drinking genuinely fun, before the consequences began piling up. I can see the consequences piling up in others around me, folks of my generation who never stopped, or younger people who will have to or else.

I came by the *straight edge* the hard way, but I'm glad that "I've got better things to do / Than sit around and smoke dope / 'Cause I know I can cope."

"In My Eyes" is the strongest straight-edge screed, as the singer gently mocks the justification for using that he hears in the scene: "You like the taste," "It calms your nerves," "You want to be different," then explodes into furious screaming replies: "You just need an excuse," "You just think it looks cool," "You just hate yourself." Harsh toke, but he nails the self-delusion inherent in addiction.

"Out of Step (With the World)" is probably my favorite, because I can now totally relate to what it's like to "Don't drink / Don't smoke"—although I do "fuck," and even Mr. MacKaye has figured out how to work a wife into his ascetic lifestyle. Still, applause for calling out fornication as the *real* opiate of the masses. "I can't keep up / I can't keep up / I can't keep up / Out of step with the world" goes the chorus, and it's in this song that he lets in a bit of the sorrow that can come with sobriety, the reality of living a life so different and so mysterious to so many of the people around you. At the end of it all, he consoles himself with "At least I can fucking think."

And then, with a *screeeech* like the actual needle going off the actual record, MacKaye's consciousness tanks with "Guilty of Being White," a mocking song wherein he tries to weasel his way out of white privilege because, like, slavery happened "a hundred years before I was born." A lyricist whose work focuses on ripping on clueless dudes, perhaps it was too difficult for MacKaye to climb over his ego to locate his own clueless dude, cop to it, and write a song about it. As a teenager trying to figure out what the fuck was happening with race, this song did not help. I lived in New England, a region that prided itself on being progressive but in fact was horribly racist, in a family that spoke racist slurs at the dinner table, in a subculture (goth) whose beauty standard was literally having the whitest skin you could possibly have. I knew the world was fucked and I wanted to fight it and be on the right side of things, but I was also pea brained and conflict averse. It would be nice to shrug off the legacy of white supremacy as having nothing to do with me; I could feel the allure of that. But the song nagged. The tone is sinister and mean spirited, and it hasn't aged well. In a *Los Angeles Review of Books* essay on the anthology *White Riot: Punk Rock and the Politics of Race,* Sara Jaffe digs into a 1983 *Maximum Rocknroll* roundtable in which MacKaye doubles down, defending "Guilty of Being White" and his right to deal with people as "individuals, not black and white" and basically whining like a baby that he shouldn't bear any responsibility for the racist legacy of slavery. Jaffe calls bullshit on "the desire that punk culture could truly be a place where race just doesn't matter anymore," asserting that "the problem is that the real first step in ending racism is for people with privilege to recognize the ways in which they benefit from the system, even if they agree that that system is broken." The work of white people is not only to look inward and ferret out all the ways we have internalized and benefited from white privilege but to *continue* to do this, every single day for the rest of our lives. Like a sober alcoholic who checks herself daily and is given a reprieve from binge drinking, only a regular, honest evaluation of oneself as a product of white supremacy can help keep white people consistently woke enough to not add further damage. As a rock icon known for his fearlessness in calling out small-mindedness and hypocrisy within punk and mainstream cultures, MacKaye's defensive inability to check himself is a bummer.

In an earlier version of this essay I all but let MacKaye off the hook for "Guilty of Being White," guilty as I am of the same white laziness that he continues to suffer from. As woke as I may think I am, my blind spots are wide, they startle and shame when recognized. But it is a white person's job to feel around for these blind spots, to respond with humility and appreciation if someone does you the perhaps painful favor of calling attention to it. MacKaye, interested, I think, in acting the hero, could really be one if he publicly acknowledged his own white privilege; he'd be role modeling to the gazillions of white punks who worship him. Doing so could possibly heal some of the damage caused by "Guilty," a piece of propaganda it's easy to imagine bigoted listeners embracing as an anthem of white pride. I started revisiting this album, and this essay, in the campy spirit that nostalgia engenders, interested in reconsidering straight-edge music in the wake of my sobriety, but the dumpster fire of white privilege—MacKaye's and my own—has blocked my enjoyment, for the most part. I'm cool with leaving some albums to the past.

A version of this piece was first published on *xoJane* in 2012.

SONIC YOUTH'S MAGIC

I have this memory of a lost night in the 1980s. For a moment I'm in the home of some kids I don't know, kids old enough to have their own place. Don't ask me where I was before or after, or who brought me there. I just know it was someplace like Allston, and the place was cold like maybe they didn't pay their heating bill. Boston in the winter. These kids were really cool. One guy was named maybe Darryl and he was just so beautiful. He had this careless mohawk, his hair was light brown, shaggy/curly, shaved down the sides, and it just tumbled into his face where his eyes were blue and his nose turned up cute like a rabbit. He wore a leather jacket with band insignia painted all over it. The girl that was there was really cool too, she wasn't trying *so hard* like me and my friends were, with our carefully dyed hair and our intense makeup—one smudge, watch out. Goth is such drag. These kids were lazy punks. They didn't have to try, 'cause they were it. I think they thought we were fussy, and young. We didn't stay long. There wasn't anything going on at their place. Just low light and no booze, a haze of cigarette smoke unmoving in the lamp beams. And Sonic Youth on the stereo.

They *would* like Sonic Youth. Sonic Youth wasn't so much a band to pine after, they were like a *philosophy*.

There was something advanced about them, the way these kids were advanced. It felt like it was too late for me to get into Sonic Youth. A weird attitude toward music, right? But shit was competitive. Me and my friends were always scrambling for an obscure, awesome band we could get into before anyone else, claim with psychotic enthusiasm, and have ultimate dibs on. I owned a few bands—Gene Loves Jezebel was one, but also Christian Death. My friends could like them, maybe even love them a little, but they were *mine*. My best friend Guen owned the Sisters of Mercy and their spin-off, the Mission UK. But who could own Sonic Youth? You'd have to be a scholar. They were deep like ancient Egypt or something. There was something spooky about them, dirge-y. Were they a cult? I learned about life from the music I listened to, I took lyrics really seriously. It seemed like I could learn a lot from Sonic Youth, but I honestly didn't know if I was ready. I think on some level I knew that the bands I was obsessed with were just another kind of pop, even if I was getting my ass kicked in the street for being so into them.

I bought Sonic Youth's *Sister*. Even the cover felt coded, a photographic rebus. The title and band's name looked to be written in gold Sharpie. Oh, look: "Sonic-Youth," it read. Is that how you wrote it? With a dash? This was crucial. I didn't want to fuck up and write it wrong on my notebook or my Catholic school skirt because people would call you out for that and it was embarrassing. You had to play it off like *who cares?* but you did care, you cared deeply. Everyone did. Then, look on the other side, it says, "The Sonic Youth." *The* Sonic Youth? Clearly this band didn't give a fuck. They were all over the place, deliberately messy.

What could I learn from these pictures? A comet

shooting through outer space. A woman sprawled on a wooden floor, short hair, tight little shirt, no underwear. No *underwear*? That's intense. Something is written on her leg, what's that on her ankle, a tattoo or, like, is she cuffed to the floor or something? Is this saying something about the subjugation of women? No—the girl doesn't look upset. She's a little sexy for sure but not as much as you'd think with no pants on. How about those cows on the other side, with the bangs that flopped onto their faces like cute Darryl's mohawk? A picture of a small town, long-ago Main Street, USA. Americana. Were they dissing suburbia? All I knew about suburbia was that punks liked to dis it. There's a little baby naked on a lawn with his little baby-penis. Then the planet Saturn. A series of houses that all looked alike. And some crazy object, a black-and-white photo of it, like a drill maybe. It seemed atomic. Some gears at the bottom.

I put on the record and guess what? It's the musical equivalent of the pictures on the cover. There's something cosmic and spacey and lonely and lost. Simple, primal drums, and wailing, weirdo guitars. This was *not* pop. Or was it deconstructed pop, ripped apart. It was haunting, the way Kim Gordon murmured. She sounded like she knew everything—you could hear it in her voice. She knew everything but was too bored by it to tell you. You'd have to figure it out for yourself. Thurston Moore seemed to give up his secrets more readily. Something in his voice was earnest.

The little sheet that was slipped inside the cover was typewritten xeroxes of their lyrics, and this was before zines. On "Schizophrenia," Thurston said, "I went away to see an old friend of mine / His sister came over she was out of her mind." I liked how it was like a story. One of those weird nights when you wind up at someone's house and some strange person is there being creepy or sad. Like when we wound up at the home of that guy who was supposed to be some big gay witch and he had an actual crystal ball that he twirled and then tossed at you saying, "Catch the light!" When I found out it was a quote from *Labyrinth* I couldn't tell if that made it more or less embarrassing.

Whereas a lot of the goth music I listened to tried to conjure a melodic romantic fantasy, I felt like Sonic Youth was playing it like it really was. Their music sounded like life to me, which maybe scared me a little, or depressed me. I was looking to escape. But I was captivated. "Come on get in the car," Kim insisted on "Pacific Coast Highway," "I won't hurt you." Really? I wasn't so sure. She sounded so tough and sinister. I respected her authority intuitively.

What about now? Well, *Sister* is only a million times better today. It's so atonal and wild and sexy. I really think more than anything this is music to fuck to. And I had been a virgin! There are some things you can't get until you've cast off your innocence. No wonder it tripped me out. "He's got a fatal erection home in bed / . . . / He's got a hard tit killer fuck in his past," Thurston singsongs in "Tuff Gnarl." Excuse me—"hard tit"? Blow my mind! I hadn't known tits could be hard.

Oh my god—"Kotton Krown"! "Kotton Krown"! "Kotton Krown"! How could I have forgotten that this is *the very very most beautiful song ever recorded*, how it became my *favorite* song, how it satisfied all of my dreamy gothy uberromantic teenage needs. "Angels are dreaming of you / Angels are dreaming of you . . ." This is when you're cuddling after crazy sex and you're flying high on druggy dopamine in *love*. What did I know about such things? Someone should make a documentary about this song. Listening to it now I get a full-body memory of what it is like to long for something you have no words for. A craving for things you haven't experienced, things you might not even know exist. "You're gonna manifest the mystery," they promise in tandem. I feel like someone just presented the inside of my brain with the biggest most luscious bouquet of otherworldly flowers. What a gift a song can be!

Being a virgin, sitting on my bedroom floor, listening to *Sister*, trying to decode it. I beheld the cover, its pictures. Each side contained a pitch-black square amid the images. I ran my fingers over it. It was raised, not flat like the others. I scraped it a little, and it began to loosen from the cardboard. *NO WAY*. The most mysterious band with the most mysterious sound had an *actual mystery* on their album cover! My heart raced, I felt like a girl in a book, like I'd found a secret drawer in the back of a desk, or a secret room that opened up from a bookcase. I tugged the blackness—a sticker—from the cover. There was a picture of Disney's Magic Castle, the blue-and-white palace in the center of the theme park. Drawn over it were a series of magic-marker circles, like radar being emitted from within, a secret broadcast.

Panting, I tore the sticker off the other side. A girl glared out from beneath. Young, maybe my age. She looked pissed. She wore overalls and stared straight into the camera. She was covered by a psychedelic wash of color, yellow and red blobs, like a strobe was passing over her, or she was trapped inside a lava lamp. I now know it to be Richard Avedon's 1980 portrait of Sandra Bennett, I saw it in person at his retrospective at SFMOMA. Dick and Disney must have threatened the band with a lawsuit! I wasn't savvy enough to pick up on the practical reasons for the stickers. I just thought it was another spooky gift from these witchy wizards. The only sad thing about my new copy of *Sister* is that those stickers are gone, and the black space is real, a void on the cover. I still sit fingering it anyway, waiting for a trap door to open—and it does. The record has come to an end in my apartment, but somewhere else in the building, someone is now playing Sonic Youth! Loud! Like I just was! Music is magic.

First published on *xoJane* in 2012.

LOVE
&
QUEERNESS

TRANSMISSIONS FROM CAMP TRANS

Unless you've spent some time as a lesbian or perhaps are the sort of straight lady who enjoys the music, politics, and occasional abandoning of the menfolk that a particularly earthy strain of "women's culture" offers, you've probably never heard of the Michigan Womyn's Music Festival (MWMF). It ran for forty years, taking place each August on a lush chunk of woodland in northern Michigan, planned to coincide with summer's final full moon. While womyn's music is the festival's alleged purpose—the guitar stylings of folksters like Holly Near and Cris Williamson as well as post–riot grrrl acts like Bitch and Animal, the Butchies, and Le Tigre, to draw in the younger generation—the real purpose is to hunker down in a forest with a few thousand other females, bond, have sex in a fern grove, and go to countless workshops on everything from sexual esoterica to parading around on stilts, processing various oppressions, and sharing how much you miss your cat. The festival aims to be a utopia, and in most ways, it hits its mark. Performers are paid well and all are paid the same amount, regardless of whether they're the Indigo Girls or some virtually unknown girl band. You can come for free as a worker, taking on jobs like childcare, kitchen work, or driving shuttles on and off the land, but even women who pay hundreds of dollars to attend are required to pull their weight by picking up a couple of work shifts. The only dudes allowed in the space are the ones who rumble in late at night in giant trucks, to vacuum the sludge from the hundreds of porta potties, called porta Janes. They are preceded by a woman who hollers, "Man on the land! Man on the land!"—a warning to skittish nymphs to hop into a tent or bush. I've been to the festival four or five times and can attest to the deeply stunning feeling of safety and peace there. The absence of guys does make for an absence of threat; everyone's guard is down, finally, and a relaxation level is hit that is probably impossible to access in the real world. Pretty much everyone who attends bursts into tears at some point, saddened at all the psychic garbage that females are forced to lug around and grateful for a week of respite. It's no wonder the women who come to the festival are zealots about it, live for August, and get totally obsessed with and protective of the culture that springs up within its security-patrolled boundaries.

In 1991 a transgender woman named Nancy Jean Burkholder was evicted from MWMF. Nancy Jean's eviction is famous in Michigan lore, for it sparked a fierce debate about the inclusion of trans women, which has been raging for decades. A lot of cis women inside the festival want to keep them out. Some staunchly insist that these individuals are not women but men in dresses trying to ruin the feminist event. Others concede that trans women are women, but because they were "born boys" and may still have penises, the festival is not the place for them. Trans women and their growing number of allies say these "feminist" justifications are straight-up discrimination and no different from the rest of the world, which routinely denies that trans women are "real" women and bars their access to everything from jobs to housing, domestic-violence counseling, and health care. Off and on for the past decade, a small group of trans people and their supporters have set up a protest camp, Camp Trans, across the road from MWMF, in the hopes of changing the policy that left Nancy Jean stranded in the Midwest twelve years ago.

IN HER WORDS: NANCY JEAN BURKHOLDER

"I appreciate women's space, and after checking with festival literature, I couldn't see that I wasn't welcome. I had talked to people, and their opinion was, if you think of yourself as a woman, you're welcome. I'd gone with a friend of mine, Laura. We drove out together, and we were number thirty-three in line. We got there early; we were really excited about going. We set up camp up in Bread & Roses. It's kind of the quiet area. Then we each did a work shift, shuttle duty. Hauling people from the front all the way back. That evening Laura was having a friend come in on the shuttle bus from Grand Rapids, so we walked down to the gate about nine p.m. to meet the bus. Turned out the bus was late and didn't get there till about eleven. We were hanging out at the fire pit, [we] just kind of joined the group of people who were hanging out and talking. When the bus came in at eleven, Laura went up to the gate to meet her friend, and I waited by the fire pit. At that point a couple of women approached me and asked if I knew that this was a festival for women. It kind of surprised me. I said, 'Yeah, uh-huh.' About that time Laura was coming back, so I asked her to come over; something didn't seem right about what these women were asking. I think one of them asked me if I was transsexual. I said, 'My history is none of your business.' I asked, 'Why are you asking?' and she said that transsexuals weren't welcome. I think I remember saying, 'Are you sure? How do you know?' And so she went at that point and talked to the festival producers. She came back in about an hour; it took a while. She said that transsexuals were not welcome at the festival, and was I transsexual? At one point I offered to show them my driver's license, which said female, and also to drop my drawers, and she said, 'I wouldn't be comfortable with that.' Which I thought was kind of off, given the amount of nudity at the festival. She asked again, 'Are you transsexual?' and I said, 'It's none of your business.' At that point she said, 'Well, I'm empowered to expel any woman, at any time, for any reason. You have to leave.' I knew there was no arguing with them.

"They wouldn't let me leave the area around the main gate. Instead, Laura went with a couple of festival security guards back out to my campsite, scooped up all of my equipment, and brought it back to the main gate. It must have been about one o'clock in the morning by then. They arranged for us to stay at a motel in Hart [Michigan]; I think we got there around two o'clock. And it was a dump. It was cold, there was mildew in the carpet, [it was] wet, trucks running by on Route 10. I couldn't believe it. I was devastated. The next day, Laura took me down to Grand Rapids, and I paid for a plane ticket and flew home to New England. I flew to Worcester, Massachusetts, and Laura's partner arranged for a taxi to take me back to their house, where my car was. Laura went back to the festival for two reasons: she was doing a workshop, and also she went back to tell my friends what happened to me. Otherwise I would have disappeared without a trace. One of the friends she told was Janis Walworth. Janis and Laura spent the rest of the festival talking to people and telling them what happened. I was back in New Hampshire, and I called *Gay Community News*, a newspaper in Boston, to tell them what happened. I think they were a little taken aback and weren't quite sure what to do with this. They did say, 'If you want to write an editorial, we'll publish it.' So, Laura wrote a letter to the editor, and they published it with my editorial, and we took up a whole page in the newspaper. That kind of started the whole controversy.

"The important piece that doesn't always get reported is that Janis organized a bunch of people to go back in 1992. She brought her sister, a male-to-female post-operative transsexual, and also an intersex person and a butch female. They distributed buttons and leaflets and did a survey. The survey indicated that seventy-two percent approved of transsexuals being at the festival. Twenty-three percent did not, for a variety of reasons. Out of that, Janis categorized the reasons why people didn't want transsexuals, and she compiled gender myths, twenty-four of them."

TWENTY-FOUR GENDER MYTHS:

1. Although male-to-female transsexuals have surgery to change their anatomy and take female hormones, they still act like men.
2. Male-to-female transsexuals are not women-born women (or womyn-born womyn).
3. Male-to-female transsexuals have been socialized as men, and this socialization cannot be changed.

4. Male-to-female transsexuals are trying to "pass" as women. They try to make themselves as much like nontranssexual women as possible.

5. Male-to-female transsexuals take jobs away from women because they had access to better training when they were men.

6. To lessen the power of patriarchy in our lives, we must purge our community of everything male, including women who once had male anatomy.

7. Most women can easily prove they are not male-to-female transsexuals, if they are challenged to do so.

8. Male-to-female transsexuals have been raised as boys, have never been oppressed as women, and cannot understand women's oppression.

9. Women's space is not "safe" space if male-to-female transsexuals are allowed in it.

10. Transsexuals have surgery so they can have sex the way they want to.

11. Male-to-female transsexuals are trying to take over the lesbian community.

12. The sex assigned to a person at birth is that person's "real" sex.

13. The lesbian and women's communities have nothing to gain by including transsexuals.

14. Nontranssexual women have the right to decide whether transsexuals should be included in the women's community.

15. Transsexuals are guilty of deception when they don't reveal right away that they are transsexuals.

16. Male-to-female transsexuals are considered men until they have sex change surgery.
17. People can be categorized as transsexual or non-transsexual—there's no in-between.
18. Women who want to become men have bought into societal hatred of women or are hoping to take advantage of male privilege.
19. A person's "true" sex can be determined by chromosome testing.
20. Transsexualism is unnatural—it is a new problem brought about by sophisticated technology.
21. "Real" women, certainly those who belong to the lesbian community, rejoice in their womanhood and have no desire to be men.
22. Since festival policy was made clear, there have been no transsexuals at Michigan.
23. Transsexuals have caused trouble at Michigan, resulting in their expulsion.
24. Nontranssexual women at Michigan don't want male-to-female transsexuals to be present.

AIRPLANE OVER THE SOUTHWEST, AUGUST 15, 2003

I'm reading *Jane* magazine because my plane could, of course, crash; this could be my last moment alive, and I will not deny myself the small delight. *Jane* is the most innocent of the guilty pleasure that is women's magazines, as it at least aspires toward a sensibility affirming that women shouldn't look starved for cheeseburgers and that gay people are cool. Printed beneath a small column in which the actor who plays the exchange student on *That '70s Show* gives advice to lovelorn teenage girls is this bit of information:

> Wesleyan University now offers the nation's first "gender-blind" dorm for students who don't label themselves as male or female.

I am headed to Camp Trans, now in the tenth year of its on-again, off-again standoff with the Michigan Womyn's Music Festival across the road. Started by Nancy Jean and friends in the years after her eviction, the protest camp faded away in the midnineties. A new generation of young transgender activists picked up the torch in 1999 and resumed the confrontational face-off. In the scant four years since, there has been an unprecedented boom in people openly identifying as trans, mostly female-assigned people transitioning to male or staking out genderqueer territory. Flocking to Camp Trans for both the political struggle and the party, these new activists have changed the outpost in significant ways. The focus of the Camp Trans struggle in recent years has drifted from its original intention of getting trans women into women-only and lesbian spaces. Trans men have generally been welcome, if not totally fetishized, by contemporary dyke communities, particularly in young, urban enclaves. The same is not true for trans women, even lesbian trans women. This influx of trans guys and their lesbian admirers at Camp Trans has not only alienated many of the trans women there but it's also blown up attendance so high they can no longer set up across the street from the festival gates. The encampment is now located up the road a bit, in a forest-lined field between the music festival and a nudist camp.

I've never been to Camp Trans, though I stopped attending MWMF a few years back, too conflicted about this exclusion of trans women. Today I'm picked up at the airport by a girl named Ana Jae who volunteered to get me so she can get the hell out of the woods. Ana hates camping; she says the bugs are attacking like mad and it's really bad when you drop your shorts to piss and they start fluttering around your bare ass. Ana can't use the porta potties because she's been traumatized by the 1980s B–horror flick *Sleepaway Camp II*, in which terrible things happen within one fetid plastic chamber, so she is forced to piddle among the bugs. I'm antsy to hear about the mood at Camp Trans, and Ana confirms that trans men far outnumber trans women. She also complains about a general devaluing of femininity in the young, post-dyke queer scene, and tells me about a sex party the night before that somehow went awry, which is this morning's main drama. Our immediate drama is that we get outrageously, wildly lost on the way back to the woods, careening through quaint Michigan townships for hours, hopelessly passing farm stands selling fresh vegetables, rows of exploding sunflowers and corn-stalks, trees and trees and more trees, gigantic willows with long whipping branches that drape and swag, and large single-family homes with porches and pools and tractors in their front yards. We know that we've unscrambled our cryptic directions when we pass a gas station that has a flapping sign that says, WELCOME WOMYN in its parking lot and loads of sporty females loading cases of beer into their cars. We follow a camper with a bumper sticker that reads SEE YOU NEXT AUGUST down a road so heavily traveled that the foliage lining it is coated with a thick dusting of brown dirt like an apocalyptic snowfall. We pass the front gates of MWMF and see its huge parking lot crammed with vehicles, women in neon-orange vests directing the flow of females through the entrance, and we keep going. It's a disappointment not to see Camp Trans boldly stationed there at the mouth of the festival, and I wonder how saliently its political point can be made tucked out of sight, around the curving road. The former vigil has turned into a sort of alternative festival, one that's free of charge and that a lot of MWMF attendees mistake for a happy, friendly, separate-but-equal campsite. A place for dykes who think trans guys are hot to spend a night cruising and partying and then return to their gated community up the road. For the trans women relying on Camp Trans as a site of protest, this new incarnation—as a sort of spring break for trans guys and the dykes who date them—has been infuriating. Which is why Sadie Crabtree, a trans woman and activist from Washington, DC, has emerged as the sort of leader this year. It is her intention, backed up by the other organizers, to bring the focus of Camp Trans back on the trans women it was originally meant to serve.

CAMP TRANS WELCOME STATION

Everyone who comes to Camp Trans, either to camp or visit from MWMF on a day pass, has to pause at the welcome tent and check in, and the MWMF attendees who arrive tonight for entertainment are charged three dollars. Behind a table made from boards and sawhorses sit a couple of Camp Trans welcomers, women doing their work shifts and acclimating visitors to their new environment. Like the festival across the way, everyone here is expected to lend a hand. The camp isn't nearly as large as the music festival—MWMF's parking lot is bigger than Camp Trans's entire area—but it still takes a lot of work to make it run. I spy a kitchen tent with a mess of pots and pans and water jugs strewn before it. Another tent is garlanded with Christmas lights that are beginning to shine as the hot summer sun sets. This is the performance area, bulked out with DJ and other sound equipment. There's a medic tent and a roped-off area for "advocates," armbanded individuals whose job is to answer touchy questions, listen to complaints, and defuse conflicts.

At the welcome tent, I sign in on a form that doubles as a petition to drop the MWMF's womyn-born-womyn policy. I'm handed a slip of paper welcoming me to Camp Trans. It reads:

> Camp Trans is an annual protest against the Michigan Womyn's Music Festival's policy that bars transsexual women from attending. MWMF's so-called "womyn-born-womyn" policy sets a transphobic standard for women-only spaces across the country, and contributes to an environment in women's and lesbian communities where discrimination against trans women is considered acceptable. For trans women who are consistently refused help from domestic violence shelters and rape crisis centers, this is a matter of life and death.

Some poster boards are stuck with Post-it notes that outline each day's workshops and meetings, another is cluttered with bright notes soliciting amour in the woods. One bemoans a throat atrophied with lack of use and another is looking for couples to participate in a Floridian-retiree role-play. Interested parties can respond by slipping scrawled replies into corresponding envelopes. There are zines for sale, silk-screened patches that say, "Camp Trans Supporter" in heavy-metal letters, buttons that squeak, "I ♥ Camp Trans," and T-shirts that say, "Not Gay as in Happy but Queer as in Fuck You." There is also a notebook labeled "Letters to Lisa Vogel."

Lisa Vogel is the sole captain of the SS *Michigan Womyn's Music Festival.* There is no one but her behind the wheel; she wrote the policy, and she is the only one who can lift it. Of the many rumors I hear this weekend, most involve her. One says that she offered Camp Trans a sum of money somewhere between $7,500 and $75,000 to start their own damn festival. This is totally unlikely, as her own festival is suffering financially. Another rumor quotes Vogel as saying trans women will be allowed into her festival over her dead body, an extreme pledge. Who knows what's true. Vogel is famously tight-lipped about the whole controversy and has never made an attempt to negotiate with Camp Trans. In the face of past protests, she has simply reiterated the policy, which, I also hear, has suddenly been removed from all MWMF web pages. There is a lot of speculation on what this means, but no one is naive enough to believe that the policy has been dropped and trans women are now welcome. More likely the immense controversy, which now involves not only a boycott of the festival but also of the performers, is wearing on festival producers and targets for attack are being shuffled out of the line of fire.

Behind the tree line is the campsite, and the arc of green has been segmented into "loud substance," which means campers are getting bombed and fucking right outside your tent; "loud no substance," meaning sober people lashed to trees and moaning loudly; and "quiet no substance," which means everyone sleeps. This is where I camp. I actually unknowingly plop my tent right in the center of a sand patch being used for AA meetings. Next to me is a camper van all tricked out with a sink and a fridge, the outside painted checkerboard. It looks straight out of *Fast Times at Ridgemont High* and, lo and behold, is occupied by my friend Chris, who is out on his makeshift patio smoking a lot of pot and triggering the substance-free campers. He's sharing his pipe with a lesbian named Mountain, who lives on a women-only commune in Oregon that has successfully integrated trans women into their home. Essentially, it is no big whoop. Life goes on, wimmin are still wimmin, they still tend their organic garden and print their lunar calendars and life is good. Mountain is one of those women who live for Michigan, so it's a real big deal that she's not there this year. She's here at Camp Trans in solidarity.

People are scurrying around, full of excited purpose. Tonight is the big dance and performance, and an influx of girls from MWMF will increase the number of people on the land. Camp Trans's population, which hovers at around seventy-five, will shoot up to over a hundred with the visitors, which is nothing compared with the eight thousand or so women hunkered down in the vast woods across the way. Sadie is dashing around, all stressed out. She's got a sweet, kind face with sparkly eyes and short hair; her all-black outfits seem like military gear, especially with the big, black women's-symbol-clenched-in-raised-fist tattoo on her shoulder. She's still dealing with fallout from last night's sex party, and now she's just found a note from a Camp Transer looking to host a Camp Trans workshop inside MWMF, where trans women can't go. There is a feeling that the action is spinning out of the organizer's hands, and she's upset that a so-called Camp Trans event would happen somewhere trans women aren't allowed. Sadie, needing a drink, bustles off with tears in her eyes.

IN HER WORDS: SADIE CRABTREE

"One problem was that some festival attendees were unclear on the mission of Camp Trans and didn't see it as a protest but rather as a part of their Michigan experience. Kind of a suburb of MWMF where fest attendees could go to hang out with hot tranny boys. That's another problem—the fascination with and fetishization of FTMs in some dyke communities makes trans women even more invisible. At least one fest attendee last year spoke openly about how she totally supported Camp Trans and loved trans guys but just didn't like trans women. We tried to solve some of those problems this year by having a very clear mission statement on all of the Camp Trans materials, providing suggested talking points for all campers, and having discussions about the experiences of trans women at Camp Trans. We had volunteer advocates whose job it was to listen to people's concerns—especially those of trans women—and help organizers plan solutions. Another thing we did was designate certain workshops and decompression areas 'wristband-free zones' where MWMF attendees were asked not to go. Having a space to retreat from interactions with fest attendees was a need that had been expressed by trans women last year, but it also sent a message. It wasn't to stigmatize festival attendees, but to help people think a little more critically about what it means to give hundreds of dollars to a transphobic organization for permission to do activism inside, what it means to speak in a space where others' voices are forbidden, what it's like to have a space that specifically excludes you. When people asked about the wristband-free spaces, we offered them scissors. You have that choice. Some people don't."

LEMMY AND OTHER PROBLEMS

Another MWMF policy forbids male voices on the land, meaning no one is allowed to slip a Michael Jackson tape into their boom box and start moonwalking. Perhaps it also means the porta potty men take a vow of silence when they roar through the gate, who knows. This rule has been broken, or bent, with the rise of drag kings—female performers who costume themselves as men, both lampooning and celebrating masculinity in a sort of burlesque, often via lip-synchs. When, some years back, the Florida drag king troupe House of Ma took a MWMF side stage during a talent show, the audience was given warning that a male voice would boom from the sound system shortly. Offended women hightailed it out of the vicinity, one step ahead of Neil Diamond. This, of course, is not an issue at Camp Trans, so the music is a little more varied—better—on this side of the road. The dance party under way on the patch of sandy brown earth designated as both "stage" and "dance floor" is shaking to Dr. Dre and Gossip, Motörhead and Peaches, Billy Idol, Northern

State, Ludacris, and FannyPack. I'm standing beside Benjamin, a genderqueer boy. His hair is an architecture of multiple pieces that look like feather dusters protruding from his scalp in feathery pom-poms. "Everyone is so beautiful," he muses at the crowd, and he is right. Mostly young, like late teens and twenties, they are kicking up Pig Pen–sized clouds of dust as they dance in their silver plastic pants and marabou-trimmed spandex, their starchy crinolines and pink ruffled tuxedo shirts, their neon-orange nighties, push-up bras, and outfits constructed from shredded trash bags and duct tape. Everyone is gleeful, happy to be smashing the gender binary, to be partying down for a cause, to be part of a revolution of good-looking gender-ambiguous people. In the process of deconstructing gender identity, I muse, sexual preference may become obsolete. Maybe I'm just trampy, but I'm attracted to pretty much everyone here.

Showtime starts with an introduction by an organizer named Jess who instructs the crowd—part Camp Transers, part festiegoers—on proper behavior while in such an unusual space, a space where trans people outnumber cis people. Because last year's visitors didn't understand how to act, this year we get a tiny schooling. Do not assume anyone's pronouns. There's really no way of guessing at who is a "he" and who is a "she," and besides all that, there are loads of genderqueer people promoting the use of a third pronoun, "ze." Others say to hell with pronouns altogether and dare us to be more creative in how we refer to them. Also, Jess instructs, do not ask anyone rude questions about their bodies. If you're bursting with curiosity or just freaking out, please see an armbanded advocate.

First there are skits, one of which demonstrates the

simple cruelty of turning trans women away from the festival gates. Another enacts the traumatizing experience of
having perfect strangers trot up to you and inquire about
the state of your genitals because you are transgender and
expected to answer this. Last-minute creations, the skits
are shaky but effective. The audience ripples out from
the spotlighted performance area, sitting in the dirt, getting hopped on by grasshoppers and crickets and weird
brown beetles with little wings folded beneath their shells.
A moth as big as a sparrow keeps charging into one of
the light dishes glowing up from the ground. A gang of
women come out, all dressed in trash bags and duct tape.
They are the Fat-Tastics, and they deliver a smart performance about fat power and fat oppression, ending in
an empowering cheer replete with pom-poms fashioned
from more shredded garbage bags. A duo of either trans
boys or genderqueers dressed like Gainsborough's Blue
Boy enact a randy ballet. Nomy Lamm, an artist who has
organized a petition for artists who oppose MWMF's
policy, howls heartbreaking songs into the warm night,
accompanied by a honking accordion. The camp feels like
some medieval village on a pagan holiday, bodies close in
the darkness, being serenaded by a girl in striped tights
and crinoline, harlequin eye makeup shooting stars down
her cheeks. Benjamin is a total trooper when the CD he's
lip-synching to keeps skipping and skipping and skipping.
Eventually Julia Serano reads. Julia is a trans woman and
spoken-word poet. She's got a girl-next-door thing going
on, with strawberry-blond hair and a sprinkling of freckles. She performs a piece about her relationship with her
girlfriend. It's got sweet and honest humor, and it charms
the crowd. Then she recites another, "Cocky":

and if i seem a bit cocky
well that's because i refuse
to make apologies for my body
anymore
i am through being the human sacrifice
offered up to appease other
people's gender issues
some women have a penis
some men don't
and the rest of the world
is just going to have to get the
fuck over it

Julia gets a standing ovation, everyone hopping up and brushing the dirt off their asses, brushing crickets from their chests, hooting and hollering at the poet as she leaves the "stage" and falls into a hug with her girlfriend and Sadie.

IN HER WORDS: JULIA SERANO

"As part of Camp Trans, so much of our work is dedicated to convincing the women who attend MWMF that trans women won't flaunt their penises on the land or that we won't commit acts of violence against other women. I have yet to meet a trans woman who has acted violently toward another woman and/or flaunted their penis in public, but I know I need to take the MWMF attendees' concerns seriously in order to gain their trust. At the same time, to borrow an analogy, it's like someone of Middle Eastern descent having to convince every person on a flight that s/he won't hijack the plane in order to be allowed on board.

"Having talked to several festivalgoers, I was distressed at how often people centered the debate around 'the penis.' Everyone talked about the significance of penises' being on the land, without much acknowledgment that these so-called penises are attached to women's bodies.

"Like most trans women, I have a lot of issues surrounding both my penis and the fact that I was born a boy. I have worked through too much self-loathing about these aspects of my person to allow other people to throw salt on my open wounds. It has taken me a long time to reach the point where I can accept my penis as simply being a part of my flesh and tissue, rather than the ultimate symbol of maleness. I find it confusing that so many self-described feminists spend so much effort propagating the male myth that men's power and domination arises from the phallus.

"It was surreal to have MWMF festivalgoers talk to me about their fear that transsexual women would bring masculine energy onto the land one minute, then the next tell me that they never would have guessed that I was born a man.

"I also found it distressing that so many women would want to exclude me (a woman) from women's space, under the pretense that my body contains potential triggers for abuse survivors. That line of reasoning trivializes the abuse that trans women face day in, day out. I have been verbally and physically assaulted by men for being who I am. Like other women, I have had men force themselves upon me. In addition, I can't think of a more humiliating way to be raped by male culture than to be forced to grow up as a boy against one's will. Every trans woman is a survivor, and we have triggers too. The phrase 'womyn-born-womyn' is one of my triggers."

DAY TWO

One thing I made damn sure to do before leaving civilization was to brew a two-liter container of coffee, and it is this I reach for when I wake up. My tent is already starting to bake as I scramble into some jeans, grab my toothbrush, and stumble out into the searing sunlight. I am the only camper—the only camper!—who did not camp in the shade behind the tree line. I set up in front of the trees—the scary trees that I imagined were dripping ticks, ticks poisoned with Lyme disease, the disgusting trees where many spiders live, the trees with their carpet of old leaves slowly rotting away, where mice no doubt burrow and any number of things that bite can be found. No, I arranged my borrowed tent right in the direct sun. Not so smart.

The smart campers are emerging from their shaded glens, getting right into their cars, and driving the fuck to the lake. There's a lake nearby and a creek too, and everyone I speak to confirms that going to the lake is definitely part of the "Camp Trans experience" I am hoping to document and they urge me to hop in for a swim. I am beyond tempted to ride along, to float in the lake in my underwear under the guise of journalism, but I am too scared of missing out on some crucial bit of drama. The vibe at Camp Trans is intense, flammable like the parched ground beneath our various feet. Something is bound to happen, and I can't be splashing around like a fool when it does.

I'm standing at the welcome tent when two MWMF workers show up. One is a femme girl with curly red hair, a cowboy hat, and glamorous sunglasses; the other is a butch girl in thick horn rims and a baseball hat. They carry a box of zines they've made, a compilation of the various opinions held by the women who work the festival across the road. The femme girl hands it off to the Camp Trans welcome worker. "It's our effort at having some dialogue," she says, or something like that. She seems a little shy, scared probably, and I have a few thoughts watching the welcome worker accept the gift, a caul of skepticism on her face. I think the festies are brave to come over with a box of MWMF opinions, I think the opinions are probably already well known to Camp Trans campers, I think shit is going to hit the fan and these workers and their good intentions are going to get creamed. The two festival workers walk off to the side, lean against a parked car, light cigarettes, and hang out. I stick a zine in my back pocket and head over to a tent for the morning meeting.

The morning meetings are a rundown of what's happening that day, a space for people to make announcements. A sort of exhilaration is blowing through the crowd as word of the zine, or the zine itself, hits them. People are hunched over, their faces stuck in the xeroxed pages, gasping. It doesn't look good. Simon Strikeback, a camp organizer and one of the activists who resuscitated Camp Trans after Nancy and company let it go, is facilitating the gathering. He says yes, there can be a circle to process the zine. He announces some other events—a workshop called "Feminism and the Gender Binary," which I plan to check out despite its terrifying title. A dreadlocked white girl with facial piercings announces that she has anarchist T-shirts for sale and is looking for partners to hitchhike to Mexico for an anti-globalization rally. Someone else holds up a silk screen emblazoned with a Camp Trans image designed by the cartoonist Ariel Schrag and asks for help screen printing T-shirts. I announce that I'm attending the festival as a member of the press. It's a good-faith thing I did at Sadie's request, so that everyone knows what's up and people who think it's terrible and exploitative that I am writing about their camp can glare at me from afar and not wind up in my story without their consent. I'm even wearing a dorky sticker that says PRESS in red Sharpie. I try to remedy suspicious looks by volunteering to help clean up breakfast over at the kitchen tent.

OVER AT THE KITCHEN TENT

There's not much to do until the water gets here. There are various pans covered with muck swiftly getting baked on by this relentless sun of ours. There is a giant bucket of beets that people are wondering what to do with. I move it into the shade, sure it'll keep a bit longer. In another bucket a whole bunch of beans soak, plumping up for tonight's chili dinner. I'm told to cull the rotten vegetables from the vegetable boxes, so I join the others inside the tent. There is an abundance of vegetables, mostly donated from a co-op several states away: cardboard boxes of squash, zucchini, bulbs of garlic. I deal with a plastic bag filled with liquefying basil, pulling the top leaves, still green, from the blackening herb below. The stuff that's no good—the dried-up rosemary and yellowed cilantro, the split tomatoes and the peppers sprouting cottony tufts of mold—all get tossed into the compost. A woman is picking beets as large as a child's head and slicing off their wilting greens with a knife. When she discovers a mouse inside the beet box, she shrieks. "Oh, that's no good," says the person culling squash beside me. "You can get really sick. I ate food contaminated with mouse shit once, and I got really, really sick." We try to scare the mouse away, but it just burrows deeper into the beets. I leave the tent, walk behind it, and pull the beet box out backward, into the grass. The mouse leaps out and scrambles into the forest. We look for visible mouse turd, but everything is sort of brown and crumbly from the dirty beets. I decide not to eat a bite of the Camp Trans food while I'm there. I'm too worried about getting a tick in my armpit to take on the additional neurosis of hantavirus. I've got six energy bars stuffed in my suitcase, two packs of tuna, and a few cans of chili. That's what I'll be eating.

Deciding that I saved the day by ridding us of the mouse, I retire from my cleanup duties. It's too hot; I need some tuna or I'll get heatstroke. I stop by Chris's stoner van to glob a bit of cool, refrigerated mustard into my tuna and listen to his instructions that I gulp down at least fifteen gulps of water each time I hit my bottle. That's the number: fifteen. "Till your stomach's all bloated," he advises. I do as he says. His little dog Poi, who looks just like Benji, has burrowed a cool hole beneath the van and lies there, panting.

BULLSHIT

I am very glad I didn't go to the lake. Now we sit in a ring, in a small, shaded clearing not far from where I've camped, a bunch of Camp Trans campers and the two festival workers who delivered the box of zines. The zine is called *Manual Transmission*, and people hate it. It's an anthology, essentially, of festival workers' opinions on the trans-inclusion issue. There is talk about throwing the box of them onto that evening's campfire, a good old-fashioned book burning. Ana Jae is set to facilitate the discussion, and Benjamin is by her side, "taking stack," which I think means keeping a list of everyone who raises a hand to speak so that everyone gets a chance to.

Excerpts from *Manual Transmission*:

Let's be clear about what womyn born womyn means. It's not about defining a goddamn thing. It is about saying this is what I'm gathering around for this particular moment. It is saying that this festival, this period in time, is for women whose entire life experience has been as a girl and who still live loudly as a woman. Period. How is that defining you? Why do you think we are so ignorant as to not "get" that, to not figure out that we also have privilege for not struggling with a brain/body disconnect? But can you be so obstinate, can you be so determined to not understand that we have an experience that is outside yours? And that that experience, even though we have greater numbers, still entitles us to take separate space?

Dicks are not useless signifiers. Even unwanted ones. You who I love and call my community of political bandits, you who grew up being seen as, treated as, regarded as boys (and perhaps miserably failing that performance) you did not grow as I. You did not experience being held out as girl and cropped into that particular box. You gotta understand, you are my sister, but you don't have that experience. And taking my experience and saying it is yours don't make it yours, [it] makes it stolen.

"This is bullshit, in my opinion," Ana Jae states. The over-all feeling about the zine and its arrival is, first, "We know this already," and second, "How dare you bring it into this space that we are trying to keep free from such hurtful sen-timents?" People take turns expressing themselves.

HITCHHIKING ANARCHIST GIRL: takes issue with a passage defending MWMF's $350 entrance fee, calling it classist.

SIMON: is frustrated, only open to discussing chang-ing the policy, sick to death of back-and-forth arguing about penises and girlhoods.

GUY TO MY LEFT: generously concedes that the fes-tie workers had good intentions but delivered a flawed product.

FESTIE WORKERS: admit they were rushed and that, though they specified no submissions degrading or attacking trans people would be published, they did not get to read all of the writings. They feel bad for the discord their zine has caused but maintain that these are the opinions of workers inside the festival, like it or not: they didn't feel it was proper to censor anyone's thoughts—who can dictate what is right and what is wrong?

SADIE: maintains that, as an activist, it's her job to declare her views the good and right and true views; she is only interested in talking to people who agree and want to help further the cause.

FESTIE WORKERS: weakly remind everyone of their good intentions.

GIRL TO MY RIGHT, IN A WHEELCHAIR: offers that she is hurt every day by people with good intentions.

FEMME FESTIE WORKER: cries; doesn't know how to help this situation.

GIRL I CAN'T SEE: says that it's everyone's responsibility to educate themselves on trans issues.

GIRL WITH CAMOUFLAGE BANDANNA: sympathizes with how painful the education process can be; urges please don't let that stop you from learning.

There's a lot of fear here, people afraid of each other, afraid of their own ability to do the wrong thing from simple ignorance, their own ability to bungle a peace offering, to offend the person they sought to help. It starts to rain. Light at first, and then heavy. The weather out here can turn violent in a finger snap, the dust suddenly flooding into muddy ponds, the sky cracking thunderbolts and sending threads of lightning scurrying across the cloud cover, occasionally touching down and setting a tree on fire. I run back to my tent and fling the rain cover over it, and by the time I get back to the circle it's over—the process, the rain, all of it. I talk briefly with a girl I know from my previous Augusts at the festival where she's usually been a worker. Last year she caught a lot of shit for taking a festival van over to Camp Trans for a date, so this year she's camping here, back in the trees where everyone seems to have gone. I go back to my tent to grab a notebook. Inside it is hot and smells strongly of sulfur, like hell itself. I take my notebook back to the now-empty clearing, sit in someone's abandoned camp chair, and write some notes.

HERE'S GEYL, THEN PAM

Geyl Forcewind is a lanky punk rock trans woman with a red anarchy sign sewed onto her ratty T-shirt. A good radiance sort of shines off of Geyl. Her combat boots are patched with gummy straps of duct tape; she spits a lot and cracks jokes. She collapses into the chair next to me and asks how my "project" is going. She's teasing me, I think, but her timing is perfect because I wanted to talk to someone about the proliferation of trans men and the small numbers of trans women or genderqueer people who enjoy the trappings of femininity. I love girls, I love girl-ness, and though I love trans men—my boyfriend is trans—I wish there were more females around these genderqueer parts. The face of the trans revolution is, presently, a bearded one. "Riot grrrl made being a dyke accessible," Geyl reflects, "and now those people are seeing that they can be gender-queer and it's not so scary. There's none of that for MTFs." Pam, a trans woman who had been quietly strumming her acoustic guitar in the woods behind us, strolls up and joins our conversation.

PAM: Trans women get abused a lot more in our society.

She's right, of course. Because it's often harder for them to pass as women in the world, and because they're likely to get way more shit for it, lots of would-be trans women just don't come out.

GEYL: Being a girl is not as cool. I actively try to recruit.

PAM: Yeah, there must be something wrong with you if you want to be a woman.

GEYL: I tried to be really butch when I first came out.

MICHELLE: I tried to be really butch when I first came out, too. It seemed cooler and tougher, and safer, to be masculine.

Pam looks like just the sort of woman the music festival across the way embraces—smudgy eyeliner, long brown hair, rolled bandana tied around her forehead and that acoustic guitar in tow. She's even a construction worker, and isn't that one of the most feminist jobs a woman can work? After Pam came out as a trans woman, her coworker threatened to toss her from the very high building they were working on. When she complained, her foreman said, "You should expect that sort of thing." She was soon fired from the job, for "being late."

PAM: If I watch *Jerry Springer*, I don't want to come out.

GEYL: All the trans women on that show aren't really trans. They're a joke.

PAM: I think Jerry is a tranny chaser. And I think he's resentful of it and wants to take it out on the community.

Soon we're informed that we're sitting smack in the middle of the space reserved for the "Feminism and the Gender Binary" workshop.

GEYL: I'll feminize your gender binary. If anyone quotes Judith Butler, I'll punch them.

THE RALLY

There's that girl Mountain again, on the mic this time, letting everyone know that if her feminist separatist farming commune can let trans women in, anyone can. "I always have said that if I didn't go to the festival each year I'd die," she tells the crowd. "Well I didn't go, and I didn't die, and I'm not going until they change the policy!" Everyone cheers. Sadie's on the mic, revving everyone up by insisting that we're going to change the policy. I guess it's impossible to engage in any sort of activism with a fatalistic view, and who knows, maybe MWMF will surprise us all and roll out the trans carpet, but I just don't see it happening. I remember glimpsing Lisa Vogel in the festival worker area years ago, after Camp Trans had brought a protest onto the land. They'd been kicked off, of course, and a reiteration of the womyn-born-womyn policy was swiftly typed up, xeroxed, and distributed throughout the festival. Lisa was smoking, and she looked pissed. Someone told me that she saw it as a class and age issue. Camp Trans was made up of a bunch of teenagers freshly released from liberal New England colleges, with their heads full of gender theory and their blood bubbling with hormones and rebellion. Lisa Vogel is loved by the women who attend her festival the way that saints are loved, and why shouldn't she be? She's provided them with the only truly safe space they've ever known. She's a working-class lesbian who built it all up from scratch, with her hands and the hands of old-school dykes and feminists, women who claim, perhaps rightly, that no one knows what it was like, what they went through, how hard they fought. It has taken a lot of work to create the MWMF that's rocking across the way, sending its disembodied female voices floating into our campsite. It's taken single-mindedness and determination. Lisa Vogel, I fear, is one severely stubborn woman.

Emily is speaking and she's saying things that could turn around some of the more stubborn festival women. Unfortunately, I don't think anyone has come over from the fest who wouldn't love to see the policy junked. Emily is preaching, as they say, to the choir. She's talking about her girlhood, how the girls all knew she was a girl like they were, and how powerful and lifesaving it was to be recognized like that, your insides finally showing through. A young friend wished Emily would get a sex-change operation so she could come to her slumber party. It's a great response to the festival's insistence that trans women didn't have girlhoods. Anna speaks next. (Not Ana Jae—this is a brand-new Anna you haven't met yet.) She's got big, dark eyebrows and wide lips painted red; she's holding the mic, and she's come to lecture the lesbians for dating trans men but justifying this shades-of-hetero behavior by saying, "He's not really a guy." Sacrificing trans men's maleness so that their lesbian identities can stay intact, sheepishly explaining, "He's trans"— again invalidating real masculinity so as not to be confused with a straight girl. For fetishizing, as a community, this sexy new explosion of trans men, but remaining unwelcoming to trans women. It's all so true my frickin' eyes well up. I'd spent the first year and a half of my boyfriend's transition explaining to everyone—women on the bus, strangers in line at Safeway, people I sit next to on planes—that my boyfriend, he's transgender. So don't go thinking I'm some stupid straight girl, the confession implies. I'm QUEER. OKAY? It tended to be more information than anyone wanted. It's all so fucked up and heartbreaking and overwhelming. Or maybe I'm just really sleep-deprived from a night on bumpy ground, sleeping atop sticks and hard mounds of dirt. Before me are the Gainsborough Blue Boys, lying side by side on separate chaise lounges, now in wiggy tennis outfits. They clutch paper bags concealing what I assume are beers and make out. Seriously—who are they? I love them. I wipe my soggy eyes, grab Anna as she shuffles past with her boyfriend, and thank her for her speech. I confess my past as an ashamed FTM-dating lesbian; I heap upon her how sad and scared I get when my dyke friends start talking shit about trans women. I want Anna—beautiful, strong Anna with the microphone—to absolve me and also solve all my social problems. She seems so capable. I think I overwhelm her. She gives me her contact information, including her phone number and email address. "She loves being interviewed; it's her favorite thing," her boyfriend encourages. Of course she does, she's a genius. She walks away into the darkness, her beaded, sequined shoulder bag glinting in the night.

I HAD THE TIME OF MY LIFE

Two people—girls, trans guys, genderqueers, I can't really tell in the light, so bright it turns them into silhouettes—are whirling across the dusty makeshift dance floor, doing a dance routine to a medley of songs from the movie *Dirty Dancing*. Here is my proof that this gender-smashing revolution is a generational thing: someone walks across the stage holding a cardboard sign reading NOBODY PUTS BABY IN A CORNER and everyone roars. I have no fucking idea what they are talking about. Patrick Swayze? Come on. But I like watching these two spinning into each other, knocking each other down, and crawling all over each other. At the very end of their act, after dancing close, they pull apart and draw the audience in, and everyone responds; they move into the brightness, becoming silhouettes that dance and raise their hands into the light and it's beautiful like a dark kaleidoscope, all the bodies coming together under the light. My eyes well up with tears again, Jesus. Chris asks me to dance, but I can't. I'm a mess. It's been such an emotional day, and I'm spent. A trans man is giving a lap dance to a girl in a bright green dress, straddling her lap as she sits on a folding chair. Two others are making out on the dance floor, and many booties are being freaked. It's time for bed. I hike back to my tent, following the small spot of light my flashlight tosses into the weeds.

DAY THREE

"I asked you to dance and you disappeared," Chris complains. We're on his patio. He's making real hot coffee on his camp stove, but I had to swear I would tell no one about this luxury because he's almost out of gas. He starts talking about how confused he was about Camp Trans, how he thought it was a bunch of trans men trying to get into the women's festival, and he wasn't down with that. "You gain a few privileges, you lose a few," he laughs. "Go cry on your own damn shoulder; get over yourself." Once he realized it was about getting trans women some women-only privileges, he was down for the cause. He's glad he's here. "I'm so comfortable," he says. "My tree keeps getting closer." He means the tree he pees on. Maybe he also saw *Sleep-*

away Camp II and is scared of the portas, maybe he's lazy, or maybe it's just such a rarity to be a trans person who can take a piss in the woods without fear.

It's the last day of Camp Trans and things are unraveling before my eyes. Cars and trucks are rolling out of the parking lot, which is just a different part of the field we've all been living in. People wave out of their windows as they pull onto the road. All day long the population shrinks. The planning meeting for Camp Trans 2004 is repeatedly interrupted as vacating campers lavish goodbye hugs on their friends. I am sitting back and listening to participants who raise their hands and offer compliments on what they felt went well at this year's gathering, and what needs to be fine-tuned for next year. Everyone is generally pleased, and the renewed focus on trans women's needs and overturning the policy was a success. There are concerns about how white Camp Trans is, but no one is naive about seeking out token people of color. Geyl suggests travel scholarships for trans people who want to come but can't afford the time off work or the travel expenses to the Middle of Nowhere, Michigan. People are happy about trans women being in charge, are happy that there was essentially no rain in a region known for violent summer thunderstorms, and want greater accountability from women who say they are organizing within the MWMF gates. There will be greater fundraising this coming year, though Camp Trans did come out ahead by $500. Incredible, really, since at the start of the week Ziplock baggies had been duct-taped inside the portas asking for spare change each time you took a whiz. It cost the camp eighty dollars each time those monsters got cleaned.

Everyone is called to help dismantle what's still standing

of Camp Trans. Intimidated by the architecture of the tents and lean-tos that need to be torn down, I busy myself gently untying the neon plastic ribbons that have been knotted, for some reason, around a rusting cage which, for some reason, contains a stunted apple tree. Perhaps there's a hornets' nest in the crook of its branches. A large swath of our field has been roped off all week with that same neon plastic, to keep everyone away from a burrowing hornet encampment. That's being torn down now as well.

Over by the portas is a structure made of tarps that all weekend I'd thought was someone's wicked punk rock campsite. Tarps spray-painted with anti-policy slogans, tied and duct-taped to stakes driven into the ground. I'd had a brief fantasy that it was Geyl's squat-like queendom. But as I pass it, Chris sticks his head out from the plastic, and asks, "Did you know there was a shower here?!" He is delighted. The shower is a little pump with a thin hose attached; it looks like the pesticide tank an exterminator lugs around. You pump the top like a keg, click a switch at the end of the hose, and a fine stream of water mists all around you. It looks like a feeble shower, but a great way to cool off. Later I'll help Geyl and a person named Cassidy tear the whole thing down, and have great fun squirting myself with all the leftover water in the little tank.

THE FINAL CAMPFIRE

Later that night the final campfire roars, with Cassidy—somehow an expert on the various ways wood can grow—strategically loading branches into the flames. Chris is burning marshmallows on a long stick, Simon is shaving pieces of potato and garlic into an aluminum foil pouch to be roasted. Someone passes around cold pizza, someone else passes around a bottle of Boone's Farm. It's the first time alcohol has been visible all week, though many revelers have been visibly under its influence. Another of the national forest laws.

I don't want to leave the circle, 'cause I know this is it. In the morning I will ride into Grand Rapids with a girl named Katina, a festiegoer who has spent basically all of her time over at Camp Trans, much to the dismay of the girls she's camping with. "You know how every time you leave Michigan, you think, I'm coming back next year?" she asks. "Well this year it wasn't like that. I know I can't come back next year."

We don't know it at the time, but the Michigan Womyn's Music Festival is doomed. Over the coming decade the trans rights movement will grow, and the amount of male-assigned individuals who begin to publicly identify somewhere on the trans feminine spectrum will increase. The exclusion of trans women from the festival will become more and more absurd and upsetting, with headliner acts such as the Indigo Girls withdrawing their support from the festival. It could, I believe, be perceived as a victory, but the institution's decision to implode rather than shift with its culture feels like one last kick in the jaw before expiring. The Michigan Womyn's Music Festival *was* magic, there could be no denying it from anyone allowed to romp within its hallowed forests. That it committed suicide rather than sharing its magic with some of the most deserving of safety within our culture is bitterly spiteful. One can only muster a *good riddance*, I suppose, and hope that as the TERFs (trans-exclusionary "radical" feminists—quotes mine) age and die off so will their fearful, reactionary points of view. But the earth, goddess willing, will be slower to go, and so the land—the open, accepting, magical land—remains, awaiting whomever might have the gumption to create an ambitious, enchanting, and truly inclusionary festival for all of us who need it.

A version of this piece was published in the *Believer* in 2003.

HOW TO NOT BE A
QUEER DOUCHEBAG

Dear People,

Hi, you are all so cute. I just added that part after being
here for a few minutes and seeing everyone's excellent hairdos and raggedy fashions. Good job being adorable. I am
here to give you advice you have not asked for. Because I
am forty years old and you are not.

This probably sounds repugnant to some of you, insult-
ingly ageist to both you and me. It is true that most younger
people have their shit stunningly more together than me
at whatever age, in fact, let's prove this. How old are you?
(Explain what you were doing at that exact age.) Okay. So,
we know now that you are very ahead of the game. It is
worth noting that I am a sober alcoholic. That means I'm,
you know, an alcoholic—just out of curiosity, has anyone
read any of my books? Okay, then you may have an idea
of what I am talking about. I began drinking in earnest
when I was fifteen years old, and I stopped when I was
thirty-two. There is this idea that alcoholics stop emotionally maturing at the age you start drinking, and then you
pick back up again when you quit. This makes me emotionally twenty-three years old, which feels correct. There
are a *lot* of people in their thirties and forties who are about

twenty-three years old emotionally. That is why I just cut to the chase and date twenty-three year olds. Kidding! I really don't do that anymore.

Anyway, I think it is clear that none of you needs anyone to tell you how to live your life and, *in fact*, we of the older generations could greatly benefit from you telling us what to do, so if anyone would like to tell me how to live my life at the close of this "speech," I am totally into it. For real. Meanwhile, I am here, and I enjoy telling people what to do, so here we go.

Stop policing each other like little queer police officers. I have never seen a quadrant of people so ready to tear each other's faces off as queers. I'm going to actually narrow my focus here and say queers who were assigned female at birth. Are we all on the same page here? Okay, good. Listen, we're sensitive! I understand, I am SO sensitive I have to take a fantastic SSRI called Celexa to keep me from bursting into tears *all the time*. I'm not kidding. And I'm not ashamed. There is no shame in any of my games. If you also have a hard time not bursting into tears all the time, I heartily recommend it. Do not be afraid or embarrassed to do whatever you have to do to take care of yourself. But back to this policing thing, we're all so sensitive, right? And we have been our whole lives and, let's face it, no one cared. If you grew up in my family—and you didn't, none of you—but if you had grown up in my family and you burst into tears all the time, people mocked you, threatened to give you something to cry about, and called you "Chelsea Waterworks." I'm from Chelsea, but you can substitute your own crappy hometown. If you grew up in New England, it's especially brutal because everyone is hard as nails and they want to throw rocks at whatever exhibits weakness. So, what do you do? You go to a super-gay liberal college where you can major in sensitivity and then move someplace like Portland or San Francisco where you can make a career out of all your unhealed triggers. That's what happens! And listen, I get that being *called on your shit* is a special and important part of becoming a good, healthy, socially conscious person. We're all good-hearted people, right, but we grow up with these huge blind spots because we were raised entirely among white people or rich people or rich white people or we've never heard of transgender people before even though we are about to realize that we, in fact, are transgender by the end of this conference.

It's important to point out to people when they are fucking up. What I ask is, can we not *enjoy* it so much? I think we've all had the experience of telling someone that what they said or did is wicked sexist/racist/ageist/biphobic/what have you. And it can feel really *good* because, if you're like me, you probably feel like your head is up your ass all the time, and it can feel so awesome to be like, "YES! I KNOW that is fucked up! Hey you, don't say that! Now I am the HERO! I am the CHAMPION of knowing how to BE in the world!" But you know, you're going to fuck up too, I'm going to fuck up. I think it's really important to be humble and forgiving, and not, like, totally get off on shaming a person for not knowing everything yet. Because I am an alcoholic and I hang out in a lot of sort of self-helpy environments where people love to create acronyms, I will share with you that SHAME means Should Have Already Mastered Everything. Get it? Amazing. Let's be gentle with each other. Let's try not to be defensive when someone steps up and schools us. Let's listen to the schooler, and, Ms. Know-It-All Schooly Pants, let's be compassionate toward the more ass-headed among us. I guarantee that in your long career as a queer you will have many occasions to be on both sides of this dynamic. Let's make it as pleasant and helpful as possible, shall we?

Don't fall in love with a person you have never met but only know from the internet. You guys, this happened to me! I was so embarrassed, but then I learned that it has happened to others too, so now I'm all empowered and speaking out. I don't mean, don't meet someone on the internet, go have coffee with them, and *then* fall in love. That's great. I mean, don't meet someone on the internet, never have coffee with them because in fact they live across the country in their mother's sewing room because they are recently out of rehab and taking opiate blockers so that in case they relapse on heroin for the sixteenth time they don't get high from it, and their license got revoked for driving the getaway car for some drug addicts who were holding up a liquor store with dirty needles, and oh, they are also on probation and can't leave the state of Massachusetts— and *then* fall in love. I know there are some of you in this audience right now thinking, *Oh my god that sounds like my dream girlfriend*. Am I right? Holler if you hear me. You are sick people. Why do queers like gigantic disasters so much? I blame seeing the fine film *Times Square* when I was twelve years old.

Here are some people whose problems I have romanticized and involved myself in: girls who like to bang their heads on walls, depressed people not on medication, people who like to pop Xanax for their anxiety—a.k.a. pillheads who think they are being healthy—surly genderqueers unable to find employment, suicidal trans men, handsome rascals with borderline personality disorders, unfaithful potheads, cranky people who are annoyed all the time and talk to you (me) like you're stupid, anxious people who get angry, angry people who get anxious, radical activist socio-paths (they make *great* activists because they don't care about hurting people), and *more!* In every instance, I sort of hugged these problems to my scant bosom, thinking: The poor things! They have had such a hard time! Because they are queer/genderqueer/female/not really female/too smart for this world/too sensitive for this world/need therapy so bad but will never, ever go because why should they when I am here to deal with their bullshit all day long? Some of these people were sweet messes and some were actually sort of abusive. I see people (mostly but not entirely femmes) stay in relationships like this because they don't want to be a bad ally. They don't want to betray someone, not stick around for the hard stuff. They know how hard it is to be queer, and they want to be loving and supportive.

Right. Listen, love makes everyone go against their own best interests and I know we all have our own process with this stuff, but next time you find yourself having a moment with some hot, troubled individual who is being a total asshole and then giving you some sort of sob story about why you don't understand what's going on for them, remember this moment. Wonder, *Is this what Michelle was talking about?* Yes, it is. And you, hot, troubled individual, next time you are trying to make your date pay for all the genuinely horrible and inexcusably fucked-up things you have survived, may you experience a moment of clarity in the midst of it and think: *Oh my god I really have to go to therapy.* May you both go to therapy. May you both go to therapy *and* Al-Anon, a lovely place people go to learn how to be in healthy relationships, to not be doormats or tyrants. May you break up with one another. Not because you don't deserve love, of course you do! But because there are times in our insane queer lives when it is better for us to be alone with ourselves, figuring out our own shit, not putting another person through it or allowing ourselves to be dragged around, boundary-less, crying all the time. Just break up. Awesome things happen because of breakups. Here are some things that I have done specifically because a breakup gave me the time, energy, space, and/or money to do it: I went to Paris, started smoking, quit smoking, bought a really expensive purse, started a writing retreat, had affairs with Parisians, went to Paris Fashion Week. Basically, the best thing you can do for yourself when you're going through a breakup is go to Paris. Do it. The queers in Paris are so into you, I promise. Go and have sex with them, they are all very promiscuous. French people are like, "Sex? Pfffff." That's what they do when something is like not a big deal. *Pfffff.* It's like *whatever*, but more sophisticated. So, okay, the point of this tangent is, stay away from painfully dramatic relationships, and if it's too late and you're already in one, break up and go to France. And if you are the painfully dramatic person, go to therapy and start getting better. You don't need to be in so much pain all the time.

You are not the only person in the world having sex. Dudes. I know, it's exciting—sex is pretty much my favorite thing in the whole world. I am with you. But there is this phenomenon in the queer world, I think maybe because being sex positive has been so important to us, right, because people try to oppress our sexuality and they pretty much force us to rebel and shove it in their face which is *fun*, I get it, but sometimes it seems like queers think no one else is having sex and guess what? They are. Totally normal-seeming squares are getting it on. Sometimes very perversely. My first real boyfriend, who I dated when I was eighteen, before I even knew I was queer, he liked to be fisted in the butt. Can you believe it? I mean, I wasn't queer yet so I didn't know about such practices and I was *freaked out*. But I did my best to accommodate, because that's what friends do. Friends who are having sex with each other. Of course, it's worth noting that you don't have to do anything you don't want to do, sexually speaking, ever. But it's nice to be open minded and to not have, as they say in some of my self-helpy groups, contempt prior to investigation. That means hating on something before you've ever tried it. To be real, I was horrified at the thought of sticking my hand up my boyfriend's butt. He was horrified at spanking my ass. But that's what we both wanted—we were both freaky perverts but in totally mismatched ways! So tragic! Perhaps some of you are in this situation right now. What's great about life is that you can absolutely find someone who is into the same twisted fun time you are into. You don't have to put up with someone sort of mopily fisting your butt like I did to my first boyfriend. I hope that he has found happiness and is right now with a girl who wants nothing more than a bend-over boyfriend, just as I have found a darling individual who is *so* nice but still wants to slap me around. Awesome!

Like Madonna said, "Don't go for second best, baby," stick it out for someone you're compatible with. Because check it: Eventually your relationship will come upon hard times, eventually the love chemicals that are flooding your system and causing you to be totally obsessed with this person, they will fade. This person will start to annoy you *just a little*. Every now and then. But if you have rad earth-shattering mind-blowing consciousness-expanding sex, you will be able to stick out these gloomier moments. But what I really meant to say is being all sex radical, in your face all day every day, frankly, it gets tedious. Just know that really, everyone is having sex. And if you are an artist or a writer, a performer, please, let us know all about your sex life, but also understand that sex alone does not hold up a story. Sex work alone does not hold up a story. Since the winning of the lesbian sex wars in the late eighties and the cresting of feminism's fishnet-clad third wave, there has been a *lot* of art and writing about how radically sexy and strippery and hookery everyone is, and I think we've hit critical mass. Give us that, but give us *more* than that. Give us your goofiness and your dark depths and your weird family and when you stay up eating cheese on the couch watching bad TV and crying, give us when you feel stupid and the big angry fight you had, give us *everything*, and then you can give us all your bathroom interludes and the weird tricks you turned and the dance party that turned into an orgy and how cool you are. You *are* cool! You really are. I am just speaking from the position of a jaded forty-year-old who has seen too much burlesque. My apologies.

Polyamory is not better than monogamy. There, I said it! No doubt many of you in the audience are relieved. Guess what, a lot of people don't like for the person they're in love with to be screwing eight other people and that's okay. It's also okay if you need to screw eight other people, that's awesome, I want everyone to screw as many people as they need to screw! But this thing happens in queer scenes where it's like the most unconventional way becomes the *only* way and frankly it's just as rigid, punishing, and unrealistic as enforced heteronormativity—which, really, some people are just into. It's just their way. They're super into being heteronormative. You'll never be able to change them, you'll only succeed in making them feel bad about themselves, which is sort of sad because they're just trying to, you know, live and whatnot, be happy. Some people are totally wired to be polyamorous and some other people will always want to die in the midst of such arrangements. They are not less evolved or intelligent or *fun*, they are just *different*. Let's not pathologize each other's differences. This tendency to want to champion the most radical way while tearing down or deriding the many other ways is *such* a bummer. It makes people feel stupid and insecure, which is so weird, right, because as queers and people who are sort of activist minded, aren't we wanting a world where people can be happy and safe and healthy and feel confident and whole in their lives? The amazingly smart writer and poet Julia Serano talks about this in her book *Whipping Girl*, which you should all read. She talks mainly about how binary trans people like herself get all this shit from gender-radical queers because they are, you know, not visibly subverting the gender binary. It makes me think about living in your body, having an embodied experience of yourself, versus living in your mind, having this primarily intellectual design on life. Not that you can't do both, hopefully we're all thinking and feeling, but it does seem obvious that even if we all want to break up the gender binary, and I hope we all do, not everyone is able to become a third gender to make this happen. It's so interesting: I have a lot of trans friends who have been sort of called out for being *men* and *women*. You know? For being *feminine* or *masculine*. And yet I get to be a totally feminine woman, and no one really cares because I'm cisgender. It's like there's this pressure for trans people to be visibly trans all the time, but that is just not going to be everyone's bag. So yeah, I highly recommend, you know, trying polyamory, but just know that if you sort of hate it and it makes your life miserable it's not because you're less evolved, you're just differently wired, so go find another monogamous person and settle down and have cats together.

Femininity is not an aberration and masculinity is not the norm. I can't *believe* this still happens but it really does. In the fight to destroy sexism, we turn on femininity. It seems like there is this subconscious belief that left to our own devices, without television or the gender binary or Barbie or patriarchy, all female humans would be sort of androgynous or masculine. A belief that anyone engaging the trappings of femininity and enjoying them—I'm talking about feminine dress for sure, and makeup and heels, and I'm also talking about the way little girls play, like, with dolls and shit—is under the sway of false consciousness. No one checks in with boys to make sure they *really* want to be wearing corduroys and throwing a ball around, or if they've been brainwashed by our culture to think they *have* to climb a tree when maybe they would like to be having a very fussy tea party. I hate that masculinity is seen as the norm and femininity, even and especially high femininity, is seen as this deviation, a sinister imposition on girls who *really* want to be wearing sweats but just don't *know* themselves, poor brainwashed dears. This is *so* annoying. My fight is to get *everyone* in tutus, metaphorically speaking. Let's be aware of the tendency to want to just get rid of what stresses us out. Femininity stresses a lot of people out, so there is a real movement in queer and feminist culture to undermine it, rather than see it as the rich, creative, fun, *deep* expression of gender that it is.

Oh yeah, while I am on this particular tangent I will mention that when I was dealing with a lot of class issues—dealing with being poor, having grown up in such a way, seeing my struggling family, aligning myself with all impoverished people everywhere—money stressed me out so I wanted to get rid of money. I mean, ideally this actually would be really awesome. But I'm really into keeping things real, and really right now, for the moment, we are all deeply entrenched in a money system that isn't going anywhere for a while, and to be against money as a way of being for poor people and for myself? Well, it pretty much guarantees that you're going to stay stuck in your struggle, that all impoverished people stay trapped in poverty. Is this radical? It's a scarcity model. If anyone is poor then everyone must be poor! How about, if anyone is rich then everyone must be rich! From where I stand, it looks just as challenging to make all rich people poor as it does to make all poor people rich—both are pretty impossible. But as an ideal, a rallying cry, as state of mind: Gender for everyone! Riches for everyone! The sexual relationship of your dreams for everyone! I really just want us all to be happy, and I want us to all help each other to get there.

Don't be an alcoholic. Okay, if you are, you probably can't help it. I mean, I couldn't help it. Enjoy it while it lasts. It *is* fun for a while. But really, there is no douchebag like a drunken douchebag. Here are some suggestions: if people have implied that you're too drunk all the time, if people have broken up with you because of it, if you've smashed a front tooth or gotten arrested or fired from your job, if you fucked up something you *really* wanted because you were wasted, you indeed might be an alcoholic. Don't wait for your drinking to go back to when it was fun because it won't. Deal with it.

Don't doubt that people are where they say they are. Like if someone says they aren't gay, maybe they aren't. If someone doesn't want to transition, maybe that's real for them. If someone is telling you they are actually a man, they probably are. If someone is claiming to be bisexual, it is entirely possible they are not a timid and self-loathing homosexual, they're actually bi. I just stayed in this house where three girls live. Two are butch girls with girlfriends who are super into being hot lesbians. They are really hot lesbians. The third I guess used to date girls for a minute, but now she's just into hooking up with hot male hooligans. The lesbians would not get off her ass. They wouldn't stop trying to get her to date a girl. It was so weird! I was like, this person is more into guys than most gay men I know. Who cares? Let her hit it with her dream hooligan. I think it's because her gender is sort of butch, she's sort of a boy, so then the lesbians think she ought to be a lesbian. Which is so weird and problematic, right? If masculine girls are inherently lesbians then are feminine queer girls really straight? I know so many femme queers whose lesbian-ism gets challenged by more masculine queers, like, it's so dumb. And listen, this boyish girl, the roommate, she has to put on this dumb girlish costume, like she puts her hair in a ponytail and wears a little sparkling necklace because she's afraid hooligans won't like her regular gender. Oh my god, I just feel like the world is so fucked up right now! No wonder we're all fighting with each other, it's all so stressful! But it's sort of fun too, isn't it? I mean, I love that this girl who totally reads butch is out there cruising these beefy dudes. And I talked to her and she sort of loves having to put on the hoop earrings, she's sort of into the whole process. She's experimenting with her gender, which we queers are really comfortable supporting when it's a girl playing with being masculine but not when one of our boys starts getting all girly. Maybe it's dumb for me to want queers to be less rigid and less controlling and policing than the rest of the world. My point is that we *are* the rest of the world, we're not so different, so let's lighten up, but I also believe, really believe, that we're special. We occupy a special place in our cultures, we always have and we still do. I think we have a greater opportunity to transcend bullshit and be generous people, I think we have a greater awareness and that this can bring about transformation on all levels of our lives and culture. I want us to begin by being nicer to one another.

Now, if I may talk about my dating life. There are trans men who maintain there is no difference between themselves and cisgender men, and there really isn't. I mean, really, there isn't, and it's important to know that—but then, for me, someone who is dating and sleeping with both cis and trans men, I have to be honest with myself and *yes* there is a difference. It's subtle and sometimes there often isn't any difference and then *poof*, there it is, that something. Don't ask me to explain it. I'm practically terrified to look at it, there is so much sensitivity and I'm sure about fifteen people are hating me right now. It could be just sexual, in that trans men are more likely to have queer sex, by which I mean good sex, whereas cisgender guys tend to be duds. Sorry but it's *true*! Queer sex tends to last at least one full hour longer than straight sex, if not more. I tend to have more orgasms in queer sex as opposed to straight sex—where it is always possible that I will have no orgasms if I don't see to myself because, guess what, it's true some cis guys don't seem to know that I have a clitoris! I am so sorry for sounding like *Cosmopolitan* right now, but I was shocked to learn all the complaints straight women have had about men forever are *true*. They really *do* want to fuck without condoms! It really *is* all about their penises! They really *do* come really fast and then guess what—you're done! *Boring!* The best sex I had with straight guys was this boy who hangs out with no one but lesbians and was on too much cocaine so his dick was useless and he just pulled my hair all night; and then this other dork who didn't have a condom *plus* was drunk and thus uninhibited and wanted to get spanked. Cool! But then the next time we did it, he had a condom and it was really dull. I wonder, do straight girls ever get fucked by their manfriend's hands? I mean, I just think that is the funnest, best sex ever, and I truly feel anxious on behalf of my hetero sisters that they are not getting the most out of their vaginas. Straight sisters, have your boyfriend use his hand! Straight dudes, fuck your girlfriend with your hands, okay? It's so awesome! Another thing I don't like about sex with cis guys is how they act like my body is this fragile female thing and they're all gentle with it. I think being with trans guys, there is an understanding of what my body is, what it can handle and take, what it wants to take. There is more understanding of all the possible ways to have sex and I'm not treated like, you know, Sleeping Beauty or something, unless we're having a Sleeping Beauty role-play, which sounds awesome. For me, sex is very athletic and I like to see how far things can go, and so to be treated like a soap bubble is exasperating.

I guess I really do hope for a time when the whole world understands that there are cis men and trans men and neither are validated or prized more than the other, and trans men can just be trans men, and I can just be a person who dates trans men and also mannish women. But that time, if it ever comes, will not happen in my lifetime, so on my identity label maker I will punch out the letters *Q–U–E–E–R* to explain my proclivities. There is also the sensually seductive *bisexual*—which makes me feel like Jane Fonda at a key party in 1972, which is groovy in its own way *for sure*, but it is also either campy or strangely sexless despite the word *sex* right there in the middle. And plus, *bi* is for *binary*, which really hits a wrong note, as many of the folks I want to get with are very much not engaging with the gender binary. That's my job! My friend Sara suggested *slider*, which I guess some British bisexual people call themselves, but I am not British I am American and in my land, sliders are tiny hamburgers and that is not my sexual orientation. The reality is that everything is imperfect and evolving, we are making up whole new lives and identities, new ways of being human and new ways of relating to each other as humans, new ways of having sex and talking about sex, we are making all of it up right here right now and isn't it an exciting time to be queer? To be a smart, kind, intelligent, sexual queer person engaged with the world, alive in our genders and our costumes, playing and experimenting along the way to a deepening authenticity that we'll spend our whole happy lives excavating? Isn't it just the best time to be queer and aren't you glad we all are? I am.

Keynote speech, Five College Queer Gender and Sexuality Conference, 2011.

POLISHNESS

I was miserable in Poland.

I was sick, a burl of yuck in my lungs that kept me coughing, and coughing meant no smoking, and that made me miserable too. The cat who pissed on the mattress I was sleeping on made me miserable, and how my heart was broken but not yet *officially*—that was a special kind of misery, edged with stupid hope and paranoia. And I couldn't distract myself with sex because the heartbreak was not yet official, plus I was so sick and lethargic with the ugly coughing—when your face stays in that prolonged contortion, *honk honk honk*. My miserable, heartbroken sickness sat on my face like a film, making me very unpretty. I had let myself get too skinny and my head sat upon my neck like a bobble toy, the wrinkles in my face deeper with no cheeks to plump them. I looked sad and I felt sad and I brought it all to Poland.

I arrived in Warsaw from Nice, where I had been vacationing with Olin, my boyfriend-not-boyfriend—he just didn't like being part of a couple. As in, it really freaked him out that time we found ourselves both brushing our teeth in the bathroom *at the same time*; see also, the greening of his complexion when I once asked to wash myself off in his shower. He did not want to encourage acts that would allow one to get dreamy about possible future domesticity and yet had taken me on a cruise of the French Riviera. Mixed messages, yes, and I had packed my decoder, determined to make it work because he was so funny and well dressed and our sex was so good. I found his belly, which embarrassed him, kingly and the orange hair that furred his shoulders very animal. All of him was noble to me, even the tarred places within him that made him so skittish and terrible. I imagined I could lure him out of himself and into some new version that was generally happier and eager for love. This is a particular feminine fantasy, and it is odd how much I clung to it and even odder how oblivious I was to my own patterns, but that is the way of them, isn't it? These gears that churn inside us and we barely notice them, no matter how many wooden shoes and metal hammers get tossed into the works.

We'd boarded the boat in Spain, a giant yacht that raised its sails to very dramatic music each night. You would be sitting in the hot tub and suddenly the soundtrack to a Viking ambush would blare and the white canvas would ascend. For one week, we were at sea. I would walk up to the deck for my morning coffee, excited to see what the morning's view would be—look, a terra-cotta castle! It was grand, this was Europe, the Europe where fairy tales come from, rolling hills and the sky and the sea blindingly blue. It made me feel glorious; there is nothing more spectacular than traveling. Except love. Olin was moody, snappy, and mean, but I was in love with him. I experimented with being this way or that, timid or cool, exuberant, funny, intimate or aloof, all along shaking on the inside, and none of it having any effect whatsoever. At the end of the trip we would go our separate ways, him to Budapest, me to

Poland. I had gotten an organization to give me a grant to teach writing to feminists in Warsaw.

I am English and had spent a week in London at eighteen, drunk, dancing all night in goth clubs, drinking shandies in pubs, and falling in love with everything, just like the psychic who'd told me I had lived there in a past life assured me I would. I am French and had spent three weeks in Paris, chain-smoking and eating cheese, involving myself in a ménage à trois and falling in love, as one does in Paris. And, I am Polish. How would I experience my Polishness in Warsaw? Not by getting drunk or dancing or smoking or eating cheese or falling in love. In Warsaw, I would suffer. Perhaps that was what one did in Poland.

My flight from Nice landed at night. The French sun was gone and would never shine in Poland anyway. How could it have been so warm and now be so cold? Was Poland so very far from France? Being American, I thought of it all as Europe. I wore a tight gray dress that wrapped across my chest, with no sleeves, made from the thick cotton of a sweatshirt. It was a good outfit for Nice, for turning my back on Olin as I hopped into a taxi, crying behind my shades like a real French lady. In Warsaw the dress was ridiculous. Night fell earlier in Poland; the airport was stark and roomy, yellow lit against the dark outside, pierced with the fleeting red and white lights of cars. My friend Anu was late to fetch me. Anu was a rogue, I knew, and I feared he would never come for me. What would I do? I would get a hotel room, I thought. In every city of every nation there were hotel rooms by the airport. I would check my emails, surely someone would try to find me. I would email Anu, email Agnieszka, whose queer organization had helped me get the grant to teach writing. If only they offered travel grants to the estranged daughters of alcoholic Polish men, so that they might learn how their own estranged Polishness operated within them. A grant to study the pieces of themselves that were Polish even when their Polish kin were unknowable, a grant to fund a pilgrimage to the inscrutable homeland of their deadbeat dad. But such grants do not exist, so one must teach writing to feminists.

I understood I was English because I loved music and fashion, the weirder the better. I had two Union Jack T-shirts by the time I was thirteen; I lay in bed listening to Billy Idol's growl and cried. I tried to feather my shitty hair like Def Leppard's Joe Elliott. Later I would fashion it after Robert Smith and Siouxsie Sioux, and lie in bed listening to Depeche Mode and the Smiths and cry some more. I understood I was French because of Jean Genet and Violette Leduc, because of Anaïs Nin's involvement with Henry Miller's crazed wife June. Also, I loved to smoke cigarettes and cry. But Poland? I loved kielbasa. I called it "the sausage of my people," making friends laugh. I loved the Polish eagle tattoo on my uncle Stashu's bicep, golden crowned, claws flexed. My own heraldic pigeon tattoo, with its crown and claws, is an homage. Poland was founded by a man named Lech, one of three brothers, descendants of Noah—yes, *the* Noah, the one with the boat and all the animals. The three brothers were hunting, each following his prey in various directions, and Lech, in pursuit of the bow he'd sprung, stopped short when he came upon an eagle guarding its nest, huge and fierce. The setting sun lit her feathers gold, and Lech, sensitive to omens, decided to stay, called the place Poland, named the eagle Golden, and made it his protector. A hunting people, open to the mystical powers of feathers and sunshine. To allow such poetry to determine life's direction. I always believed the witch inside me came from my mother, the alcoholic from my father. But maybe it is more complicated than that.

I met my friend Anu years ago at a queer club in Paris, where he was studying photography. I was in love with a blond boy named Killian whose girlfriend would not allow him to dance with me, and so I twirled alone in the hot pink light of the club until I found myself dancing with Anu. Killian was pained to see me dancing with Anu, and pulled me aside and begged me to stop, to not take him home. Home was the apartment above the Shakespeare and Company bookstore. I had meant to sleep inside the bookstore like all the eighteen-year-old boys, the Tumbleweeds in their velvet blazers and rumpled Rimbaud hairdos, rolling cigarettes on the stone steps outside. I had meant to sleep among them and write about it, but the owners learned I was a writer and gave me the writer's apartment, a single room with a flat twin mattress resting on a board that rested on stacks of books. Books lined the walls too. Tumbleweeds left their diaries on the desk during the day, and everyone traipsed through to use the only bathroom. Of course I took Anu home, to spite Killian, who loved me, and also because he was very attractive—olive skin and dark hair—and Polish, which was exotic to me, more so than France even, because Poland was the mystery inside me.

I bought Anu beers from a café in the Latin Quarter and we sat outside, the stone buildings crowding us. He told me all about his family, that his father was a salt magnate and he was the heir to a salt fortune. After the fall of communism, his mother had opened the first Chanel store in Poland and Anu grew up looking at the photos from her stash of *Vogue* magazines. Anu's tales seemed like lies, but lies tailored to my particular interests, so they were like little gifts from Anu to me. He told me he would write me a mermaid story about the mermaid tattoo on my belly; he would write me a bluebird story about the bluebird on my hand. He would send me a vial of pure Polish salt. Of course, it was only pillow talk. I smoked his cigarettes and took him back to the apartment, where he opened a Tumbleweed's diary and wrote inside it. I was scandalized. I was already afraid I hadn't worked long enough in the bookstore downstairs, hadn't typed out my biography in the typewriter niche as requested, hadn't impressed the White Witch, the Irish poet who presided over the weekly tea party in George's apartment, where the bookstore's elderly owner lay on his twin bed that he shared with a pan of cat litter and a small black-and-white TV, his dresser overrun with papers and old food and at least one cockroach. Perhaps I was pushing the boundaries of the bookstore's hospitality bringing someone back for sex on the scrawny bed, both of us freezing midgrope, feigning sleep when Tumbleweed boys crept in to use the bathroom. And now here was Anu, gleefully vandalizing their diary. He did not vandalize my body. He was very gentle, turning it like an artifact in his palms, studying my tattoos, fascinated. I played PJ Harvey and the Smiths, and he hadn't heard of either of them, nor had he heard of Patti Smith. I didn't understand how this attractive, genderqueer person who had danced so well to M.I.A. in the club did not know this music, but later, when I came to Poland, I understood better.

Agnieszka was chosen to host me in Warsaw because she had the nicest apartment. It is true that the building sat on very green grass. The neighborhood seemed sedate.

Inside, it felt like public housing. Isn't all housing public under communism? Agnieszka's sturdy *panelák* was surely built by the state after the war, after the Nazis had burned the whole of the city to the ground and the Soviets brought it back. Housing. What could be more of a uniform, human need, so why not create these uniform blocks? Agnieszka had a tremendous number of locks on the door, like a joke about old New York City. "Don't let the cats out," she requested. And don't let them into the room I was given to sleep, because they would pee on my things. I forgot many times and would rush into the room, urgently smelling my suitcase, relieved that they hadn't pissed there, until, of course, they did.

There was no beauty inside me at that time, and it was hard to connect with Warsaw's beauty, so unlike other places I'd seen. I had thought myself expert at locating difficult beauty, a happy consequence of growing up in my slummy New England town, but here I'd become an ugly American, the worst, my heart cold to the brutalist buildings punched into the city. The heavy gray skies, the directive from Anu not to smile at strangers, lest they think I was simpleminded, a fool, or else gearing up to rob them. I found it very hard to board a train car, pass an old woman on the street, and not reflexively smile. Olin, too, had had a problem with my smiling; my relentless positivity had aggravated his depression. This insanity had hurt my feelings, but later, with distance, I could see my happiness for what it was: aggressive and manipulative, as if the radiance of my personality could burn away his sadness like a fog. My mother had employed a similar tactic with my depressed Polish father, and wasn't Olin so very much like my father with his chronic grumpiness and his cigarettes and alcohol? Did this weaponized positivity, calibrated to offset cynicism and despair, drive them both away?

What was brilliant about Warsaw was how the Polish resistance fought the Nazis for sixty-three days. Ordinary people fueling the uprising. These are the people I liked to imagine myself descended from, not the other, evil Polish, who killed their neighbors and moved into their homes. The Warsaw Uprising was urban combat, espionage, and sabotage, the largest armed resistance in World War II. The Polish Home Army raided a military prison that had been turned into a concentration camp, freeing almost 350 Jewish prisoners. Women fought, were involved. Like Anna Smoleńska, an art student who won a sort of contest to design an emblem for the resistance. The *Kotwica* is all over Warsaw, a *P* growing out of the middle peak of a *W* resembling an anchor. Anna was a girl scout at the time, and in Warsaw, the Polish boy and girl scouts comprised the Gray Ranks. Anna was twenty-three then and she looked queer. Short hair slicked sideways across a broad forehead, a pleasant, open face, sweet. Wearing a necktie. She engaged in sabotage and worked for a resistance newsletter. The Nazis wanted the editor but found Anna, and took her and all the women of her family to Auschwitz. A photo shows a shadow of the stout lesbian she would have grown into had she been allowed to live. Her round glasses, her bloody nose. A virus infected her chest there, and she died.

Certain things give my body dopamine. Sex, shopping, smoking. Text messages. Possibility, anticipation. I recently learned that talking about yourself triggers a dopamine release, and my entire adult life made a sad, new sense. I am an alcoholic, and I think that this grasping for sensation, this need for dopamine, for a high, is what turned my drinking sour. I don't know if I have less dopamine than you have or if I am simply greedy. Having taken away alcohol, I'll lunge toward fucking instead or find myself dizzy, sweaty, from the sight of a perfectly designed shoe. I'll eat cigarettes. In Poland I had nothing. I got little bolts of *something* from the iron *Kotwicas* bolted into the bricks of buildings here and there, marking the place where the uprising was fought. Mystery gives me dopamine too, and history, sometimes, and revolution. I thought about the mermaid Syrenka, said to protect the city of Warsaw, what a shitty job she had done. I imagine it was beyond her capacity. The Soviet army was meant to join the uprising, but had stopped short on the other side of the river Vistula, allowing the Nazis to destroy the resistance in hope that the Polish would later need Russia. And they did. And they did. I imagined Syrenka, a dark-hearted, tangle-headed mermaid gone furious with grief.

While I was in Poland, Olin's plan was to explore Budapest with an old friend, a long-ago girlfriend. The two of them stayed with mutual friends, a couple, both of whom had eating disorders and so had little energy to show their guests around town. The old girlfriend was terribly mean to Olin, and he'd had a moment, stuck inside her bad temper, when he wondered if that was what it had felt like for me, traveling with him.

It was hard for Olin to enter bodies of water. He would go slowly, wincing. I would jump in, like a dolphin or mermaid. I would splash and frolic, and if I were to be honest, I would admit I was also performing the part of a free-spirited young woman, at one with the elements. I knew he was not like this, and I hoped my spirited splashing would cheer him. I thought maybe it could jolt him out of his dour state, a revelation, *Yes, I can jump in the ocean too!* and he dives in, peeling off his depression like a T-shirt. Olin had metal rods where his shinbones ought to have been. The cold of the metal immersed in the seawater was terrible. Years ago Olin was in a car accident and everyone died. Olin died twice, but was the only one to live. He recovered at home, on morphine, slowly becoming addicted. He was fourteen years old. I leapt from the sea, droplets shooting off me like crystals.

In a smoky bar in Poland, filled with interesting-looking people chain-smoking cigarettes and sipping drinks, Anu asked if I was faking my happiness. Was I really like this all the time? Was I putting on a show? I didn't know how to respond. I was miserable, but I didn't need to talk about it. Anu knew I had just ended a terrible trip and that my heart was broken. I had sadly told him that I would not be able to sleep with him because I felt so ill, a presumptuous thing to say; he may well have had enough of me in Paris, plus I wasn't looking pretty and he had a new girl, young and plump faced and devoted. They wore matching leopard socks and Anu wrote love notes on her skin with a marker. I can be miserable and happy at once, I explained. Once, when I was newly sober but had no recovery, nothing to help me navigate the mindfuck of life without alcohol, the writer Mary Woronov also asked me if I was always happy. She was not curious like Anu, but a bit more scornful. There is something dopey about happiness, as the Poles know. Woronov is a Slavic last name; Russia was founded by Lech's brother, Rus. "Are you on Prozac?" Mary demanded. I explained to her that I had just quit drinking and I wanted to die, but I didn't see the point in making it anyone else's problem. She laughed. "Well, of course you want to die. Life is miserable without drugs."

In Warsaw Anu pointed to the Palace of Culture and Science. They called it the syringe because of the decorative spire on top, 150 feet tall. The building used to have "Stalin" all over it; a gift from Russia, it had been named the Joseph Stalin Palace of Culture and Science, but after Russia began its de-Stalinization, Poland too wiped the brute's name from its buildings.

The year of my visit was the fortieth anniversary of Solidarność, and the scrawled red logo radiated from a banner draped over the palace's facade. My Polish father was a union organizer, and he loved Solidarność; I had a pin of that logo when I was nine. It was the first time workers in a Soviet country had come together to form a union; it was Warsaw's latest uprising. Over nine million people joined; it was more than a union, it was a resistance, and it toppled communism. Possibly my father too wondered how Poland lived inside him, and with Solidarność he felt an answer, a shared and raging blood, fighting for freedom. First there had been the Polish pope, Pope John Paul II, who I also had a pin of—a large round pin of his face dangling from a purple ribbon—from someone who had gone to Boston to watch him pass in a parade. Born Karol Wojtyła, he'd resisted the Nazis in Kraków doing guerilla theater, working at a chemical factory by day. The day he was shot my depressed Polish father was even more so. "What is this world, when someone shoots the pope?" A spring day, his sadness bathed in sunshine as he unlocked the door to the home he would soon kick us all out of, my mother, my sister, and me. His heavy trudge up the stairs. I was maybe excited that the pope had been shot. I've always had a hard time distinguishing between excitement and anxiety, and have wondered if my body enacts a strange alchemy on my emotions, turning one into the other, maybe fusing them into a whole new chemical. It made me proficient at stressful relations, the excitement of infatuation morphing to a nearly identical, persistent panic. My capacity for love had always amazed me, but now I see that it was only generalized anxiety disorder. Medication helps.

I didn't visit the Solidarność exhibit at the Palace of Culture and Science. I had to manage my nostalgia for a father who was not dead, but was in fact working at a health-food store in Clearwater, Florida.

Past the Palace of Culture was the saddest H&M in the world. It was as if a post-Soviet collection had been designed especially for this location, and the store had agreed to sell those and only those clothes. I was hoping to buy a coat, I was freezing, but I couldn't. Later Agnieszka would take me to a thrift shop, because I was sure that a country whose history was so close to the present would have wonderful secondhand shops full of old lace and artifacts, but I simply did not understand communism, or history. I found a pair of striped pants that tapered nicely at the ankles, and a strange old makeup bag. We went back to Agnieszka's, me hacking my Polish cough. We passed tiny fruit and vegetable stands, where people bought whole heads of sunflowers and carried them home, plucking the seeds to eat along the way. I was careful not to smile at anyone. Inside her home I waited for my nose to adjust to the stink of cat piss. I petted the animals and boiled frozen pierogis. Inside my room I read *The New Yorker*. A man had written in to comment on an article about dying. He wrote that his wife had died of cancer and briefly described what it had been like to sit at her bedside and love her as she passed over. I burst into tears. *All I want*, I thought wildly, *is to be loved. I want to be loved so badly*. The thought humiliated me but it was true. I allowed myself to weep for it. I wanted someone to die with. Probably it wouldn't happen. Every time you think that it is going to happen and then it doesn't actually happen it deconstructs your heart a little, until something once lush and scarlet has the brutalist architecture of a formerly communist country. I signed my computer onto Agnieszka's shaky internet to see if Olin had sent me a missive from Budapest; he hadn't. I did have an email from my friend Peter. I had visited Peter in New England at the start of the summer; we'd gone to Provincetown and played bingo with townies, rode bicycles through the cemetery, shopped at Marine Specialties with its barrels of glass balls and discontinued airline plates and German army shirts. I had bought Olin a magnifying glass, the handle an animal horn. "I just want to be loved so badly," I typed to Peter. It embarrassed me so horribly, this need. It seemed the only way to fix that was to tell someone.

I visited the mermaid statue in Warsaw's Old Town Market Place, an exact replica of the original town square the Nazis blew up. I went there with Anu and his sweet-faced girlfriend, with Agnieszka and another Agnieszka, this one a schoolteacher who was recently fired for being a lesbian. Someone let rats inside her classroom so that when Agnieszka returned to gather her things she was faced with the rodents and their shit and the damage they had done. It was very hard to be gay in Poland. It didn't used to be so, at least not legally. Whenever Poland was free and self-governing, queerness was allowed, but the country was always being invaded and partitioned and overtaken, and homosexuality would be outlawed. When the communists took over it was illegal again, with the state taking down the names of all queer and queer-adjacent individuals. Queer activists have petitioned the Institute of National Remembrance, the body that prosecutes crimes committed under communism, to begin an investigation into crimes against queer people, but they declined.

The mermaid in the square was small breasted and thick waisted, with a sort of leafy drapery growing down from her hips and unfurling onto her scaled tail. Anu told me they called this statue the toilet because the fountain released its water with a sound not unlike a toilet flushing. The water flowed weakly, which seemed an insult to the power of the bronze mermaid, her countenance placid, noble even, as she raised her sword above her head and brandished her shield. I liked her as much as I liked any mermaid or armed female, but I looked forward to visiting the bigger statue on the banks of the Vistula.

On my last night in Nice my Olin spoke to me cruelly, and so I stuffed my *New Yorker* into my bag and stormed out of the hotel. The hotel was around the corner from the ocean; for a fee you could rent one of their loungers and lie there, sardine-packed against the other guests on their own blue-and-white striped towels. I thought this was bullshit and had resolved to simply lie on the beach like a normal person, until I saw that the beach was made of rocks, smooth gray rocks with distinct white bands. The people who tried to rest upon them looked poor, miserable. I knew Olin would pay for our loungers, as well as the inevitable lunch and drinks we could order, and I couldn't allow this with the vibes so bad between us, which meant I would have to pay, and I couldn't pay for only mine, that would be too dramatic of a statement, one I was too scared to make for I was still hopeful, somehow, that things weren't as bad as they were, and so I would have to pay for us both, and I cringed at the cost.

Later, once Olin had joined me, I lay on my lounger and stared at the breasts of the women in front of us, a mother and daughter, the mother's breasts large and wide, the daughter's taut and round, both of them deeply tanned and hung with gold jewelry. I enjoyed looking at them. I thought about taking off my own top, but I feared my breasts were odd, blobby triangles with no real shape or allure. Having grown up in America, one has to muster a sort of bravado to remove one's top in public. This is easier at a protest or pride march or queer disco than at an upscale beach resort in France where one already fears they are a bit of a dirtbag, plus is having low self-esteem due to romantic troubles. I wondered aloud what to do. "Take off your top if you want to," Olin said without looking at me, and went back to reading *Just Kids*. After this day at the beach, Olin spoke cruelly and I flung myself outside, stopping at a café to buy a pack of cigarettes. I walked and walked until even if he were moved to find me I was beyond where his legs could comfortably take him. I smoked and drank espresso and limonata and read about the fine-dining scene in Las Vegas. Tourists came and went. Across the street was a Petit Bateau and I was thankful it was closed because I would have liked to soothe my anxiety with clothes I couldn't really afford. Down the street, an elderly woman played a violin and sang in French, a giant rock of amethyst somehow pinned in her thinning gray hair. She was clearly insane, but touched, and I considered becoming her, considered ruining my sobriety of seven years by getting drunk at the café, following the path of ruin wherever it took me. Ultimately, to my golden years where I serenade the public, soliciting coins, stones stuck to my head.

Every now and again I would look up to see if I had caught the imagination of anyone handsome, the way women alone in public often can, but nobody cared. I left the café and wandered down narrow streets, stopping at a restaurant for some food, sitting outside with my book and my magazine. I ate swiftly, eager to smoke again. The thought of Olin weighed on me. He would be hungry. The fight, if I remember, was about where to dine. Low blood sugar probably had made a contribution to the day's misery. I ordered him a pizza and walked it back to our room. He knew he didn't deserve it, which was nice. He asked if I was going to stay elsewhere, but we were leaving so soon that it didn't make sense. Plus, I hoped we'd have sex again, and we did. I didn't know if it was me, or him, or us together, but something happened when we had sex. How can he loathe me so and yet—*this*. It didn't make sense. So, of course he didn't loathe me. It was something else. A mystery, eking dopamine from my brain like water from a rock.

I taught writing to the feminists in Getto Żydowskie, the old Jewish ghetto, the brick buildings pockmarked with gunfire. Much of the neighborhood was destroyed, the new one built right on top of the rubble, but some original buildings were still standing. We wrote together at a bar that hadn't opened yet, out in a courtyard where sausages were cooked on a grill nightly and plants grew from brightly painted industrial containers. When we got cold we moved inside, sitting on armchairs in the ghost haze of old cigarettes. When I say I taught, I more mean that I inspired. Created a space where the feminists' stories mattered, where the only thing to do was write them and so they were finally forced to do so, rather than cleaning their house or jumping in the shower or turning on the television or whatever anyone does instead of writing their memoirs. Once upon a time, when I was twenty-three years old, I believed powerfully in the importance of telling your story, and I told mine with vengeance and did what I could to encourage everyone else—well, the girls, anyway, the poor people and the people of color, the queers—to tell their stories as well. That was seventeen years ago, and anyone would get sick and tired of doing the same thing for seventeen years. When memoir is what you've been doing, it means you've become horribly sick of yourself, of your narrative, and I had. I was sick of excitedly telling everyone to write their stories, and as bad as it felt to be so annoyed with my own tale, this was worse, to be bored with an activity I still knew to be powerful and important. But knowing and feeling are two different things. Even as I felt such affection for the women who came, and did love their stories, wanted them to write them, some part of my heart was missing. I tried to overcome it but still longed for the workshop, the official point of my visit, to be over.

The bar kicked us out sooner than they'd agreed. Everyone was upset. It seemed maybe the space didn't value feminist art or females or girls or gay people. Everyone decided to meet back at Agnieszka's to share work and drink wine, and I got a ride with an older lesbian who told me about the days of rations when she was a child, how mothers would stand in line for theirs and then send their children later, for more. Children could earn coins standing in ration lines on behalf of various adults. In the seventies, the average Polish person spent over an hour in lines each day. Later, when I tell my mother that I found Poland depressing, she laughs and wonders what I'd expected. My father's family would sew secret pockets into their coats when they went back to visit, so when they were inevitably mugged the thieves wouldn't find their money. But, of course I couldn't have known this. I didn't know these relatives, I had nobody to tell me to sew secret pockets into my clothing, to warn me not to smile, to tell me I would connect with some ancestral sadness in the clouds that sit on top of the city.

Agnieszka's gloomy apartment was enlivened by the feminist writers. One woman, with the plucky, un-Polish energy of a young Renée Zellweger, set up a tiny phonograph spinning Elvis, turned out the lights, and delivered her piece in a storm of glitter, dancing around in a vintage slip. She had gone to school in London and so spoke English with a perfect British clip. Another woman was more traditionally gloomy, with the long, beautiful face of a silent movie star. She was also the bass player for a popular all-girl metal band, and the rest of the workshop whispered excitedly about her presence. I wrote too, as I always do when I teach, to stress that we are all just writers among writers, but my piece was terrible, the worst, all about Olin and my heartache, who cares. These women had real problems. Romance, yes, but also they lived in the ashes of communism, raised by defeated people, in a country scarred with atrocities and failed resistance. They were fired from their jobs for being gay. Abortion was illegal. This didn't inspire me to count my blessings; it just brought me a little lower.

I met a gay boy photographer at Czuły Barbarzyńca, a bookstore that made me think I simply hadn't been seeing the right parts of Warsaw. It was minimalist and brainy, intellectual and cool, with good coffee. I had feared the coffee of Poland, and so I had brought my own French press and two bags of Blue Bottle coffee with me. This had made the narrow cabin on the ship stink like a coffeehouse, but once at Agnieszka's I was glad I'd been so obsessive, for she drank only tea. I was working on my computer, and when the photographer came we walked together to the Vistula to see the statue of the Syrenka Warszawska, the mermaid of Warsaw. I don't know what he was taking my picture for. When you travel as a writer people often ask you to participate in various things, visits and lectures and parties and interviews, and I tended to say yes to everything. We walked through Powiśle to the gunmetal sculpture, where a bride in a fat white dress was having her picture taken. We waited for them to leave and then I scrambled awkwardly across the statue, posing like this and that, my hair scraped up, my face bony and creased, my mouth too big. Thick wool tights pulled under the cutoffs I'd worn in the Mediterranean.

The mermaid was powerful. Thick and angular, with a hint of a smile, as if she took delight in her power. Maybe it's a smirk. Surely she's defiant. It's the face of Krystyna Krahelska, changed somewhat because the artist didn't want her to feel too embarrassed or exposed, her face the face of Warsaw's eternal protector. It's true the mermaid's eyes are wider, with a different cast than Krystyna's; her nose is sharper, to correspond to the angles in the design. But I believe the defiance is hers. Krystyna Krahelska was a poet. Her songs were the songs of the Warsaw Uprising. Like Anna Smoleńska, she was twenty-three, a girl scout who had become part of the Gray Ranks. Like Anna, she reads queer to me in photos. Maybe Polish women just strike me as queer. In my favorite photo her hair is pulled back into two braids, and she looks deeply into the camera, sexy and sure, her eyes burning, no smile on her face, and a necklace pulled tight against her throat. In another she sits very close to a friend, almost cuddling, her hair stuck under a cap, butch to her companion's femme, whose head is covered with a fringed scarf. Krystyna was a messenger and a nurse; she transported weapons and taught other women how to treat battlefield wounds. Rushing to help a soldier, she was shot in the chest three times by Nazis. She lay down in a field of sunflowers, afraid to rise lest she give the other fighters away. She waited for nightfall, and died.

The day I left for home I dropped my French press in Agnieszka's bathroom sink and it smashed. It had served its purpose and was done. I swept up the glass, worried about the cats and their tender paws. I applied lip gloss in the bathroom mirror and was glad I was returning home to the rest of my clothes. It took a day or so to see Olin and know he truly did not belong to me. We met outside a coffee shop, and shamelessly I tried to go back to his house for sex, because in sex everything made sense, my anxiety obliterated by the force of it. He said his stomach was upset. *The person you love just avoided having sex with you by faking diarrhea*, I told myself, just to make sure I was getting it. That it was over. At home I sat on my back porch and smoked cigarettes. My illness was gone and I could smoke again. In Poland I'd eaten a last meal of kielbasa and potatoes and the lines in my face had softened. A flirtatious Gchat would soon turn pornographic; I would have another person to get dopamine from. "Don't use people to get high," my AA sponsor had told me. I would get on medication and it would be easier. I would try to call my father in Florida and his line would be disconnected and I would never talk to him again; even when he was dying and I found him, he would decline my call. I would write a book about the Warsaw Mermaid and another one and another one. Above my head, a flock of pigeons blacked out the sun with their flight.

HARD TIMES

The emails roll in and there is a lesbian magazine that wants to know what I have to say to all the women out there, the formerly lesbian females whose girlfriends have morphed a slow and deliberate morph, whose relationships are now something altogether different. Are now something that makes them feels vaguely—no, acutely—uncomfortable when they take it inside a queer bar. When they nuzzle like they always would, unthinking, and there's a dyke in the corner staring a little—no, she's glaring. And suddenly our girl, the former lesbian, pulls back from her now-boyfriend, afraid she's being disrespectful, taking up space in a gay bar. But she's not straight. Is she? Now on the streets when they hold hands or kiss nobody gives a shit. In front of the scariest dudes, passing by strip bars, the throng of men ignore them. They don't care. The girl thinks, *If we were queer they'd have said something. Might have even done something.* Never mind that for years she has held hands with girls, kissed them on sidewalks, in defiance of or oblivious to the danger, and nothing ever happened. Now, inside the queer bar, she will feel guilty for the woman's glares upon her, and on the streets, she will feel guilty for the lack of glares and this will be her world. For a while.

The dyke in the corner of the bar does look pissed as

she takes a swig from her beer and leaves her seat, swings by the couple on the way to the pool table. This stranger has become something larger, everything has become larger since the transition commenced. Everything has become tender, become symbolic. Clearly this woman, this dyke, hates them, would throw them from the bar if she could. Instead she channels all her irritation into her pool game, every sunken ball a smack. Our girl wants to grab this woman. She's seen her before, hasn't she? I mean, they've both been coming here for years, to this queer bar, surely they've been shoulder to shoulder on weekend nights when the place gets packed. Surely they've shifted their weight back and forth beside each other, in line for the bathroom, pressed up against the wall by the crowds of females, maybe they'd turned to one another—*What are they doing in there, fucking? Shooting up? Talking on their cell phone?* Maybe just a grimace of shared discomfort, dancing a similar jig on the wood floor, the dyke in her work boots and our girl in her heels, in her patched-up sneakers, in her tall boots, or her sandals. The dyke looks a little familiar, with her hair damaged from years of bleaching, crusty up around her ears, on her forehead, her crinkled, handsome face. Maybe, our girl thinks, she could run up to the woman, could meet her at the bathroom when she goes to piss. She could say, *It's not what you think. He's—he used to be like us. He's trans.*

Our girl bites her lip. Her boyfriend's hand grips her thigh—why'd she just pull away from him? Her energy has totally shifted. She feels gone, preoccupied. He could ask her why but decides not to. He decides to pull away too. To entertain himself with his thoughts. Like how much he hates this bar, to start. Why was he even there? He knows what straight men look like in a queer bar. They look stu-

pid. They're closet fags or they're looking for a lesbian to
shove their girlfriend at. They smile too much, at everyone.
They're like dogs. Just dying for someone, some gay person, to come up and place a friendly hand on their shoulder and say, *It's all right, pal. It's okay that you're here. Thanks
for stopping by.* The boyfriend keeps his eyes on the floor.
Careful not to look at the pool table, the only action in the
place, where the balls clack and roll and there's that woman
who was looking at them funny. She stabs the orbs with her
stick, chewing the side of her cheek like there's a wad of
tobacco stuffed behind her teeth.

Back to our girl. She thinks the bar dyke thinks she's
stupid. The way dykes always think straight girls are stupid—sort of lost, weak maybe, playing it safe, unimagina-
tive at the very least. At the very least we should feel sort
of bad for them, be ready to move in when the boyfriend
becomes an asshole, when his ego flares up and he hits her
or maybe just humiliates her in public. She watches the
dyke strut around the pool table. Maybe once she would
have thought she was hot. I mean, she *was* hot. Maybe
once she would've cared, would have been moved by that.
Our girl thinks her posture is a little smug. She sinks the
ball, stands up straight, chest out, tits poking up against her
T-shirt like armor. Cocky.

So, am I supposed to go to a straight bar? she thinks. She
imagines pulling the dyke aside, confronting her. Cor-
nering her in the back, by the pay phone, *What, I don't
belong here now?* She imagines going to a straight bar.
Which one would she go to? There were so many. She'd
have to figure out the kind of straight they were, she and
her boyfriend. Aesthetically speaking. What other kind
of straight people did they want to be around? She thinks

about it. Thinks she doesn't really want to be around a lot of straight people. Feels bad about it. She knows her boyfriend wants to be near other guys like him—straight guys. But inside a straight bar, he'd be just as quiet. They both know this. He's not going to make any friends. People don't really make friends in bars, they go there to meet the friends they've already got. Maybe they should just forget the whole bar thing. They can have a glass of wine at home if they want. They barely drink anyway. Her boyfriend turns to her and says, "Want to go?" Their glasses have long been empty, soggy cuts of citrus slumped along the bottom. They put on their coats. They go home and have a fight. The boyfriend hadn't wanted to go there in the first place. Had done it for her. Is pissed she wanted to tell the dyke, that stranger, that he is trans. What difference would it make? It shouldn't make any difference. Any difference it makes would be in her head. The thought of them, his girlfriend and the dyke, standing in the corner talking about him. Like they know him. He seizes up with anger like an overheated car. He sputters and freezes. She doesn't get it.

She's crying, our girl. She doesn't get it. She's in the middle of something large that she doesn't understand. She wishes she could levitate, rise up, hover above this thing, her relationship. The lesbian magazine thinks I can help this girl. Thinks I know something that can give her direction, comfort. I tell her, "Girl, no one will understand you." Your dyke friends will not understand you. They will allow your boyfriend in but only if you all agree he is special, he is the best boy, some sort of elfin, fairy, magic boy, the boy who was once a girl. They will let him in only if you all agree that this marks him: his former girlness, the thing he hates. Some will approve of your boyfriend's maleness because he passes, and he will be the exception when they say ignorant things about other trans people. Some will tell you about how they like trans men but they just don't like trans women. Because they're still male. But then doesn't that make your boyfriend still female? Well exactly. That's why he's okay, that's why he's in. Have some fights with your friends. Or don't, just walk around with a stone in your stomach. Feel your feelings, like the Buddhists tell you. Feel how similar it feels to when you were young and your family said racist things about the Puerto Ricans who lived in your city. Feel how similar it feels to when you were in high school and boys talked about beating up faggots. What's the feeling? You feel afraid. You will feel afraid a lot. It's okay, girl. It's okay, not everyone is like this but the ones who are will exhaust you, will break your heart, will not understand why you take it all so personally.

Your boyfriend? He's busy. He's figuring out how to be alive, how to talk and walk—he's staring at himself in the mirror more than he's looking at you. He's learning how not to ask the men he works with their astrological signs. He's learning not to like bunnies so much. He's learning how to lie to other guys about his history, because telling people he's spent the past eight years doing lesbian activism doesn't make sense. When you don't understand him he lashes out. He doesn't understand him, either. That's the point. He's mad because you always tell him nobody meant to hurt his feelings. You tell him people are ignorant and just don't know. He hates it when you say these things. It's as if you're on their side. He wants you to hate them—the ones who say inappropriate things about trans bodies, the ones who call him his old name when referring to the past. He'll say,

"Why are you always defending them?" And the girl will shut up. She didn't know that was what she was doing. She was trying to make all the bad feelings go away. The knot, the one in her stomach. A dense, nautical tangle. "Why can't you say, 'What an asshole, what a jerk'? Why can't you just say it for a minute?" But they're her friends. The girl wants to believe that everyone is good, that they just need time to get it right. The girl understands this is a luxury, this attitude. If they were chipping away at her like this, would she be so kind? But the girl is exhausted. I tell the girl: Prepare to be exhausted. And lonely. Your boyfriend is exhausted too, and probably does not want to hear about your strain, probably cannot bear it. You will wonder if it is worth it. You will wonder what it would be like if there wasn't all of this. You will feel guilty for your thoughts. Your thoughts of leaving him to it. It's his and you would leave him to it, you would go off and do other things and maybe you would never have to ponder such problems again. How in the subway you said, "Never again." You said it with a smile but it hurt, you knew it would and you didn't care, just for a minute, you really didn't. You were crying, you were a deserter. Magazines would stop asking you for advice to give to girls like you. Girls you cannot help at all because you are too busy sitting on your back stoop in the mist, smoking cigarettes, in pain. You remember a friend whose butch girlfriend was having gender issues. The friend said, "I'm going to go out with a straight guy next. A white, heterosexual man, not trans. I don't want to be with someone more oppressed than I am." You were shocked by her comment, but now you understand. It is a guilty understanding.

At night the couple wind themselves together. They sink into their lousy bed and twine all the parts soft enough to bend. Her nose is in the boy's hair, her face pressed into his scalp, all the sour-sweet smells. Soon she'll have to move. She can't breathe, her arm will fall asleep beneath his weight, but she will stay there until the discomfort is too great. She hopes that the morning will be different. That they learned something from the fighting and that tomorrow will be easier. A good day. *These are the hard times*, the girl thinks as her limbs grow heavy. These are the times they will look back on. They will measure their progress and know they are happy. They will be grateful to each other, for having come to bed each night, for surrounding the other with their body. The girl is optimistic. These are the hard times. In the future, they will name the moment and be glad it has passed.

From *TransForming Community*, a 2005 National Queer Arts Festival performance.

HAGS IN YOUR FACE

Throughout the majority of the 1990s my evenings were split between working at a nonprofit call center, where I bummed money off strangers for good causes, and getting drunk and dancing at any of San Francisco's queer punk clubs. I didn't know the town was a hotbed of these two particular and generally separate subcultures, and I didn't know how badly I needed this particular hybrid in order to discover myself in my entirety, but when I walked into a club called Junk, formerly a gay club called Paula's Clubhouse, it was like I had walked into my own best-case scenario of life. Up in the DJ booth, a scrawny punk with a bright blue mohawk spun Nina Hagen. Soon enough she would be my girlfriend, but that night I made out with a different girl entirely, when the centrifugal force of a broken mosh circle sent us flying into one another. I never saw her again, but no worry. The Mission District in the nineties was a promenade of fierce young dykes, each more shorn, more intriguingly pierced, more gender ambiguous than the last. Reigning over all, at least to my starstruck eyes, were a motley crew of surly twentysome-things resembling Peter Pan's Lost Boys if the Lost Boys were girls, the sort of girls who look like the sort of boys who might break a beer bottle over your head at a club.

Youthful and sweet cheeked, their tender faces topped with hair matted into dreadlocks with spray adhesive, or glued into a mohawked plank, or dyed black as coal and worn to the waist not in the way of a maiden but in the way of, like, Lemmy from Motörhead. I'm talking about the HAGS, and if you were alive in the Mission during this era you saw their tags everywhere, at bus stops and in bar bathrooms, on phone booths and brick walls. HAGS SF, HAGS IN YOUR FACE, in a black Sharpie scrawl. You knew a HAG was a HAG because they moved in a pack, as all wild animals do, and the backs of their motorcycle jackets and denim vests all proclaimed their affiliation: HAGS. More than the presence of a women-only bathhouse soaking with lesbians, more than the women's bookstore selling Dorothy Allison novels and feminist newsletters, even more than the Bearded Lady, the dyke café that hosted late-night art events attended by Kathy Acker, the HAGS were evidence of the mad freedom to be found in San Francisco. Yes, the city was still plagued by fag bashings and other antiqueer hate crimes, but if this was the place this group of magnificent and terrifying dykes thought best to call home, it was where I wanted to call home too.

The HAGS were formed by Tracie Thomas, a queer Colorado punk who followed her band, Feminine Deodorant Spray, to the Bay Area at the start of the decade. A photo from the era shows Thomas posing before what looks like a fuzzy zebra-striped wall. Her mohawk is as stiff as plastic, her denim vest covered in studs. She wears a bullet belt and a Misfits T-shirt and a handkerchief knotted around her neck. There's a tattoo on her forearm and her head is slightly tilted as she looks warily into the camera. She seems to be trying to radiate classic outlaw toughness while simultaneously wondering if the photographer is going to kick her ass.

Sometime after this photograph was taken, Thomas was grieving a breakup by flinging plates out the window of a friend's fourth-floor apartment down by Fisherman's Wharf. She was not alone. "I had a couple of friends who were like, 'Let's hang out and support each other,' and it was a kind of tough, get-your-energy-out, girl support togetherness thing." The inspiration to codify the energy struck Thomas. Influenced by filmmaker and misfit icon John Waters—"Cookie Mueller and the girl gangs, Divine strutting around beating people up and rolling people"— she dubbed her posse the HAGS, after the auteur's obscure black-and-white film *Hag in a Black Leather Jacket*.

The HAGS' primary activity—and this remained constant throughout their existence—was roaming in a protective pack around San Francisco, getting drunk, going to punk shows, and committing the light vandalism known as "tagging," leaving your gang's name or your own inked somewhere it shouldn't be.

"We'd spray-paint tags all over the city," Thomas recalls. "I remember we spray-painted this van and it turns out it was the Breeders' and they wrote the song 'Hag' about it." Indeed, the lyrics begin, "Hag! Coastal cutthroat!" and a bit further down Kim Deal speak-sings, "You're just like a woman / Hag." In this lost country of the 1990s, where such a "dirty switch" is "everything right," HAGS seemed to rule by an almost cosmic decree. "We would climb over fences at night and hop into public swimming pools and drink beer and be this girl unit." Like the alluringly bad boys of my youth, only girls. Like *The Outsiders* come to life, the teenage girl who wrote them into existence now showing all the way through.

"Just being a lesbian in this world you're going to have somebody messing with you, or even just being a woman. There was a lot of fag bashing going on in San Francisco, so we would take the streets and walk, and it was like we were an entity, like, *You're not going to do this type of thing to us.*"

When the HAGS began, it was five dykes. One of them was Johanna Lee, with her shorn red hair and nerd glasses. She rode her motorcycle up to Alaska and made scathingly perverse comics lampooning both the dyke culture that was her home and the Christian values of the abusive family she had left behind. Like everyone in the HAGS, she was young, in her twenties. It was Johanna who "tagged in" a HAGS member by painting the back of everyone's denim and leather jackets. "Each time someone got tagged in Johanna would take acrylic paint and draw that person on the back of our jackets. The jackets had 'HAGS' on the back and then there were little stick figures."

Another original HAG was Stacey Quijas. Originally from Colorado, she too was running from an abusive family; she quit school after eighth grade and had been on her own since age fourteen. Quijas wore her hair long under a backward baseball hat or up in a massive mohawk. From her nose dangled a ring, like a baby bull. Her legs were famous. On the back of each calf sat one-half of the L7 logo, each a skeletal green hand making an L or a 7. There is no overplaying the importance music had for the HAGS. In particular girl bands who shredded and killed and murdered as hard as dudes, bands like the Lunachicks and 7 Year Bitch, Tribe 8, and Malibu Barbi. The all-female grunge-metal-punk L7 was Quijas's favorite, and a photo of her tribute tattoo graced the cover of the *Pretend We're Dead* single. It's also how Quijas met Kelly Kegger.

"Green mohawk, leather jacket, combat boots, spikes, piercings, rings, covered in tattoos, tiny, loud, in your face, laughing, crying, yelling, stoic, tough, pretty, kind, selfless, selfish, self-conscious, insecure, obsessed, girl crazy, loyal, chaotic, serene, supportive, judgmental, rude, accepting, but most of all wild—as in untamed, danger- ous, mind-blowing." That's Tobi Vail, founding member of Bikini Kill, the person who literally put the *grrrl* in *riot grrrl*. She spent a season on the road with Quijas, who acted as the band's roadie during a tour in 1992. They had all met a bit earlier, through the networks that bring bands cross country and into congress with other bands, crashing on floors, giving lifts to transient fans. The tour stopped at Jabberjaw, a coffee-shop-cum-music-venue that hosted all-ages shows for the likes of Nirvana and Elliott Smith. In attendance was a nineteen-year-old metalhead from Torrance, named Kelly. Now a man, back then Kelly was a dyke, into metal, sporting super-long, dyed black hair. Recently out of high school with no plan for college, not much going on, a loner, she'd come to the Bikini Kill show out of desperation for some sort of counterculture that got close to her queer punk self.

"Oh, your legs are on the record!" she said to the band's roadie. "We were standing out front, and me and her started talking about music. I had a little Honda Civic, we went out to my car and I had all these cassette tapes. We were listening to songs, metal songs. Like, this old demo from Metallica. And Corrosion of Conformity. We were listening to this band Born Against, and Rorschach, and she was like, 'Oh yeah, I like this music, I'm not into Bikini Kill! I'm just touring with them.' She said that I'd like San Francisco."

A few months later, Kelly packed up her Honda Civic and set off for San Francisco with three thousand dollars she'd gotten in a car-accident settlement. "That was like a million dollars back then," she says. She arrived in town without knowing a single person, located a place to live by word of mouth, and found her way into the Mission's growing queer subculture by showing up at the Bearded Lady and Junk.

"I remember walking in there and everyone was into SM. Everyone was, like, bald. And just, like, leather. And people were having sex out in the open, like, everything was a sex party. I was like, 'Whoa, this is a total Judas Priest song! This is wild!'" Appreciative of the spectacle, the young queer did not swing in that particular direction, and was often clueless when being hit on by racy lesbians. "They were like, 'What are you into?' and I was like, 'Well, I like Italian race bikes. Music, I'm really into metal.' And they were like, 'But *really* what are you into?' And I liked Pepsi and espresso. I'd get an espresso over ice, and then pour a Pepsi in it. And they were like, 'Whatever, this guy is useless.'"

The night wasn't a total bust; Quijas was also at the club that night and the two reunited. Later, she took Kelly to meet the HAGS at a house party following a Lunachicks show.

"They had 'HAGS' written on their jackets," Kelly recalls. "It was just all these crazy fucking dykes that weren't into kumbaya music, you know what I mean?" For Kelly it was a revelation. "I tried to be gay in Los Angeles, and it just wasn't working out. It was like Farrah Fawcett dykes hanging out at the Palms. The South Bay punk scene was Black Flag, Circle Jerks, just *dudes*. But then when I met the HAGS, they were into music and going to shows. We didn't just go to queer shows. We went to straight shows too. None of us were mousy at all. If some dude was going to fuck with us, we'd fight back with them."

It wasn't only the macho landscape of punk rock that held potential brawls; antiqueer violence could pop up on a Muni bus, as it did when a man spit in a fellow HAG's face and called them both "crazy dykes." They knocked him onto the floor of the bus and kicked him until the driver threw them off. Then, high on adrenaline, they lit up cigarettes and got kicked off again for smoking. "It's hard to think about being proud of that. Being this person who fucked shit up all the time."

But that's a thought conjured from the comfort of 2016. Although San Francisco had been a safe haven for queers since World War I, when the military began dumping their "blue discharges"—gay soldiers—at its port, inadvertently creating a gay community, there have always been violent bigots in the city, as seen from the recent murder of the popular transgender DJ Bubbles, who was gunned down near the record store she worked at in the Tenderloin, or the fatal bashing of Radical Faerie Feather Lynn in placid Duboce Park in 2014. Queer people are never safe, and in the 1990s that knowledge was acute. I recall driving by Esta Noche, the city's first Latinx gay bar, and seeing a patron getting walloped with a two-by-four on the street outside. I spent the night leaving hysterical messages on the answering machines of various nonprofits; it hadn't occurred to me to call the police—police weren't friends of queers. Like the HAGS and most other queer females, I lived in the Mission, not yet a neighborhood of innovating restaurants and boutiques selling thousand-dollar retro sound systems; the Mission, in the nineties, was the neighborhood that folks from the rest of the city were too scared to come to. Much of that was simple racism; the Mission is the city's Latinx neighborhood. But it was really the city's *impoverished* Latinx neighborhood, and the tension of white queers—the first wave of gentrification—added to the friction of a place already contending with gang activity, a brisk street market of drugs, and sex for sale nightly. Packs of inebriated and aimless young men raised in an American culture of homophobia roamed this gay city. My best friend was assaulted when a man ran out from the Valencia Gardens housing projects and clobbered him on the head. A gang of bicycle thieves jumped out at me as I rode home from work on Mission Street one night, almost knocking me off my seat as they seized my rear tire and proclaimed my bike to be theirs. I fought them off with wit and outrage, tools I also used to scare off the single men and packs of boys who harassed me as I made my way home, though I was on occasion inspired to use my purse as a weapon, when the advances were especially relentless. Once, when my girlfriend and I were held up at gunpoint at a bus shelter on the corner of Sixteenth and Mission, I dissuaded our attacker with tales of our poverty and an offer of beer from the six-pack I was carrying. This was the landscape the HAGS gathered in; though they were not consciously gathering for self-protection, they understood, as we all did, that us broke, female queers may be called upon to protect ourselves at any minute, and the safety of numbers was always more effective than a pocketbook.

Silas Howard directs for film and television now, but in the nineties he ran the Bearded Lady café and, as the bass player for Tribe 8, was the focus of much HAG adoration. "The city was much more violent," he remembers. "I got a gun pulled on me several times. Harry (the Bearded Lady's co-owner) got gay bashed at a taqueria on Twenty-Fourth Street. There were way more neo-Nazis going into the punk scene. All of that tension was on the surface—we were at war. It felt like that." At war on the streets of our neighborhood as well as in the culture at large, where Senator Jesse Helms famously called us "degenerates . . . weak, morally sick wretches," and was backed up by Senate Majority Leader Trent Lott, who compared queerness to alcoholism, and Bill Clinton, who we thought maybe liked us or something, signed the Defense of Marriage Act. "I believe marriage is an institution for the union of a man and a woman," he stated. For a certain segment of the queer population, the answer to such hostility was not to be respectable, to continue working to convince these bigots we were "just like them," but to become the degenerate beasts they accused us of being, to take delight in our monstrous power, to say fuck you and goodbye to the possibility of living a "normal" life in this culture. Enter the HAGS.

Marya Taylor is a sober fortysomething queer female with beachy blond waves who is frequently accompanied by a pack of dogs. In the 1990s she was a drunk twentysomething with jet-black hair and silver piercing jewelry that arced from her chin like little fangs. The abstract, black tattoos that spill down her body like ink are still there. The city she inhabited is not. "It was a different San Francisco," she remembers. "Not a day went by that I wasn't verbally or physically bashed. I remember riding my bike as I stopped at a gas station to put air in my tires and a carload of dudes came up. Then a second car came up, and they were there to bash on me too." Taylor purchased a gun, choosing a semi-automatic 9mm over a .38 or .44 because it held significantly more bullets per clip, enough to take out a carload of dudes. Taylor had been in the same queer punk orbit as the HAGS, thrashing around at the same clubs and performing onstage with Tribe 8 while the gang moshed in the front row. The responsibility of gun ownership spurred her to become sober, taking her out of the HAGS orbit and into recovery.

"The people who were sober had this light in their eyes, and the HAGS were great but I had this really sick feeling in my stomach, like it was the dark path. It was the time before they got super strung out. It was a gut thing."

Tracie Thomas worked things out with the long-distance lover who'd inspired her to fling plates out of the window. She moved to New York, starting a HAGS chapter in the city and attempting to control the San Francisco chapter from afar, having final approval over who was allowed to have the HAGS tag on the back of their jackets. It wasn't happening. "After I left they were making everyone a HAG. It turned into chaos, and everyone was on drugs."

Meanwhile, a teenage dyke on the run from the stultifying environs of Monroe, Louisiana, was hanging out in Austin, Texas, with a fake ID. Kids in junior high had named her Joan for her shaggy hair and Joan Jett T-shirts; she modified it to Joan of Anarchy, her tag. When Bikini Kill played a dive bar in town, Joan showed up with her phony identification, and like Kelly before her, noticed the L7 tattoos on their roadie's legs. "I was just taken aback, 'cause there were no other dykes like me. She was the first punk-rock-type dyke I ever met. I was really taken with her. I wished I could just go with her wherever she was."

Soon enough Joan would. She caught a ride to Seattle for a bit, then hitchhiked down to San Francisco for an anarchist fair. Homeless, she met up with other gutter punks crashing on the streets of the city, and found her way to Turk Street Studios, a rehearsal space in the Tenderloin that had become infamous for the amount of debauchery taking place within its warrens. "It was actually kind of like a big headquarters for crystal meth." Joan fell in with a member of Tribe 8 who'd been ejected from the band for her drug use; the musician was shacking up with a drug-dealing HAG in a practice space. When Joan pointed out a bag of meth that had slipped from the dealer's stash, she earned the HAG's trust and began working as an apprentice of sorts. "A guy would come over and sell us eight balls and we'd take it and bag it for resale. I was the watchdog, I guess. I made sure people didn't rip her off." In return for her duties Joan was permitted to crash at the practice space and gifted with free drugs.

Joan's heart was outfitted with a pacemaker, making all drugs, but speed in particular, a poor choice of recreation, even for a gutter punk. But Joan was under the illusion she had about two years to live. Back home in Monroe, Louisiana, hepatitis B had broken out at the café she worked at. A blood test came up negative, so she received a vaccination. When the café's insurance company later requested their own blood test, the antibodies from the vaccine created a false positive. Mistakenly believing she had two years to live, Joan abandoned her college enrollment and hit the road.

"I was living on the street, doing drugs. I wasn't worrying about it because I was like, I want to do what I want to do, because I thought I was going to die tomorrow." A visit to Larkin Street, the Tenderloin clinic that cares for homeless youth, eventually verified that Joan was free of hepatitis B, but by then she was living a certain life.

It took Joan a minute to prove herself worthy of HAGdom. "They were very selective about who they let into that circle," Joan, now Johnny Ray, recalls from his comparatively sedate life in Vallejo, California. "I think it was because of that strong love they had for each other. They were looking for their sisters from another mother."

At a punk festival in Portland, Oregon, Joan spent the day with the HAGS, but come nightfall they told her to buzz off. "I didn't want it to seem like it bothered me, but I was curious." A single kindly HAG stayed behind with Joan, and the pair ran around Portland doing drugs, eventually coming to rest in a dumpster. "It had potato sack bags in it, like the old kind you used to play with in school. We said, 'Fuck it, let's sleep in here.' So we slept in the dumpster with potato sack bags."

Joan synched back up with the gang at the festival the following day, drunk and high and skanking in a circle pit. She noticed some neo-Nazis skanking alongside her. "I didn't like skinheads much and I started beating on them in the pit. The bodyguards working the event had to separate us, and they were about to kick me out." Joan was rescued by Becky Slane, a HAG who vouched for her and promised to help her cool down. Becky made a date with Joan to kick skinheads at punk shows when they got back to San Francisco. "And after that I was a HAG, I guess." It was Slane who eventually tagged Joan into the gang, painting "HAGS" on the back of her jacket.

Maybe Becky felt for Joan because her own HAG-ness had been contested by none other than Tracie Thomas, now referred to as Scramma by the gang she left behind. "She was a figurehead," Becky recalls from her sunny kitchen in Los Angeles. "A figurehead that did carry some weight. She had to give her blessing or it wasn't official. I remember this forty-five-minute phone call to New York—and this was at a point in time when you actually had to pay for long distance. We didn't have any money. It was kind of a big deal."

Truthfully, Becky was a little suburban in comparison to her gangmates. She hadn't grown up in foster care, hadn't been a teenage runaway, hadn't suffered extreme sexual abuse at the hands of her family. Her music taste was a bit off; she embraced "sissy bands" such as Babes in Toyland and Hole. Her mom even provided her with money: "Never any more than ten dollars," she recalls. "I'd get seven dollars in the mail sometimes." Still, it wasn't the cash, it was the presence of an actual family of origin who actually cared about your well-being that set Becky apart from the rest of the gang. Everyone else's family had been split apart, by homophobia or abuse or addiction or all of the above.

And yet, Becky got her ass kicked by a couple of mulleted softball lesbians for tagging HAGS in the Castro and was a leader in intense drug use, so as far as the gang was concerned she was in, regardless of Scramma's ruling.

"I shot speed. I blew out veins inside my arm, like they

were starting to leak, because it's very caustic. If it gets in your soft tissue, like if you miss or something like that happens, it is incredibly painful." Like most addicts, she didn't go to the hospital. Like most addicts, she kept on using. For a while.

Fiver came from Ohio, the middle kid of a big, Catholic family. When she was twelve years old her mother up and left, no warning, no contact. For a while, Fiver was raised by her father, a biker who parked his motorcycle in the kitchen, taught Fiver to play the guitar, and may or may not have struggled with his own inebriations. When it got to be too much, the kids were split up into foster homes. Fiver actually got a good one. She grew close to her two foster brothers, in particular the younger one. Says Carina Gia, a poet who was in love with Fiver during their twenties, "They actually gave her a lot of stability. She really liked them a lot." At some point the two brothers were messing around with a rifle. The older brother shot the younger one in the head. It was an accident, a mistake. It was Fiver who found the boy, already gone. After, she lived briefly with her mother, but that didn't work. After that she was on her own. She made her way to California, like so many lost and restless queer people, queer girls especially, drawn to the Bay Area as if a pulsing, magnetic stone were lodged beneath the water there.

It makes sense that Fiver found her way to Berkeley, to the university, even if she wasn't a student. She'd made it through a few years of college back in Ohio, as an English major, and had wanted to be a writer. She loved Kurt Vonnegut and was obsessed with Jean Genet, in particular *Our Lady of the Flowers*. But her primary occupation at Berkeley was getting wasted and hanging around the co-ops, the university's alternadorms, each with their own personality. Carina began in La Florian, the vegetarian one, and made her way to Barrington, the more rebellious co-op, full of murals and with a roof known for launching students on acid to their death. Eventually it would be shut down by the neighborhood, but not before a blacked-out Fiver knocked on Carina's bedroom door and asked if she could spend the night. It wasn't romantic. The two had met only once before, and Carina had found her obnoxious. Any chemistry between them was further obscured by Carina's youthful obliviousness to her own sexuality. "I identified more or less as a shy person, and that was it."

Carina and Fiver stayed in touch from then on. When Fiver followed a girl to Tahoe, Carina found she was unable to eat or sleep. "I realized something maybe was afoot. In my heart. And I was like, that can't be! That weird, freaky chick who's really funny, what?" They began writing letters. Eventually Fiver returned to Berkeley, landing on Carina's doorstep like a puppy who'd found her way home. "She just showed up one day. She had nowhere else to stay. After that things moved kind of quickly."

Carina and Fiver's romance sounds like a montage from a lost John Hughes film. "We would go into cafés and eat other people's food, like the half cake they left behind. I would ride my bike and she would ride her skateboard next to me. We would steal flowers from someone's yard. We didn't have a lot of money, we were poor. But we had such good synergy that it didn't even matter what we did. It could be about taking a walk or reading books or analyzing things into oblivion or painting the kitchen. It didn't really matter. We always wanted to be next to each other."

A committed drinker, Fiver's drug use was occasional, and of substances that Carina was hesitantly accepting of—"Not to say that they were acceptable." She drew the line at harder drugs, and so when Fiver indulged in those off-limit substances, she did them away from Carina. The romance began to fray. "I was trying to get a degree," she says. "I was trying to graduate. Her addiction took hold more and more, and I was trying to walk a different path." The lovers split up. Carina went to Europe for a while; she was born in Germany. When she returned a year later, Fiver was a HAG, and her using had become merged with the group's identity.

"It was more than friends hanging out," Carina says of the scene. "There was a lot of fuck-shit-up energy, without fear of the consequences. There was a certain beauty in the recklessness." Still, she worried for Fiver's safety, and missed the bookwormy skate nerd she'd fallen in love with.

"I feel like there's a certain part of Fiver that was subsumed. People didn't know that she was a writer, or that she loved to play her guitar. All that was left was this entertaining punk rock HAG." The humor she'd cultivated as a kid, as a way of commanding attention in her overrun family, became a single note within the druggy group dynamic. "My feeling was that I knew who Fiver was outside of all that posturing. I was wary of it because I saw the results in Fiver's life. And I thought, *What are you doing to yourself?*"

Their contact became increasingly strained, with Fiver coming to Carina whenever her using spun out of control, and Carina using what few resources she had to try to stanch the downward spiral. Twenty-three years of age, with no understanding of addiction, never mind the means to send her lover to recovery, Carina did what she could. "I tried to manage by trying to limit, like you do with a child, like it's candy: 'No more than *this*.' I was trying to control the use. Obviously, that didn't work." Another of Carina's efforts was retrieving Fiver's guitar, an heirloom inherited from her grandmother, each time she pawned it for drugs. "I was very committed to being codependent."

Eventually Carina and Fiver's relationship became untenable, and Fiver drifted toward a fellow HAG who used drugs as heavily as she did. But there was a moment between her initial distrust and her eventual parting when a friendship grew between Carina and the HAGS, a sort of Wendy among the Lost Boys. She found Johanna Lee, who had formed an intellectual connection with Fiver, to be brilliant. "She seemed like she could read your mind at points, a psychic person. The way that she spoke, how fast she was, she always reminded me a little bit of Robin Williams, when he channels that fast-talking humor." She recalls Quijas, who in so many ways was the heart of the HAGS, as "a little, tiny, feisty bull. Quijas seemed like good people to me. I liked being around her a lot." She let a homeless Joan of Anarchy sleep in her living room with a similarly homeless girlfriend, in spite of Joan confessing a nightmare in which Carina made her go to a poetry reading. "I said, 'Don't worry, I won't do that to you.'"

It's uncertain if the HAGS understood what a spectacle they were in the queer/dyke landscape of 1990s San Francisco. The fact that they were rarely spotted outside the pride, how much raucous space they took up at shows, their handle scribbled all over the neighborhood suggests yes. But no one ever knows exactly how they appear to others, do they? I want to tell the HAGS they succeeded. When they poured into a bar, my breath caught in my chest. I wondered what sort of transformation I would have to enact in order to date any of them and came up blank. Yes, I knew they did drugs. I was an adventurer, gearing up for my own wild ride; I wasn't terribly put off by that. But I also didn't know what it meant, not exactly. My friend Malaina involved herself in a tryst with a drug-addled couple who hung out in HAG territory; when it all went awry, Malaina was scared to leave the house because her paramours had sicced the HAGS on her. "The HAGS didn't have any loyalty to somebody just because you fuck the same gender," clarifies Lynnee Breedlove, former singer for Tribe 8, writer of the HAGS anthem, printed at the start of his HAGS-inspired novel, *Godspeed*, and also performed by the band, though not without controversy. A fellow band member had been intimately involved with a HAG, the relationship marked by addiction and abuse; she feared glorifying their lifestyle. But to Breedlove, an "honorary HAG" who spent significant time with the gang despite a commitment to sobriety, it was deeper than that:

> I had to look at, what is so great about them, why are they my heroes? There were a lot of nice, clean-cut lesbians that were cute and dykey and young and didn't want anything to do with that kind of craziness. But what those guys were to me—what we all were—were fucking warriors. You're facing down repression that's in your face all the time because of your gender, your punkness, and you say, You know what? I'm gonna live. I'm actually *not* gonna kill myself and I'm not going to go downtown and get a nine-to-five, so fuck you. I'm gonna be fucking happy, whatever it takes. Even if I'm only happy in this moment, from a chemical or a show. I need to live my life in this

moment any way that I can, and this is *the* only way that I know how to do it right now. And it's a fucking valid way for me. And you don't get to judge.

Sitting in the Outer Sunset in the twilight fog, eating a bowl of soup, Lynnee tears up as he makes this proclamation. It will always be very close. The shirt he's wearing used to belong to Stacey Quijas: "Corrosion of Conformity."

In the 1990s my daytime hours were spent sleeping off my hangover on my crumby futon, eventually heading out to do some writing, a spiral-bound notebook stuffed into my army bag. At night I wrote in bars, but when the sun was out I wrote in coffee shops. Café Macondo was a good one. It was on Sixteenth Street, between Albion and Guerrero. Now it's a bar with pinball and one million beer options, but then it was a café with a social justice bent, a table piled with flyers for political actions, empanadas in the cooler. Their coffees were a little bit smaller than in the other cafés, and this bothered me, but there was hardly anyone ever in there, which I liked. One day some HAGS were there. I noticed them, then quickly made like I hadn't noticed them. Not so much making like they weren't a big deal, more like making that I was the sort of person accustomed to their type of big deal, like I was a big deal myself, maybe, in some parallel universe. I focused on my writing and tried not to eavesdrop on their urgent mumbles. One of them walked over. It was Johanna Lee. She'd grown her buzz cut into a long, orange mane; her friends called her Mountain Man. She had a sweet baby face and wire-rimmed granny glasses.

"Hey, can we borrow some paper?" she asked. They had just learned that Valerie Solanas, author of the *SCUM*

Manifesto, shooter of Andy Warhol, and certainly a proto-HAG, had died right here in San Francisco. It had been some years ago, but it had been *here*, under the city's nose, at the Bristol Hotel, an SRO in the Tenderloin. Johanna and her co-HAG were going to make stencils about it and spray-paint the Tenderloin. I peeked over at her table; it was Fiver. Gaunt, gray-skinned, a fisherman's cap pulled onto her head, bangs spilling out. "She was fashion oriented," Carina recalls. "She liked suspenders, and she would cuff her jeans, there were always specific boots that had to happen."

I tore pages from my notebook, thrilled to be a part of the caper. This simple interaction solidified all I had projected onto the HAGS—this gang of punk rock dykes, many of whom would transition to male later in life—that they *were* the amazon warriors Lynnee Breedlove hailed them as. That despite their apparent scorn for contemporary feminist movements—"We ate riot grrrls for lunch," quips Becky, declaring the movement to be "for fluffy little college girls that complained about stuff a lot"—that, despite this, they were in fact the deepest, wildest, truest feminists, so feminist they frightened other feminists, so feminist they could shit-talk the movement and write it off as trifling because they were living the most hardcore feminist lives that only someone like Valerie Solanas would have recognized and understood. And me. I understood too. I desperately wished they would invite me along on their vandalism art project, but they did not. And truly, their vandalism art project might have never actually happened. Nobody I spoke to knew anything about it. I heard about Fiver trying to get back into a bar she'd been eighty-sixed from, incognito in a bad wig and a pair of Sally Jessy

Raphael eyeglasses. I heard about Johanna becoming pen pals with Aileen Wuornos, the death-row sex worker condemned for killing abusive tricks. I heard about Johanna Lee pouring vanilla extract around the tents of lesbian feminists who were trying to kick the SM dykes out of the Michigan Womyn's Music Festival, calling forth a plague of raccoons. I heard about how, when Joan of Anarchy needed her pacemaker replaced, Fiver comforted her visiting mother, assuring her that Joan had a good head on her shoulders, that if any of them were going to make something of themselves it would be Joan. But nobody remembered them doing stencils in honor of Valerie Solanas. Probably a good idea got consumed by speed distraction and was eventually discarded like a torn-apart clock.

> *Mr. Quijas locked herself out and she was pissed*
> *So she thought she'd wrap her hand in a flannel shirt*
> *Proceeded to smash the windows with her fist*
> *Since she saw it on TV she knew she couldn't get hurt*
> *The blood began to squirt*
> *All she could blurt*
> *Out was*
> *I'm a hag*
>
> —*Lynnee Breedlove, "The Hag Anthem"*

That's not Lynnee's favorite story about Stacey Quijas, though. Lynnee's favorite is the one when Quijas flew to Europe with her girlfriend, both of them people of color, punk and pierced, visibly queer. They got hassled at the border. The hassle escalated into a strip search. "The scary border guard matron snaps her rubber glove all smirky-smug and intimidating, like, 'Okay! Who's first?' And Quijas jumps and yells, 'Me!' She jumps at the lady, like, *You can't rape the willing, put your finger up my ass, I like it, bitch.* That, to me, was the only way I knew how to face authorities who were telling me to do shit that didn't make any sense, saying 'Fine!' All this shit that you say is going to hurt a normal person isn't going to hurt me, 'cause I'm a superhero."

Lynnee is talking about sexual abuse. His normally fast talk is faster, but with a hushed intensity, his eyes dart with a sort of pleading desperation, looking to land on something or someone that understands. He's been preaching compassion for the HAGS for decades, though less now, since nobody talks about them very much. "What that does to people, what nobody in the nineties wanted to deal with, because nobody wants to hand over that power to the perp, is create superpowers. It gives you the opportunity to leave your body and move energy and escape the immediate situation, or deal with the immediate situation in ways that the average Joe doesn't have." He likens Quijas to a tiny baby dragon whose cute roar belies the fact that she can singe the hair off your head. He likens her to a person frozen in their childhood charm, the sort of charm possessed by a boy of eleven or twelve, or a girl who is like a boy of eleven or twelve and whose home is profoundly unsafe, who learns charm as a survival skill and rides it all the way home.

It was Fiver who got Becky to quit drugs. "We'd had the conversation before, drug addict superstition. That you could tell, by looking into someone's eyes, if they're gonna die or not. Things that normally wouldn't kill people would kill these people whose eyes went vacant and dead. I still think this, it's almost like a spiritual thing. Like drugs take you away from your soul, almost. Fiver came up to me and was like, 'Dude. You're starting to look like that.'"

Becky was spooked. The warning coincided with a birthday, always a good time to reevaluate your life. It coincided with an eviction, for not paying rent for six months. It coincided with blowing out the veins in her arms. "Something just flipped that switch in my head. If I knew how to flip that switch I'd be a very wealthy person."

There's no explaining to a nonaddict how impossible it is to change your ways, even when they are clearly killing you. That some do is a miracle. That most don't is reality. By the time your problem is a problem it has leached its way into every facet of your life. It is your identity and coping mechanism, it is how you interface with others and connect with yourself, it is deep inside your cells now, and you belong to it. Becky wasn't sure she would make it. The one thing that fed the hope that she might survive to access a greater life was Lynnee Breedlove, who cheered her on, believing in her, laying on the love and pep talks. "I credit Lynnee with being alive today, really." A few years in, after she got her footing and was incredibly, blissfully sober, she pulled Lynnee aside to thank him. "In traditional Lynnee style he was like, 'Dude, I was lyin'! I thought you were gonna die!"

"She looked really fucked up," Lynnee remembers. "She did *not* look like she was going to make it. But, that was my job. I put her in bed and was like, 'Get horizontal. Drink water.' I got her some food, got her some calm-me-down whatevers. 'Just stay here, don't do anything.' I was excited for her."

Becky kept hanging out with the HAGS after she kicked speed. But beyond a certain point, it just didn't make that much sense anymore.

"I think I just wanted a better life for myself." That's how the next miracle began, that of Joan of Anarchy hopping on a Greyhound back to Monroe, Louisiana, to kick drugs at her mom's house. On the way, a seatmate commented, "Wow, man, you're coming down hard." The revelation that she had been on speed for three consecutive months came after another HAG asked her when she'd last eaten. Joan could not remember.

Once the speed was out of her system, Joan returned to San Francisco. She got a girlfriend, a nice girl with nice friends, and they became her social circle. She became Johnny. "When I started transitioning I stopped drinking so much and doing drugs, and started feeling more comfortable with my body." Pretty much his only contact with the HAGS was when Quijas stopped him on the street to borrow money. She came over to Johnny's new apartment and complimented him on his new deal. "She was like, 'Man, you're a good-looking guy!'" Johnny had been nervous, what with so many of the lesbians in the scene shunning trans men, and the HAGS' own wonked allegiance to women. But that was it. "Last time I saw her I was like, *I can't have Stacey in my life because I'm trying to do right.* And I saw her in the street, and she saw me, and I just passed her up. My girlfriend said, 'Hey, that's Stacey,' and I said, 'I know, keep walking.' Stacey just chuckled."

Underneath Johanna Lee's drug use was something else, probably schizophrenia. Ren Volpe met Johanna in 1989, at the Michigan Womyn's Music Festival. After the fest, Ren hitched a ride out of the Midwest with a girl she'd hooked up with. When they pulled into the Bay Area, the girl introduced Ren to her live-in girlfriend. In spite of this, Ren remained in town, vulnerable to the city's "magnetic pull for lesbians everywhere." Within three years nearly everyone she'd befriended at the festival had moved to San Francisco.

Ren is a real can-do dyke; she's written a book about automotive repair for women and currently is a school teacher and, like most every lesbian in this essay, makes part of her income caring for dogs. In the nineties she helped produce a community newsletter, a sort of skill-share classifieds where women listed their talents and were encouraged to trade services with one another. She organized the city's first Dyke March. Ren made zines and became close with Johanna, whose comics were political and funny, sharply subversive. Ren still has them, part of an archive of 1990s dykephilia which should be being handled with white gloves in some institution somewhere.

At her cottagey home in Bernal Heights, where a fire roars in an outdoor fire pit and her family—a partner and two daughters—awaits the arrival of a traumatized dog who dislikes men and is thus being fostered in a lesbian household, Ren shows me Johanna's art. A zine, *Up Our Butts*—a mash-up of the stuffy feminist periodical *off our backs* and Valerie Solanas's play *Up Your Ass*—shows a mulleted leather dyke, a cross-body bondage harness on her torso, a garment for harnessing a phallus at her groin, a pair of asshole sunglasses obscuring her face and a giant cat-o'-nine-tails in her fist. She speaks in a cartoon bubble: "I hope you don't think this is WEIRD, but the GODDESS told me to give you this magazine!" In the lesbian community newsletter, Johanna offered her cartooning and drawing services, as well as motorcycle riding lessons. She was hoping to barter with someone who could teach her how to tattoo.

Because I had given her the paper for her Valerie Solanas project, Johanna always remembered me, and always
shot me a sunbeam smile from her kindly face. But I wasn't
close to her. I didn't watch her drug use and her mental
illness progress side by side; unlike Marya Taylor, I didn't
have to rescue her dog when psychosis convinced Johanna
that the government had placed a tracking chip beneath
the animal's fur. Unlike her roommates, I didn't watch her
come home covered in blood from a random SM encounter in a stranger's van; for days her roommate scoured the
city for the mystery dyke who had engaged in an intense
scene with her, fearing Johanna had actually killed someone. They did eventually find the person, another young
queer new to the city from Texas and sleeping in their vehi-
cle; all was well. Initially I ran into Johanna at the Bearded
Lady, where anyone could spend the day on a single coffee without hassle. Later, I'd see her on the street, begging
spare change of oblivious passersby. I myself had come to
the city essentially homeless, with no familial support; the
specter of life on the street haunted me. Giving coins to
spare-changers was a sort of tax one paid for the luxury of
having a home of one's own. But Johanna I'd give a dollar.
She always appreciated it.

"She'd been homeless for years," Ren recalls. "I'd be driving around and see her; she'd always get in and drive around
with me. She was in the back seat mumbling and talking to
herself, just a crazy bag lady on the street. I'm like, 'Johanna!
Who're you talking to?' She said, 'The voices in my head.'
I said, 'Well, what are they saying?' She said, 'If they were
meant for you you'd hear them too!' She was delusional,
but she also had this metacognition about her delusion.
Because she was really, really smart."

Because it was not as large a countercultural movement as all that rose and fell within the 1960s, because it was less a national movement than something occurring within specific neighborhoods in San Francisco, and certainly because those involved were not even LGBT people but lesbians—specifically dykes who were not looking to fit in so much as fuck shit up—there is no recorded history of this subculture and the copious amounts of culture it produced: politics, fashion, art, sex. But like that other decade of revolution, the dyke nineties of San Francisco began with a joyful, dark idealism that obscured the coming crash. As Ren explains, "We were all fucking nuts." She talks about gangs of dykes selecting the most passably female among them, dressing her up like a girl, and sticking her on the street as bait. When a man eventually fucked with her, the rest of them would jump out of the shadows and kick his ass. "We were all freaks that got drawn magnetically to San Francisco. Johanna was just a freak among freaks. How would you know someone was crazy when we were all pretty freaky?" There would, of course, be no way to know until the end of the decade, and an inventory of who among us was still standing.

Kelly from Torrance, HAG name Kelly Kegger, never wasn't working. She began as a bike messenger who didn't know her way around the city and, having slowly spent her three-thousand-dollar windfall hanging out and getting slowly hooked on dope, couldn't afford a Zo Bag, *the* practical accessory of choice for bike messengers everywhere. She kept her giant, sputtering radio shoved into the pockets of her cargo shorts. Eventually she learned her way around, got the necessary Zo Bag, and made enough money to pay for her weekly room at the Potter Hotel, one of the better SROs in the city, populated with fellow queers and bike messengers. She spent her nights debauching with the HAGS. "It would be four thirty, five in the morning, and I'd be like, 'I gotta take a power nap.' Then seven o'clock in the morning, everyone is still partying and I'd be like, 'I gotta go to work.'" This was a common bike messenger lifestyle at the time; a popular T-shirt read "Powered by Speed and Beer." "It was nothing," Kelly maintains. "You just ride your bike around." Come three o'clock she was done ferrying packages around the Financial District and would return to whatever communal house was HAG central. If nobody was home Kelly would grab a piece of chalk and leave a note on the sidewalk. "We didn't have phones or nothing," Kelly says. "Those were like our little text messages."

Kelly's closest friendship was with Quijas: "We had a crazy relationship. We fought like we were a couple. She was super jealous. You couldn't talk to any of her girlfriends. But she could fuck *your* girlfriend." Kelly and Quijas each had femme girlfriends, sex workers who were friends with one another. Anya had been drinking tequila in a bush outside a party when she met Kelly; she was hiding from her clean and sober girlfriend. "I saw this person with long, black hair walk up to the keg. She tried to pour beer and it was empty, she kicked the can and cursed and that was Kelly Kegger." Soon the four of them—Anya, Kelly, Quijas, and her girlfriend—were family.

"I would go to work. Kelly would take me, drive me to my trick, would be there while I was doing phone sex, buying drugs, coming home with money," says Anya. The same system was in place with Quijas and her dominatrix girlfriend; they would all pick her up at the dungeon and joke about it. Though Anya was as punk as the HAGS, and developed her own heroin addiction alongside them, "I wasn't a HAG. There weren't any real femmes in the HAGS. They were the butches. Really tough, but masculine. I was completely extreme too, I loved them because I felt exactly the same way. I was cut from the same cloth and it was hard; they didn't accept me because I wasn't butch. It was a boys' club. 'Bros before hos,' that way you're not vulnerable. The love and intimacy can penetrate the gang and make it vulnerable to the outside."

As Kelly's habit progressed, consequences began piling up. "I got fired from the bike messenger gig, which is really hard to do." She'd picked up a side gig locksmithing and managed to hang on to that one. When she burned through her stash before payday—as happened more and more frequently—she would steal the locksmith van and drive it through Oakland, using her tools to help folks on the street bust into cars for a fee. Now living in a studio in Oakland, she became increasingly isolated from friends, her days and nights revolving around scrambling for cash and accessing drugs. When there wasn't enough money for both rent and dope, dope won, and Kelly moved in with Anya, by now more of an ex than a girlfriend.

At the end of Kelly's volatile friendship with Quijas, she'd urged her to go to the free clinic on Haight Street for a checkup; she appeared dangerously swollen. "She just looked like shit," Kelly remembers. "They gave her all these tests and her thyroid was fucked up. She had to quit drinking and using drugs. They told her, 'You'll be dead in five years if you don't do this.' I was like, 'Well, what are you gonna do?' And she was like, 'Well, I'm not quitting drinking.'"

"I watched people I knew fall through the cracks," says Silas Howard. He's in a lovely wooden room, classic New England hardy elegance, in Williams, Massachusetts, where he's ensconced in an artist's residency. Many of his current works in progress come back to this point in time, this moment when the youthful, invincible glory of his friends turned on them like a black hole, crushed beneath the pressures of addiction, homophobia, family abandonment, gender discrimination, all of it. "There was a moment when there were a lot of people coming to San Francisco who were like the lost kids, no safety net, so the stakes were really high and people would rise and fall really rapidly. It got really hard when addiction became so dark. All of the anger we were putting out into the world, which seemed so liberating, was starting to turn back in. There was a political aspect to it, but sometimes they were just being fucked up, being destructive, being mean."

For all the time that has passed and the personal writing he's done about this moment, discussing it can still be painful. It's one thing to discuss your family's trauma with other family; it's another thing entirely to release their stories to a world that doesn't love them. "You want to talk about things in a protective mode, and there's the honest thing of how complicated it was to watch them all go through that. We watched our friends go through mental illness, eating disorders, drug addiction, all of that. This was a gang of people who were helping each other stay there. It was really hard when it got hard."

The last time Kelly saw Quijas was at a pay phone south of Market frequently used to cop drugs; you'd page your guy and he'd call back. "It just came to a crashing end,"

Kelly said about the friendship. Kelly had let Quijas and another HAG stay at her place, but they were so loud and paranoid, screaming that Kelly had stolen from them, that Kelly feared getting kicked out. At the pay phone they made small talk about who they were buying from. Quijas recommended a new guy whose dope was good and cheap, and who would do home deliveries, even out to Oakland, any time of the night. Kelly switched her source.

In January 1999, Kelly noticed she had tiny open wounds all over her legs and her butt. Little dots. She and her pit bull were still crashing with Anya; by day she would do methadone in hopes of getting off dope, but by nightfall her resolve would fade and she'd be back to heroin. "It was like a double habit." She'd been skin-popping black tar heroin, the sticky, rock version of the drug found on the West Coast. The workers at the methadone clinic took a look at the wounds and sent her to the hospital. At the Oakland Kaiser Medical Center, the doctors were baffled. Kelly explained she'd been using drugs. "They were like, 'Well, you can't use drugs anymore.' That was their solution." They sent her home with antibiotics.

This was on February 7, and Kelly hadn't used dope in twenty hours. Proud of herself, she kept it going, hitting recovery meetings and stealing the money from the basket, racking up a record five days clean from heroin.

By Valentine's Day, Kelly was unable to get out of bed, hadn't, in fact, left her room in days. Her pit bull had shit all over the place and Anya was pissed. When she bust into Kelly's room to bitch her out, she was shocked. "She was like, 'What the fuck is wrong with you?'" Kelly only knew that she was sick, something wasn't right. Anya dragged her from bed and brought her back to Kaiser. When reception told them they'd have to wait, Anya went ballistic, furious at them for having sent her home, certain Kelly was dying. "I was like, 'Don't be so dramatic. Jesus.'" But her fury worked. "They admitted me right away. And then they did emergency surgery."

What the doctors were saying did not quite register with Kelly. Partly it was denial, and partly she was haggard and addled from drugs and detoxing and also she was sick, very, very sick. Then, much of it was the denial native to anyone in the throes of an addiction. She worried about losing her locksmith job and the health insurance it gave her, she wanted to know when she'd be getting out. "They were like, 'We don't know if you're going to make it out of surgery.' I was like, 'Oh. Okay.'"

Kelly survived, but the doctors warned she might never walk again. This struck her as absurd, as she could feel her toes just fine. The doctors continued: If she had shown up at General they would have simply removed her legs. It had taken the doctors at Kaiser fourteen hours of surgery to prevent those amputations. Still, Kelly didn't get it. "They were like, 'You can't use drugs *ever.* Do you understand that?' I was like, 'Okay, whatever.'"

Kelly understood that she had had a bacterial infection, one that had gotten close to sending her body into septic shock. Her butt harbored deep wounds, stuffed with gauze. After three weeks the hospital wanted to send her home, but Anya had left their shared house and Kelly had nowhere to go. She was moved to Medical Hill, a nursing and rehabilitation center.

At Medical Hill, Kelly was put on methadone and taught to walk again. After a month and a half she was limping around, which bolstered her confidence that her surgeon didn't know what he was talking about. She had yet to come out of the clouds about what had happened to her. When her morphine drip was removed after two months, she put in a call to the home-delivery dealer and ordered some heroin.

Also at two months, Kelly got fired from the locksmith job. "They were like, 'You haven't been here in months.' And I was like, 'Yeah, I'm in the hospital.' But it wasn't work related, so they're like, 'You're out of here, dude.'" Cut off from her health insurance, Kelly's options were to come up with $489 a month for COBRA—impossible—or get sent to Highland Hospital, Oakland's rough general hospital. Kelly called her mom in Southern California to see if she might be able to come bring her home, but she wasn't able to get the time off from her library job.

"This nurse lady, she comes in and was like, 'I'm going to pay it.' I was like, 'What the fuck? Why are you doing this?' She said, 'Because then you'll have to do something nice for someone someday.'"

It was Kelly's roommate who helped bust her out of denial, a twenty-six-year-old mother from Richmond receiving hospice for stomach cancer. The woman, who hosted lots of visitors, was confused as to why Kelly had only been seen by her mom, her drug dealer, and Anya. For a while, Kelly refused to talk about it, and wouldn't share what she was in for, either. But eventually she talked.

"She was like, 'Oh god, you're a junkie!' I said, 'Yeah, I guess I was a junkie. Technically, I guess I still am.' I had never really said it out loud. She's like, 'Well, you're not on it now.' And I was like, 'Well, I can't walk.'" They were on the patio smoking the weed the woman's brother-in-law smuggled in to help ease the effects of her stomach cancer. "She said, 'I never heard of anyone having what you had. Usually they just OD and die.' It was a lot to hear. Like, oh fuck, I'm a junkie. You're not supposed to be a junkie."

Eventually Kelly's mom did pick her up and take her back to Long Beach, where she flushed the last of her heroin and kept on methadone. She spent the days trapped at home, tripping out on pop culture. She'd spent the past years without TV, snug inside the "queer drug bubble," and was utterly flabbergasted by rap-rock and Britney Spears. One day Anya called her from a pay phone in San Francisco; during the conversation, she spotted Quijas and put her on the line.

"I remember telling Stacey what happened. She said, 'Oh, it doesn't sound like you were taking care of yourself. You should take better care of yourself.' I was like, 'No, dude, I'm telling you, if you get these bumps or sores you gotta go to the hospital.'" Quijas blew it off. Stung by the condescension, Kelly didn't press it.

On June 6, 1999, a thirty-three-year-old woman presented to the San Francisco General Hospital emergency department with a chief complaint of two days of excruciating, sharp, and continuous pain in her left buttock after four days of fever and chills, nausea, vomiting, and lethargy. She reported five years of heroin use, black tar heroin use on the day of admission, and occasional methamphetamine use. She was alert and oriented but anxious, with pale, cool skin and pinpoint pupils.

"Clostridial Myonecrosis Cluster Among Injection Drug Users: A Molecular Epidemiology Investigation" is a difficult paper for a layperson to read. Partly this is due to sentences which contain phrases like "a crepitus area was found . . . with erythema, induration, and ecchymosis," requiring the sort of Google searches that beget infinite additional Google searches. Lacking that mysterious detachment required of surgeons, it is difficult also to read such sentences as: "Deposits of a black tarlike material were present in the tissues with pock marking and scarring on both lower extremities." Having actually known Fiver, having felt inspired and emboldened by her time on this planet, and having been close to Carina Gia, the poet who had loved her so, it is difficult, too, to read: "She developed refractory hypotension while being treated with intravenous epinephrine and dopamine and died intraoperatively seven hours after admission." People I spoke with were under the impression that Fiver died in the elevator at General without ever being seen by a doctor. It was hard to obtain information. Says Silas Howard, "We all knew each other, but going to hospitals—we didn't know each other's legal names. We weren't family. All of a sudden it got very real. Access." For the record, from the records, it looks like they tried to save her, Fiver.

Five days later, Stacey Quijas arrived at General Hospital. She was twenty-eight years old. She reported skin-popping black tar heroin for the past seven months, most recently earlier that day. Can I convey the simple chaos that existed outside that room, that hospital? The chaos of people living life on drugs, of people accustomed to no access, broke people, and no one had cell phones—these were folks who communicated with one another via chalk scrawls on sidewalks. But what was the hospital's excuse? When people went to check on Stacey, they were told she'd been released. For four or five days, according to Kelly, HAGS and other queers looked for their friend. Eventually some went to the hospital and told them Quijas never came home. "Oh, she's still here." Stacey Quijas was in the ICU. By then she was probably on her third or fourth surgery.

Once they could get in, a vigil arranged itself at Quijas's bedside. Lynnee Breedlove, occupied with the management of Lickety Split, the all-girl bike messenger company he'd started, came when he could. "She was knocked out," he recalls. "I think they might have done a drug-induced coma. Blood was everywhere. Her beautiful body that was all tatted up everywhere—they had to cut away the rotting parts, and there was no way to stop the bleeding." A day or so after her friends found her, Quijas died. Says Silas Howard, simply, "It was a horror movie."

Dr. Andre Campbell is the San Francisco General attending surgeon who operated on Quijas and additional people who contracted the flesh-eating bacteria through probable exposure to black tar heroin. He is the coauthor of the medical paper detailing the cataclysm. In the wake of the deaths, he helped create San Francisco's Integrated Soft Tissue Infection Service, a special clinic catering to people with abscesses and cellulitis. They treat about one hundred thousand people with soft tissue infections each year, overwhelmingly IV or intramuscular drug users.

"You can actually watch the infection go up someone's back, their arm," he explains from his office at General. "The only way you can control it is by cutting it. Debride. It means cut away, cut off the skin, the tissues underneath, the fascia and the muscle. You have to get control. It's a race between the bacteria and you."

The day before Quijas died, a third HAG came to the hospital. She lived with Fiver and Quijas in a dilapidated warehouse where chickens ran amok and which was destined to be shut down very soon by health department workers in hazmat suits. The third HAG had come to visit her friend, but while she was there she spoke with a doctor about her worry: she had been skin-popping the same black tar as Fiver and Quijas. The doctors examined her, found nothing of any concern, but gave her 2.4 million units of intramuscular penicillin just to be safe. The HAG went back to the soon-to-be-condemned warehouse and promptly shot a bit of the contaminated heroin into her stomach. This will likely baffle and even enrage anyone who has not been touched by the powerful insanity of addiction; even I, who was grabbed by the undertow of my own habits so many times before somehow getting clean, even I spoke aloud the phrase "What the fuck?" in a condemning voice upon reading this in the medical paper. The third HAG, unable to resist the pull of a piece of dope currently killing her two best friends, did some, and returned to the hospital the following morning. After ten surgeries, 20 percent of her body surface was removed. She was in intensive care for over a month. After forty days, she was released to a rehabilitation facility. She is alive.

"People just want to get better," says Dr. Campbell, who cared for the third HAG throughout her time at General. "It was tough going there for a bit. It's our job to be compassionate."

The papers picked up that some "addicts" had been cut down by a sensationalistic "flesh-eating bacteria," in part

because Dr. Campbell himself conducted a press conference. Two other drug users had been admitted with the same
lethal bacterial stew, one on crystal meth who'd reported his
drugs looked especially "dirty" and lost his arm, and a black
tar heroin user who survived three debridements and was
released after twelve days. Between 1992 and 1997, General had treated only seven cases of necrotizing fasciitis; in
less than one month they were seeing five. Dr. Campbell
feared a bad batch, and who knows how much of it, could
be on the street, killing people. Getting the word out was
crucial. "The problems get bad when people wait and they
don't come in," he explains. Needle-exchange programs
were kept in the loop by the health department, helping
spread the warning to IV drug users.

The story became more lurid with speculation that the
heroin had become contaminated while being smuggled
up from Mexico in cadavers. Dr. Campbell has himself
heard of drugs being brought through customs this way,
but it's impossible to know how this batch made it into the
US. What the doctor thought he could learn was whether
the contaminant was present in the drug itself, confirm-
ing that a batch was tainted, or if the bacteria had come
from another source: dirty needles, contaminated water,
chicken shit. Dr. Campbell's medical sleuthing failed to
prove beyond a doubt that the infections came from the
drugs, though the evidence is suggestive, in particular when
you consider that Kelly—who fell sick across the Bay and
was not included in the study—had likely bought her drugs
from the same dealer as the others.

Silas Howard found the media's sudden interest in his
friends angering and heartbreaking. The world turned its
back on the HAGS while they lived, but in death, cut down

by such a grimly newsworthy event, they were the talk of the town. "The way they were just reduced to being addicts, the way they were treated, it was really intense. Still to this day, if I look up Stacey Quijas, the first thing that comes up is the flesh-eating disease that killed her." It's true. If you know how to refine your search you can find the two covers of *There's a Dyke in the Pit,* a compilation album released by the Outpunk, a now-defunct queer punk record label. In one version she wears a mohawk on her head and the leather-jacketed arm of a grinning friend slung around her shoulders; she frowns into the camera like she's issuing a dare. In the other she wears a backward baseball cap and a smirk, throwing devil horns aside two femmes with wild hair and glorious, pierced smiles.

"I remember I was so mad," Howard continues. "I was like, 'Who gave you the right to print our friend's name and label them a drug addict?' That seems slanderous. It seems, like, even if it's true, why do you get to print their name, with only this thing?"

An ex-girlfriend of Quijas had come to town upon learning of her death; Howard took her to General, where they flagged a nurse. "I said, 'Our friend died and my friend wasn't here and she just wants information.' And he looked at her and said, 'Well, you know what you guys do. You shoot up drugs. And you die.' It was just the coldest." Quijas's ex had never shot drugs, and Howard had long been clean and sober. "It's just weird the way society deals with addiction."

Stacey Quijas's body was sent to Colorado, to the family she'd run away from decades earlier, and was buried wearing a pink dress. "A lot of us people who were close to her did our best to advocate against that, saying she would not want that," Lynne Breedlove recalls. "It was an ongoing discussion and power struggle for three weeks." The family refused. Defeated and infuriated, friends organized events to honor the fallen HAGS at Ocean Beach and in private homes. "At that point, everyone just had to go, 'Fuck it. We're having our memorial over here, we're not going to that funeral.' 'Cause that's just her body. She left that a long time ago. Do whatever you want, dress it up, play your little games. We're going to celebrate her life the way she would have wanted it."

According to Carina, Fiver "was buried where she came from, Lincoln County, Ohio, which she always made fun of." Although they played Janis Joplin and Jimi Hendrix at her funeral and buried her with a bottle of whisky, she didn't escape the final marks of a culture that misunderstood her as Carina learned after speaking with the funeral director by phone. "He basically made it sound like she looked better than ever with the makeup they had put on her, possibly better than she looked alive. So," she says wearily, "I guess that happened."

In the wake of Fiver's death, Carina became determined to rescue her belongings from the condemned warehouse. At the time, Fiver was in a relationship with the third HAG, and the woman's friends were possessively guarding Fiver's belongings as the woman convalesced at General. Carina sweet-talked her way into the place and absconded with Fiver's trunk. "This was my soul mate," she says. "I'm not going to just let people throw this shit out on the curb." Carina found the trunk was full of photographs, full of Fiver's clothing, her books, and her journals.

"I think it sobered us all up quite a bit," says Lynnee Breed-love, speaking on the aftermath of the deaths. "You know that moment when you're an addict and you realize, 'Oh, I can die from this, okay.' I think the whole community of us suddenly got that."

Kelly got it. Having come up from Long Beach to attend the memorials, she moved in with Breedlove, staying on his couch for a year, healing, kicking drugs, eating ice cream, smoking three packs of cigarettes a day, watching television. "I was like, you stay here as long as you want, just do what you want. Quijas was her running dog. She had the grief of losing your best friend, to the same thing that almost killed you, that you didn't want to tell anyone about because of the shame, and then you have survivor's guilt." Eventually Kelly began working for Breedlove's messenger service, driving a borrowed truck. She moved into a spare room and became a proper roommate. She remained haunted. "Keg had trouble sleeping," Breedlove recalls. "She would have to have a fan for the white noise, and blackout curtains, all this stuff." She was unable to carry twenty-dollar bills on her person, as the sight of them was too triggering. But slowly, Kelly returned to the land of the living. Rent was cheap, and she got a second job, with AAA. With some cash in her pocket, she took off for Europe to attend a summer metal festival. She experimented with drinking, figuring at least it wasn't harder stuff, and returned to the States full of regret and hungover, with the determination to become fully sober.

By fall, Kelly had cut off all her long hair. She stopped wearing her signature vest with its many music patches, a kind of tribal identification garment, a uniform. She quit smoking. Sometime after the start of the New Year she looked around her room, essentially wallpapered with flyers for punk and metal shows. She began taking them down.

They went into boxes, alongside other metal accessories and skull decor.

"She was able to sit and reflect in that room and go, 'What's my part?'" Breedlove reflects. "The answer came back—'I'm somehow inviting this in, whatever it is. Pain, death, destruction, confusion.' What can you do different? For her it was, 'I'm getting rid of all this death stuff.'" Together they hauled the effects of Kelly's former life down to Third Street, where homeless people, some of them tweakers, live in trailers. "It felt freeing," says Kelly. On a delivery the following day, Breedlove drove past their dump spot and the items were gone. Kelly painted her dark room in light colors and took down her curtains.

It's June 17, 2016. Sixteen years ago Stacey Quijas died. Memorial posts are cropping up on Facebook. "Let me tell you how different my life is now," Kelly says. He still works in transportation, though higher up, and he managed to buy a house in Oakland when the market crashed. "Today on June 17 what I'm doing is going to the LGBT night at the A's, to watch fucking baseball. Who would have thought that in sixteen years I'd be going to some fucking gay baseball night? I didn't even like sports. I still don't like sports! But I like going to baseball games because I like hanging out with my friends and being outside."

"I think it's normal," says Joan of Anarchy, now Johnny Ray, about his own life. He lives in Vallejo, and for the past nine years has worked for animal care and control. "I go to work and I come home and drink my beer and hang out with my animals. I try to keep a low profile. I still like going to shows and getting in the pit, but the last time I hurt my arm."

Kelly's old girlfriend, Anya, was stuck in the quicksand of methadone maintenance for years before being able to quit both that and heroin. She's kept away from hard drugs, but dabbled in psychedelics until two years ago, when she became clean and sober. She raises her son in the East Bay and works as a sex educator and body worker. "I still do things that are super radical," she says. She identifies as an anarchist and as a radical mom, but has shrugged off the punk identity that shaped her younger years. "I was almost dead because of the punk scene," she says. "It's really hard for me just to go to a show."

Becky Slane spent some years traveling around the country, landing in Louisville, Nashville, New York City. Today she lives in Los Angeles and makes her living as a commercial painter. "I'm the person you call when you want some crazy, cool texture, a cool painting accent, or if you want something to look one hundred years old, like *really* a hundred years old, not like a Cracker Barrel gift center." She also does tile and mosaic work, and credits finding her artistic gifts to her time in HAGS. "We were constantly with the punk rock arts and crafts," she laughs. "We didn't have anything that wasn't altered or messed with. That was something I realized I had an aptitude for, and developed a love for."

Tracie Thomas, who unknowingly began this saga with a tongue-in-cheek John Waters homage, lives in Florida with her girlfriend, an animal chiropractor. The story of the HAGS has left her "so antidrugs now, it's not even funny." She spends a lot of time at the gym and on the tennis court, and cares for a couple of French bulldogs. She runs a clothing business called Trauma Tease, T-shirts silk-screened with designs: flaming dice, mudflap girls, ace of spades, Satan smoking a cigar. One garment reads, "Luck Runs Out." She walks on the beach every day. "The simple life, I guess."

As for Johanna Lee, the HAGS madman savant, she lived on and off the street for many years, often cared for by lovers and friends, "an army of femmes," claims Lynne Breedlove.

"I saw her before she died, she looked like she was seventy," says Ren Volpe. "I was like, 'Oh my god, this is my friend Johanna, a young, vital peer.' In her case it wasn't just drugs. It was drugs and mental illness, then all of the physical illness that come with that." What was she sickened with? "Everything," says Breedlove. "HIV, hep C." Unlike her compatriots, Johanna escaped the particular hell that is a problematic birth family having the last word on your life. She refused contact with her mother from her deathbed, and instead enacted what Breedlove calls "this whole Valhalla Viking ritual at the beach." A close friend then brought her to the hospital, and she died.

Maybe the HAGS didn't really mean anything. People live and die all over the globe; they struggle against external oppression and those parts of our human interiority we call demons. But there is something. Perhaps it is connected to how quickly and thoroughly San Francisco changes, how so much of that change is centered in the Mission, HAG central. How they would have railed against the latest gentry: how many cell phones would they have smashed on the street? Is there a place in the culture for such wild ruffians, a crew of wounded animals who bash back? And what about queer history? Will the California public school system work HAGS 101 into their forthcoming curriculum? Will they find ways to discuss the violence, psychic and otherwise, so many queer people endured? Will it explore the various and creative ways queers made space for themselves, made family, made themselves big and scary the way you're supposed to when facing down a grizzly? When facing down the drooling and ferocious wild beast of homophobia, the HAGS became gorgeous monsters. The strategy was not sustainable. Is it any less valuable for that, any less admirable, beautiful, clever? Even at a distance, the HAGS marked me, had a tattooed, silver-ringed hand in making me who I was and am. The HAGS are dead. Long live the HAGS.

HOW TO REFER TO
MY HUSBAND-WIFE

For our wedding, my person and I decided to ask a good friend to marry us. There were a few reasons for this, our friend was famously grumpy, and marriage—gay marriage in particular—really got her grump rumpled. She wished homos would put their efforts toward less bourgeois activity and was bitter about her own failed gay marriage. She was also a poet, prone to sentimental weeping, with a humorous presence reminiscent of Fozzie Bear. I told her that working-class queers were going to be getting hitched every bit as much as the upwardly mobile, and begged her to become a minister online so she could tie our knot. Being a good friend, she acquiesced, penning a stunning speech about the history of queer liberation and eking out a few of the sentimental tears we'd hoped for. She stood behind us, beneath the sagging chuppah, her eyes moist as my beloved and I spoke our vows, promising to be super extra excellent to one another for the rest of our lives. We kissed shyly before our friends and family, then looked to our reluctant officiant for the final words. "I now pronounce you . . ." The phrase hung in the air, truncated, and we all waited to see what my love and I were about to become.

The question of what to call my totally masculine

female partner (partner, ech!) had begun surfacing a month before our wedding. My sister had inquired about what her children, my fiancée's future niece and nephew, should call Dashiell after we were hitched. I was "Auntie Michelle," and my sister did her best to enforce the formality, having sweet memories of our own aunties. I knew Dashiell wouldn't be an auntie. Her hair is military short and blocky men's eyeglasses sit on her angular face. She leaves for work each morning in a button-down, sometimes a tie, sometimes not. Always men's pants and wing tips, a cardigan. She looks like a guy—like a super hot male model, and I often accompany her into the ladies' room, ready to put out any man-in-the-ladies'-room fires her presence might spark. Female titles feel so wrong with Dashiell, and pronouns are confusing—I often find myself calling her "he" without meaning to. She doesn't mind. It doesn't fit her perfectly, but neither does "she." Like so many people whose bodies, minds, and aesthetics exist in between our two-party gender system, her current options suck. When I write about Dashiell and when I speak to her or about her, I slip in and out of masculine and feminine pronouns, and that's pretty much fine.

It took months to come around to it, but Dashiell decided that she'd simply like the kids to call her "Dashiell." Great. Next came the question from our officiant: "What do you want to be pronounced as? You know, in place of husband and wife? Or, do you *want* husband and wife?" The question was a good one. And a tough one, one that Dashiell and I had both seen coming and had been casually avoiding. It wasn't just a matter of what would be said at our wedding, it was a question of what we would call each other once the rings were on our fingers.

"Can you say, 'I now pronounce you each other's person forever'?" I asked, knowing as I said it that it sounded totally weird and awkward, maybe what a beloved pet would call their gentle master. I did like referring to Dashiell as my person, and she did the same; many nights, snuggled on the couch, one of us would spontaneously turn to the other and proclaim, "You're my person!" delighting in the way we belonged to one another. But "person" sounded both too intimate and too cutesy. Still, as the wedding drew nearer, neither of us had come up with anything better.

"I now pronounce you . . ." Dashiell and I looked up at our friend, all of us with sweet-weepy faces. "Married!" Our guests all cheered. Good one! And, so we were. "You're not my wife," I said to Dashiell, later. I scrunched my face and shook my head, "*I'm* the wife." Thinking of us as each other's wives made me think of those cheesy gown-wearing, twinsie bridal cake toppers on a lezzie wedding cake. Even though I know there are women out there marrying one another in matching dresses, that completely misses the mark for Dashiell and me, making her gender—and hence, her self—invisible, and making my queer, femme desire invisible as well.

Dashiell *did* feel like my husband, but the word had too much manly baggage for her to be comfortable with it. There was "spouse," a word from government forms that reminded me of the tiny plastic pegs in the Game of Life board game. "Partner" had been so absorbed by hetero liberals that saying it suggested I was married to a stay-at-home dad who campaigned for Green Party candidates and had a feminist blog. Plus, the roots of "partner" are in the bullshit domestic partner option cowardly politicians once pushed for in lieu of actual marriage. Its neutrality sounded neutered to me—blah, bland, redolent of linty, sexless marriages.

I hit on our somewhat goofy, imperfectly perfect word accidentally on the phone with the lab at our hospital. I got my thyroid levels checked earlier that day but had forgotten to bring my insurance card, so called back later to provide my info. I recited the numbers and spelled out Dashiell's name, the primary insured person.

"Relationship?" the receptionist asked.

"Huh?"

"What is your relationship to the card holder?"

"Oh, uh, husband-wife," I said. "We're married."

Husband-wife? Husband-wife! The receptionist didn't miss a beat and I hung up the phone laughing.

First published in the *Bold Italic* in 2014.

WRITING
&
LIFE

THE CITY TO A YOUNG GIRL

Because I have written a lot about marginalized, even criminalized, experiences—my own—the title *activist* often gets applied to me. It never feels correct. Maybe because I did real activism in my youth, traveling up to Kennebunkport, Maine—summer playground for Bush the First—with ACT UP to stage a massive die-in in the quaint New England streets. A human carpet, prone beneath the August sun, queers sprawled against queers, silent, everyone thinking about those they'd lost, or their own death sentence. Not me. I hadn't lost anyone, too young and too lucky, I guess, but I'd awakened to how evil people could be, how so many of these evil people ran the show called America. I did a lot of activism that summer. When my recent ex-boyfriend showed up for a potential job at a Sunglass Hut in Nahant, Massachusetts, and was asked by the manager if he was gay—"Because we don't even let them shop here"—I assembled my ragtag group of new, gay (and newly gay) friends and we ransacked that shop, leaving piles of sunglasses, the entire store, really, heaped on top of the counter. We informed the manager of our queerness and his illegal discrimination and went on to get him fired. After sleep-deprived weeks defending women's health clinics against Operation Rescue, I found out the name of the church one of the antichoice priests preached at and another field trip was under-way, one where we homos stood outside the church with screams and signs and noisemakers, disrupting their Sun-day morning services as they had disrupted our Sunday mornings, period, for the past weeks.

I spray-painted the name and crime of the man who'd sexually assaulted my friend outside his apartment. I blocked the streets around a church hosting a famed antigay preacher, throwing a notebook full of angry poetry at the head of a lesbian cop manhandling protesters. I took off my shirt to call attention to the unasked for sexualization of my body, its freedom controlled by government and capitalism. I did all of this and more, and perhaps because I did it all so long ago, hearing myself referred to as an activist simply for my writing feels bad, a real cop-out. Activists put their bodies on the line. They risk arrest and abuse. My writ-ing—though it may have, hopefully, provided support and entertainment—has been largely a self-serving enterprise. I write because I am strangely compelled to, and because I generally enjoy it and understand it to be my purpose in this life, but also because I hope it will bring me things: money, security, compliments, fame, respect, and power, and the opportunity for increased money, security, compli-ments, fame, respect, and power. Even RADAR Produc-tions, the queer-centric literary nonprofit I created and ran for over a decade, even as much of its work could be loosely construed as "activism" for championing and providing resources to marginalized writers, even that provided me with a paycheck and access to a material world I'd never before known. There is an argument that activism can take many forms and need not only be risking everything in the streets, but to me that *is* activism, and having not done that in quite a while, the label quickly peels off of me.

And so, when I was asked to speak at a university on the topic of activist writings and the personal being political, I felt uneasy. If I'd had more psychic space, if I hadn't had a one-year-old and hadn't just relocated to an entirely new town where I was trying to build for myself an entirely new version of my writing life, perhaps I could have read actual activist texts, writings by Malcolm X and Assata Shakur, James Baldwin and Martin Luther King Jr., various suffragettes and abolitionists, and taught a sort of class, but that's not exactly what I do and, I believe, not exactly what was expected of me. Being a writer of personal narratives that do cast a light on my life's political sources and ramifications, I figured I should be talking more or less about myself. And I was less inspired than ever.

Donald Trump hadn't won the election yet, and, truthfully, I didn't believe he would. In but a few weeks, I would gather beloved friends at my home to watch the results come in and celebrate our imperfect candidate, the first female president of the United States of America, Hillary Clinton. My friend Tara wore a lavender pantsuit, my friend Gigi brought balloons and little American flags. My eight-year-old niece arrived wearing a "Hillary" barrette my sister painstakingly crafted for her. I myself made a "Trumpkin"—a small, orange gourd carved in his likeness, replete with perpetually windblown comb-over, barfing bright-green guacamole onto a platter. It was only my friend Maggie who arrived with all the grimness of Cassandra and spent the night about two inches from the television screen, her thin face growing increasingly pinched as I ran from room to room, following a parade of toddlers, pausing for a scoop of guac and to reassure poor, nervous Maggie that everything, of course, was going to be all right.

Obviously, it wasn't. When the impossible began taking shape on the horizon of our collective lives, Maggie went home, and others followed. Having been distracted by the kids, it took me a moment to catch up with where my guests had landed, a baffled acknowledgment that Donald Trump, the sexual-assaulting, racist, reality-TV narcissist, was to be our president. *There's a mistake*, I thought, as Tara began to cry in her excellent lavender pantsuit. I watched comedian Jena Friedman cry on the television, advising us all to get our abortions, now. My friends Nicole and Sandwich were sunk into my couch and stayed that way until I all but kicked them out, all the life energy sucked from them, not wanting to go out and face this world that we all already knew was horrible, right? We all were like-minded, with days of in-the-streets activism in our past, writers and artists whose political opinions are clear to any reader. We were among those who complained about the giant problem that is America even throughout the Obama years. We knew the bulk of the people in our country are misogynists who don't believe they are misogynist, racists who don't think they are racist, homophobes who don't think they are homophobes, we *knew* this already, but still, to see these attitudes manifest in this president, *this* president— we cried. Soon I would phone various legal organizations to see if they advised I begin a formal adoption process for the baby I literally gave birth to. I would hear shouting from my bathroom and dash out of the house in a bathrobe to watch the entirety of Eagle Rock High School defiantly storm out of class and take to the streets. I would succumb to a variety of Facebook fights that were, honestly, beneath me in every way. I would promise to stop and do it again, my rage in need of any outlet, no matter how pathetic. I would unfriend a cousin I'd thought I loved. I would ask one hundred online friends to please befriend my mother, because she is based in Florida and her internet experience was becoming increasingly apocalyptic.

But my talk at the university was weeks before this. I may not have believed, then, that the worst could happen, but I was still disgusted by the swell of support Trump was enjoying. It was exactly two days since the *Access Hollywood* story had been leaked. "I moved on her like a bitch. Grab them by the pussy. You can do anything." It was the last one, "You can do anything," that stuck with and haunted me. Because it's true, and we were seeing it play out writ large, as so many of us had witnessed in our personal political realm: any man can do anything, and it's fine. The consequences are minimal, if there are even any consequences at all. A man can sexually assault a woman, brag about it, and run for president, and voters with full knowledge of this voted for him. Because what is a female life, comparatively? What is a pussy?

When I was young I had my pussy grabbed. I also lived in a city that had elected a man who was rumored to be sexually aggressive toward women, decades before I was born, in spite of his known penchant for indecent exposure. A political scion—his father had been mayor decades earlier, the VA hospital was named for him—known to visit women's colleges, Barnard and Radcliffe, and lurk around the grounds, brandishing his dick at whatever unlucky student happened to cross his path. He was a young mayor, twenty-five years old, and he'd already been a senator before that, had hung out with JFK, went on to chair the school committee, to buy the town newspaper, the *Chelsea Record*, and publish his own political opinions without regard to accusations of conflict of interest. Andrew Quigley. It was through him I first learned the word *flasher*. A Ford dealership was advertising cars equipped with newfangled turn signals—it was the 1970s, and *flashers*, as they were called, were extra. WE HAVE ANDREW QUIGLEYS, the dealership advertised, making my father chuckle as we drove by. Why is that funny? "They mean flashers. Andrew Quigley is a flasher."

"What's a flasher?"

"Oh."

The idea of a flasher—sad, desperate, bottomless beneath his trench coat—is humorous enough, I suppose, but when you are a woman, alone, walking, and are suddenly face-to-cock with a strange man unhinged enough to do such a thing, well, it's terrifying. It's not having to look upon a penis that is the source of terror, that is simply gross. Most penises need to be beloved in some way to not repulse, and so gazing upon one unbidden is pretty yucky, though not necessarily horrifying. It's the implicit threat that is so frightening. A man seeking an unwanted sexual scenario with a nonconsenting woman, understanding his penis to be, on some level, a weapon, hiding behind a tree and hopping out with it unsheathed. Is this man going to grab me, chase me, rape me, kill me? He wants to inspire a sexualized terror. I saw these men around Chelsea when I was growing up. Hiding in the woods behind the VA hospital. Lurking by the creek I crossed via overpass on my way to the mall. Pulling up to the curb near a different mall, asking for directions, window pulled down, and when you get close enough to see—there it is, in his hand, being jerked as the jerk asks you if you know which direction is Broadway. You see your life *flash* before your eyes in such moments, with every gruesome story about kidnapped girls, girls dumped in dumpsters, found dead in the woods, on the railroad tracks, etc. etc. etc., ricocheting across your (my) twelve-year-old brain.

It's funny, having my pussy actually grabbed didn't inspire the total terror that a random dick on an empty street did. Maybe because I was older, eighteen, just out of high school, in Boston for the day looking for a job. I'd stopped by my post office box to see if anyone had smuggled some dollars through the mail in exchange for a copy of my new zine, *Bitch Queen*. They had! With some money and zine trades stuffed in my black army bag I made my way into Copley Place, a Back Bay shopping emporium waaaaaaay more upscale than the cruddy Mystic or Square One malls where my formative dick-flashes had occurred. I could not even tell you what the stores at the Copley Place mall sold, they were beyond my reach to the point of non-existence. But they did have an Au Bon Pain, and when I had the dollars, I liked to get a soup and a croissant and sit and read a book. Thanks to my new feminist zine venture, I had about five dollars and was looking forward to chilling out after pounding the pavement all day. I entered through the Westin, a hotel so fancy they employed a piano player in their lobby during the afternoon. I imagine he was playing that day as I boarded the escalator and was carried up into the luxe environment, deep carpet and crystal chandeliers. I was wearing pants. Baggy black pants I had bought on a trip to New York City. I had only recently emerged from the intense black lace of my goth identity. I didn't really know what to wear if I wasn't wearing black lipstick and rhinestone chokers, and I think I probably looked boring. Neutered, somewhat androgynous. The pants were silk, and something about the way they both fluttered and hid me felt cool, felt like New York or London, sort of tough. Maybe something a girl who worked in an art gallery would wear. Maybe I would work in an art gallery someday, maybe I could pop in and see if any were hiring—is that how a person got a job at an art gallery? My army bag still held a few resumes, getting crumpled against my new zines, *Not Your Bitch*, *Chainsaw*, *Outpunk*. Deep in thought, a hand is suddenly, insistently, painfully digging into my crotch.

Because the pants were so thin, it felt like there was nothing between the man's knuckles and my vulva. Knuckles, the hard bumps of them, are what I remember most, and it's why the word *knuckles* has long grossed me out a little. There was also a fleeting bafflement at my own physiology. My pussy—my *privates*, I was raised to call it—was located in the *front* of my body, was it not? And this man standing behind me, the ease with which he just reached out and groped it. I had imagined my pussy, my privates, tucked deep inside me, somehow protected by evolution, but now I understood it to be but a piece of ripe fruit dangling from my backside. The joke was on me—and what a joke!—to have walked around with my pussy so accessible all these years. This was bound to happen. It truly was. Before I could breathe again, because I had stopped, of course, the escalator had delivered me to the top. I fumbled off and the man continued on in long strides. Before I could even begin to come up with a plan, he was gone. Gone through the doors that led to the glass skywalk that led to the mall.

I wish I had done absolutely anything at all. I did nothing, which is always the worst. And I know that it is enough to withstand an assault; that in itself is enough, to have to then act in any sort of clever, brainy, heroic, witty way, with the sensation of the man's hand still clamped on your pussy—it's too much. It verges on a sort of victim blaming. It is enough that I stood there, shaking with rage, with the sudden onslaught of injustice. Enough to have spun around in hopes that someone, anyone, had seen it, was making themselves known to me, was stepping up to right this horrid wrong. I was eighteen years old and still lived at home and probably wanted someone to take care of me. There was no one. A security guard standing idly by the exit where the pussy grabber had just passed through. A man. I didn't like security guards. My friends and I had been ejected from the Copley Mall more times than I could count, for loitering or stealing coins from the wishing fountain or using the smooth metal descent between the escalators as a slide. They handled us roughly and with disgust and I was not about to tell one that a man had grabbed my privates. A man I'd only seen the back of, who could be practically any man at all. And so, my story ends. I did not grab him back, dig my own knuckles into the blob of his scrotum. I did not let a warrior yell loose from my throat and attempt to tackle him. I did not simply scream and point, I did not give chase. I stood there, stunned, until I realized I was in the way of the people coming up the escalator, and I moved out of the way and walked through the glass tunnel to the Au Bon Pain. And I had soup and a croissant and I read about a young, punk rock feminism I had not at all known was happening. And I went home. All the time, the man's hand stayed there, lodged roughly between my legs.

This was the story I was going to tell at the university, about how a man who brags about grabbing women's pussies is a serious contender for the presidency of the United States and there was nothing my writing or anyone's writing could do to stop it, to change the consciousness of the millions of people voting for him, because we *have* been writing, and before us, so too were all the others who lived and died writing and their writing didn't change anything either, did it? A big part of my personality, I know, is optimism, hope, and inspiration. If I may be so crass, I might even say it is part of my brand. I was not brought to this university to suggest that the writings of, say, James Baldwin, even as they remain perhaps the very best writings in the history of the English language, actually have done nothing to bring about change because here we are, decades after his death, contemplating the eminent rule of a famous bigot. While on a normal day I am a bit ambivalent, suspicious, about writing's ability to *change the world*, on this day I was most cynical. I decided to accept the fact that I might be a ginormous bummer to the students I was preparing to present to. It didn't feel good. Students are children, right, and children are the future, and the future is bright. But I felt so tremendously defeated, and I wanted to make space for that. It didn't feel good, but it felt honest. And why should these children be the future, anyway? They are inheriting all of this shit and somehow they're supposed to save us all? Ugh. We're all fucked, is how I felt. I sat at a café, trying to work it into a coherent essay. I did a lot of internet research, trying to find more information about Andrew Quigley's indecent exposure. Whatever happened happened before the internet, and his family probably had his record expunged anyway. I posted a call for rumors, knowing how tacky that sounded, on a Chelsea

Facebook page, and was met with outrage from the towns-
people, for speaking ill of the dead and bringing shame
upon his ancestors and also for being a lazy writer likely
suffering from writer's block. I deleted it. An acquaintance
from Quigley's generation confirmed the anecdote about
the Ford dealership and recounted a school board meeting assembled to discuss Chelsea High being the lowest-
scoring high school in Massachusetts. A fireman at the
back of the room, unimpressed with Quigley's proposal,
shouted, "Hey, Andrew! This is what I think of your input,"
and whipped his raincoat open and closed, open and closed.
I kept searching, playing with different keywords. And then
I found this:

The City to a Young Girl

The city is
one million horny lip-smacking men
screaming for my body.
The streets are long conveyor belts
loaded with these suckling pigs.
All begging for
a lay
a little pussy
a bit of tit
a leg to rub against
a handful of ass
the connoisseurs of cunt
Every day, every night
pressing in on me closer and closer.
I swat them off like flies
but they keep coming back.
I'm a good piece of meat.

This poem was written in 1970, by a fifteen-year-old New York City girl named Jody Caravaglia. It had been published in the Hunter College High School literary magazine, and from there was picked up for inclusion in an Avon anthology with the scintillating title *Male and Female Under 18*. Forty thousand copies of this collection of youth writing were published, and the book was selected by educational publishers Prentice Hall for inclusion in a reading program which bundled together a variety of books and sold them to school libraries at a discount. Chelsea High School's library participated in this program, and in winter 1976, *Male and Female Under 18* was added to the shelves. That spring, an upset parent made a phone call to Andrew Quigley, then chair of the school committee. Her teenage daughter had borrowed *Male and Female*, and maybe she was freaked out by "The City to a Young Girl," the shock of finding the word *cunt* in a school library book. Or maybe the mom was paging through it and it was she who flipped out. Regardless, Quigley made a home visit, was shown the poem, and decided the book would be removed from the library. He didn't consult the rest of the committee—three men and three women—but did arrange a meeting to discuss "objectionable, salacious, and obscene material being made available in books in the high school library." He then penned an op-ed and published it in his newspaper, the *Chelsea Record*. *Male and Female Under 18* "made me sick to my stomach to think that such a book could be obtained in any school—let alone one here in Chelsea."

Quigley shared copies of the poem with the three male members of the school committee in time for the meeting. He did not distribute copies to the women, believing the poem too "crude" and "offensive" for female eyes. At the meeting, Quigley deemed the poem "outright obscene" and "filth." Fellow committee member Anthony "Chubby" Tiro cosigned, stating, "The book is lewd and leaves nothing to the imagination. It's outright obnoxious." The committee moved to petition Chelsea's superintendent of schools, Vincent McGee, to remove the book from the school library; it had already been temporarily removed, Caravaglia's poem torn out. McGee found it concerning that the complaint was being handled in an open school meeting, and suggested Quigley was "setting in motion a chain of events that might lead to censorship."

And he was. Quigley penned another editorial, scolding McGee's thoughtful prudence and calling "The City to a Young Girl" "vile and offensive garbage." He threatened the librarian, Sonja Coleman, with the loss of her job, and she responded by defending Caravaglia's poem as not being obscene, insisting that both students and faculty should have access to it, and suggesting that the book was improperly removed from the school library—there are clear American Library Association guidelines on how to handle a challenged book, and the Chelsea school committee seemed ignorant of them. Quigley wrote another editorial, calling the poem "lewd, lascivious, filthy, suggestive, licentious, pornographic" and, again, "obscene." And he continued to call meetings. At one, a committee member called Caravaglia "a sick child." At the next, the school committee voted unanimously to remove *Male and Female Under 18.* At the next, Quigley moved that the committee consider removing Coleman from the library.

One week later, Coleman, having assembled a group of allies under the banner Right to Read Defense Committee, filed suit against the Chelsea school committee in federal court. The plaintiffs asked for an injunction against the book's removal, protection for Coleman against reprisals, and a judgment that the removal of *Male and Female Under 18* violated the rights of students, teachers, and librarians. Federal judge Joseph Tauro soon issued a temporary injunction, returning the book to the library for students whose parents issued a note allowing them to read it, and ordered that there be no reprisals against Coleman.

Here's me, in a café in Portland, Oregon, a few hours from this talk I was dreading, suddenly electrified with excitement, with rage and pride and a sense of poetic, feminist history. First of all, the poem itself: "The streets are long conveyor belts / loaded with these suckling pigs." The pure disgust of a fifteen-year-old girl, one empowered enough to call out such shit when she sees it, to not mince words, to turn the assaulters' grotesque language against them by reclaiming it—one of my favorite methods of defense: "a little pussy / a bit of tit / . . . / the connoisseurs of cunt." This was slam poetry decades before slam poetry existed. It was the sort of feminist confessional rage I myself had begun my writing with, and I was swooning backward through the ages at this fifteen-year-old girl who had so deeply pissed off Andrew Quigley. Oh, the irony, if that's what it is, of a serious street harasser trying to shut up this brave, truth-speaking young girl. The perennial bravery of librarians! The confirmation, yet again, of how lousy my hometown was! I continued to scan the trial transcripts because the trial, though I had never, ever heard of it, was actually quite important and is still taught in law schools today.

The bench trial spanned six days in the fall. Over a hundred Chelsea High School students crammed into the courtroom, missing school to watch history being made for them. They were scolded by the judge for snapping their gum and for *throwing toilet paper out of the courtroom windows* (!!!) but otherwise kept it together. It took months for Judge Tauro to deliver his verdict, and in the meantime Quigley and the school committee voted to fire Sonja Coleman, but backed off when the librarian asked the court to hold them in contempt for disregarding the order that her job be protected.

In the end, what prevailed? Justice. In his opinion, Judge Tauro speaks lovingly of libraries, calling them "magic." "The most effective antidote to the poison of mindless orthodoxy is ready access to a broad sweep of ideas and philosophies," he wrote. "The danger is mind control."

I google-image searched Jody Caravaglia, fantasizing that a tough-ass teenage girl would pop up and say, "What's up," to me between cracks of her gum. What I got was a bunch of pictures of pregnant women wrapped around yoga balls, in between black-and-white photos of Patti Smith Group live onstage, Mink DeVille on his knees, all big hair and intense cheekbones, Elvis Costello with his guitar slung around his neck. Photo credit: Jody Caravaglia. My heart raced, because I love girls and their stories, I love outsider culture, and it is truly these things that have helped me make sense of my own place in this hostile world, that somewhere there was a corner, there were people, and I belonged to them. Jody Caravaglia, who was fucking sick of men ogling her on the streets of New York City, who boldly wrote a poem about it, who pissed off a bunch of conservative men and prevailed. After the trial, Sonja Coleman said that thirty or so Chelsea High students formed their own group for students' rights as a result of their right to read being so messed with. When Quigley and Co. tried to ban their student newsletter they involved the ACLU, and the goons backed off. Meanwhile, Jody Caravaglia, now in her twenties, was pursuing photography, capturing these underground antihero rockers, getting bylines in *Rolling Stone*. Feeling like a detective, I clicked around my computer, checking out the photos of rows of pregnant women on yoga balls. A prenatal massage place in Brooklyn, begun by a Jody Caravaglia. When the creative people of my generation's need for stability grew too strong to ignore, they became life coaches. The generation before mine had become massage therapists. The trajectory from angry slam-poet teenager to cool rock photographer to prenatal massage therapist made sense. I called the number on my screen and left a message for Jody Caravaglia. And five minutes later, as I returned to my table with a refill of coffee, she called me back.

Here's why I love "The City to a Young Girl." First of all, it's true. For any young female, any city is strewn with landmines of unwanted male attention. So, it's got universal appeal. Something it probably has not been credited with because universal experiences are male. But all women know this. And the boldness of her language makes her strong, a sort of warrior on all of our behalf. That language does everything I didn't do when the man on the escalator grabbed my cunt. By simply grabbing the reins of the predatory language meant to intimidate and objectify she becomes a sort of fearless linguistic goddess. You feel the power of the words twofold—with a flinch you feel them being hurled at you, yet simultaneously she catches the bullets in her hands and whips them back at our assailants. She's also lampooning them, mightily. "Suckling pigs."

"Connoisseurs of cunt." How hilarious! To reduce the threat of men to a bunch of needy babies, grotesque and snarfling. To mock their interest in women—they're *connoisseurs*—sure they are, the poet winks. I am giddy with the daring vision of this fifteen-year-old girl when my cell phone rings.

Jody Caravaglia is as open and forthcoming as maybe you could expect from such a poem, as, I don't know, earthy as someone comfy with both obscene language and handling the bodies of pregnant women. I like her immediately. She still doesn't think her poem, her writing it, is that big of a deal. She went to a cool high school, it was the sixties, she was encouraged to think and write boldly, it's what everyone was doing. She thought the trial was absurd, but she wishes she had thought of a way to monetize the moment. Her poem had captured national attention, but she struggled the way artists struggle. She had a turbulent love life. She was terrified of Trump winning the election, horrified and disgusted by the recent *Access Hollywood* tapes. She's intense but warm, a New Yorker, I guess, though I suspect she's also a Scorpio. Through my phone her energy enters the sedate Portland café, seeming to invigorate everything. I told her I'd like to be her friend. "I don't do friends," she says in a not unfriendly way. "But we can know each other."

I have to ask, "What sign are you?"

"Scorpio."

I read the end of "The City to a Young Girl" differently than the author intended it. It closes with "I'm a good piece of meat"—a dark acceptance, I thought, a depressing moment of biology actually equaling destiny. After indulging this larger-than-life hellion vibe, a sort of linguistic revenge fantasy, I appreciated the entrance of some despair, some exhaustion. It's real. But that's not quite how Caravaglia meant it. It was more like, she's complicit. Some part of her liked the attention. Some part of her was participating. I wanted to struggle against this with her—no, this fifteen-year-old girl, *all* of us girls and women, are put into the rotten position of being sexualized and harassed by strangers and having that be somewhat *normal*—whatever we do to cope with it, we're not complicit. But I didn't write "The City to a Young Girl." It's not my poem, it's Jody Caravaglia's, and at the end of it all I do like that she complicates the story. "I'm a good piece of meat." It's grim, but smart. There's a poet behind the poet, a set of eyes watching the way that this put-upon female body gathers some sort of pleasure, or power, from the sexual attention, and that observer blows our narrator's cover. It's meta. I love Jody Caravaglia.

But I have to go. I have a lecture to deliver. I try to get all of this down in a document in the scarce time I have left. I'm feeling it, the purpose and point of our political writings, our personal struggles. It's not to change the world that can't or won't be changed. It's to leave traces of ourselves for others to hold on to, a lifeline of solidarity that spans time, that passes on strength like a baton from person to person, generation to generation. I felt enlivened by Jody's poem, which did, in fact, change the actual world if by changing the world I mean changing laws. I guess that's my issue with writing as activism: how hard it is for it to change the actual systems that oppress and limit and kill. But Jody Caravaglia did it. Her poem created increased legal freedom for what we can and cannot read, what young people have access to. This poem, with the help of Sonja

Coleman and her allies, demanded that the complicated and often violent experience of being female not be considered obscene.

At my lecture, calamity happened. My document was nowhere to be found. I found myself in the most dreaded position of being at a podium in a room full of occupied seats, department heads lingering in the back of the room, all eyes on me, all words erased from my screen. So I talked. I read "The City to a Young Girl." It was a pleasure to read it. I told everyone about Jody Caravaglia. That two hours ago I was in despair about this topic, activist writing, writing that makes a difference. I had made my peace with being uninspiring and depressed, and within this short span of time a piece of writing spoke to me across generations and filled me with hope. The discovery of this poem, this triumphant court case, and my new brio-filled not-friend Jody Caravaglia—that I had found them all through my investigations of that scoundrel Andrew Quigley—it felt like magic, a miracle. Our words and stories are so often buried, forgotten, never known, and the excavation of them may not change the world but it may make the world worth living in. I cried a little as I spoke, wondering if this current political climate wasn't effectively driving me mad, but so what if it was, I figured. Madness is always an appropriate response. Everyone in the audience wanted to know the poem, to know Jody Caravaglia. They wrote her name in their notebooks. Later, when I returned home, I typed her name and her poem into various social media sites, using the somewhat pathetic tools of our time to launch her story into the world. Somewhat pathetic, but without them how else would I have shared her work, how else would I have found it, found her, at all? I felt a rare sensation that all was as it should be, the whole awful beautiful mess of it. The feeling filled me up, sparking tears, a gorgeous flicker, and then receded. Because all is not as it should be. And we all must get to our work.

From a talk given in 2016 at Portland State University.

PIGEON MANIFESTO

The revolution will not begin in your backyard because you do not have a backyard. What you have is a back door that shits you directly onto the streets of your city, what you have is a back staircase of wood that resembles splintered matchsticks, it trembles each time a bus rolls down Mission. What you have is a patch of concrete, a splotch of weedy grass clumped with trash. This is not a backyard. What you have is a cement slab that pools with rainwater, that catches the tumble of a beer can and a sludgy condom that fall from the apartments above you. What you have is empty of anything green, but the slugs still find a way to work it out, inkiest green like mold breathed to life, they slide a wet trail across what is not a backyard. Maybe you have never had, will never have, a backyard, but you still could have slugs and always you will have the pigeons.

The revolution will begin at your curb, in the shallow pool of shade that is your gutter. The revolution will begin with the pigeon bobbing, hungry, in the street, it is now your job to love her. It is now your job to not avert your eyes from her feet, your job to seek out and find the one pigeon foot that is blobbed in a chemical melt, a pink-orange glob, a wad of bubblegum. The pigeon splashed in a pool of chemicals laid out to kill it because so many of the people hate pigeons. This is now why you must love them. We must love the nature that does not make it on the Discovery Channel, on Animal Planet, we must love the nature that crawls up to our doorstep like spare-changers and scares us with the thickness of its feathers, its mutant feet, and orange eyes. Someone could have made dinner with the rice on the corner but instead they sprinkled it on the curb with the hope that hungry pigeons would eat it, and that the grain would expand in their stomachs, tearing them open, felling them in the street, plump and feathered and dead in the gutter. I think perhaps this does not even work, because I watch the pigeons peck at the rice and fly off on gray wings. I hardly ever see them dead in spite of how many people try to kill them.

Pigeons are doves. They are rock doves, and I wonder if we began to call them that if people would hesitate to hate them, as doves have that history as messengers of peace. It is true that in my neighborhood nobody hates the mourning doves, dusky and elegant with wings that squeak as if they flap on rusty hinges. They roost on the wires like little Audrey Hepburns, while the pigeons troll the ground, tough and fat, some of them look like they should be smoking cigarettes. They look poor and banged up, like they could kick the mourning doves' asses but are wise to the divide-and-conquer tactics we use on one another, so they coo wearily at the mourning doves and waddle forth in search of scavenged delights. What you may not know is when you call a pigeon "a rat with wings" you have given it a compliment. The only thing a rat lacks is a pair of wings to lift it, so you have named the pigeon perfectly. When you say to me, "I hate pigeons," I want to ask you who else you hate. It makes me suspicious. I once met a girl who was so proud to have hit such a bird on her bicycle, I swear, I thought that it was me she hit. I felt her handlebars in my stomach and now it is your job to feel it also. The pigeons are birds, they are doves. They are the nature of the city and the ones who no one loves. When people say they hate pigeons, I want to ask them if they hate themselves, too. Does it prick the well of your loathing? Do they make you feel dirty and ashamed? Are you embarrassed about how little or how much you have, for how you have had to hustle? Being dirty is not a problem for the pigeon. You can ask it, "How do you feel about having the city coating your feathers, having the streets gunked up in the crease of your eye?" and the pigeon would say, "Not a problem." You will now stop blaming the pigeon. It is not the pigeon's fault. The pigeon was once a dove, and then we built our filthy empire up around it, came to hate it for simply thriving in the midst our decay, came to hate it for not dying. The pigeon is your ally. They are chameleons, gray as the concrete they troll for scraps, at night they huddle and sing like cats. Their necks are glistening, iridescent as an oil-slick rainbow, they mate for life, and they fly.

First printed in *Word Warriors*, published by Seal Press in 2007.

SUMMER OF LOST JOBS

It was the summer I could not keep a job. The summer I discovered vodka, an ancestral beverage somehow drawn from the pale and starchy bodies of potatoes. That summer, the New England humidity which mostly grows thunderstorms collapsed my death-rock hairdo, a coiffure like a house of cards growing improbably higher and higher, unsustainable, hit with blasts from the can, the locks rendered sticky, clumping into a solid mass one could mold with one's black-tipped fingers. The whole ratted mass of it, the back-combed glob of artificial jet black, glossy with its unnatural highlights of blue—blue-black, an impossible color. The dye would stain my neck the color of dirt for a week, Dalmatian splatters across my neck, drooling down my sternum. I was impatient and unskilled in my appearance, I was sixteen.

I knew how I wanted to appear and it was not how I appeared naturally. I had no time for my own transformation, wanted only to turn to the mirror and behold white, white skin, bloodless, the skin of girls in fairy tales, horror stories, and very old poems. A throwback to long ago when women took poisons to achieve such a pallor, when they let leeches suck away some of their hardy, living color. My technique used clown white, the thick, greasy pigment favored by circus performers, purchased at the beauty supply store in downtown Boston. You climbed a flight of stairs to get there and were served by an older girl with impeccable blue hair, the color of macaws, an electric shade, blue as a bottle of Windex. Her makeup, too, was stunning, precision lines around the eyes like an Egyptian corpse, a work of art. Thick, then thin, gliding around those big dark eyes. The place sold real beauty products, and then they sold costume stuff like the clown white, which came in a red tin stamped with the image of an old-fashioned clown. Unscrew the tin and behold the puck of shiny white, to be smeared over the skin of your face like a perverted cold cream. I would blend and I would blend, but still the irrepressible health of my cheek's apples would glow pink under the oily veneer. I would have to take a palmful of baby powder, and somehow get it onto my face. Though I'd try to be gentle, delicately sprinkling it across my forehead as though dusting a pound cake with powdered sugar, it would cling in dense patches to the slick of my skin. The best way to use baby powder as makeup was to empty a mirrored compact of its original contents and fill it instead with the scented dust, using the soft round applicator to press the stuff to your cheeks, getting rid of the sheen.

It was the summer all my goth friends got locked up for cutting their arms, and these reconfigured compacts would inevitably be confiscated by the attendants at their institutions, sent to the lab to be analyzed. The summer, the blurred summer, of my homemade beauty products. A plastic spray bottle of sugar water was supposed to make my hair even more impervious to both gravity and the water-rich air of New England, but in fact only made the hairdo fall beneath the syrupy weight of the spritz, drawing all manner of winged insect as well. Egg whites did in fact stiffen your hair, as did the Elmer's Glue the punks used to make their liberty spikes, but these formulas also made hair rigid—there was no room to fuck up a hairdo like that, and really more than anything my look was *fuckup*. My aesthetic, my nation. My work ethic.

I sat in the car outside of the Mystic Mall in Chelsea, Massachusetts, crying. This was a historic day, the day I told my mother that I hated her. My mother had a thing about the word *hate*—it was as taboo as *cunt*, a word it would take me another decade to violate in her presence. "You don't hate anyone," she would correct my vitriol. "You strongly dislike. Don't hate anyone." It was good advice but all it did was ensconce the word *hate* in a glittering dark cape and place it on the craggy mountaintop to beckon me with its evil charm. I was a dramatic teen, I was goth, the most dramatic subculture ever. All was wild and overblown, explosions of hair and frothing lace collars, passions and revulsions spilling over.

My mother was scared of me. My face was covered in what appeared to be vanilla frosting, nothing had prepared her for having a daughter who wanted to look like this. When I returned home each evening with the litany of the abuses I'd suffered—children hurling rocks at me, carloads of boys shouting "Freak!" as they careened past, girls who looked at me plainly and inquired, in the accent of the region, "What the fuck are you supposed to be?" My mother offered little comfort. I *was* a freak; what the fuck *was* I supposed to be?

"It's clown white!" I shrilled, plonked in the front seat of the little Ford Escort. Inside the mall was It's Tops, a place that sold T-shirts and rock pins and the only place in

Chelsea that would give me a job. I had PMS, was rushing on progesterone; three or so years into menstruation and the hormonal surges still caught me wildly off guard, could plunge me into despair with sudden violence. Even I could see that the clown white wasn't working. It wasn't giving me the stark, otherworldly complexion of a Patrick Nagel painting, I just looked crazy. Still, it was as close as I'd come to achieving my ideal. My mother was starting in on me, "You can't go into work like that!" and *blam* came the tears. You just can't cry and wear clown white. The salty streams cut through the grease, make the smears smearier. My face reddened horribly beneath it, puffy and bright. "Great!" I shrieked. "Great, look!" I yanked the visor down and stared at the disaster of my face in the tiny mirror. "It had looked okay," I lied, "and now it's ruined! I hate you!"

There, I said it. The word had too much power for me to resist its pull indefinitely. In the powder-blue Escort, surging with estrogen and melting petroleum-based makeup, I professed my hatred for my mother and her lack of support for my lifestyle choices, and my mother either smacked me, sullying her hand with greasepaint, or she did not—the blare of emotion distorts my memory. Sobbing I took the inside of my long black skirt into my hands and wiped and wiped the clown white from my skin, taking my shaky eyeliner job with it. Oily and fragile, a crust of clown white ringing my hairline, I climbed from the car and strode into the mall to be fired from my job.

"We like you so much," the owner said. Her voice was a plea, she was not the sort of owner comfortable with firing her employees. "We just don't need you anymore," she lied awkwardly, topping it off with a shrug. The owner lived out in Gloucester in a modest castle on the beach. Earlier in the summer they had invited me to a barbecue there and allowed me and my friends to drink beer after beer. My boss would vanish behind closed doors with her husband—a doctor who had advised me against piercing my nose lest I hit a particular nerve and become paraplegic—and emerge with freshly bloodshot eyes and a scratchy nose.

I'd known that I was about to be fired. I had been caught reading on the job far too many times; lacking any books of my own I'd resort to copies of *Mistral's Daughter* or *Portnoy's Complaint* tucked into one of the bottom drawers beneath the register. I alienated the customers with my odd appearance and choice of soundtrack—extravagantly gloomy Cure songs, the militant chant and snarl of Generation X. "I don't want to have what a steady job brings. / Don't want security / don't want responsibility / 'cause that's youth!" I never stole from It's Tops, but so many shirts were ruined in my attempts to adorn them with glitter decals and fuzzy letters, I'd have to smuggle them out of the mall to be thrown into dumpsters. Under my lazy watch the shop unraveled into disarray; it simply did not occur to me to clean certain areas, they escaped my radar. It was kind of the owner to pretend my termination was not the result of my own shitty work ethic.

It was simply not possible for me to find work in Chelsea. I could find slurs and ass-kickings, but not a job. A friend from school hooked me up with a receptionist position at a hair salon in Boston called Penelope's Place. My friend's sister was the salon's manager and a very nice person, but she, like everyone, ultimately answered to Penelope, a skinny woman with fake red hair, frantic with all the stress of running a failing regional chain of hair salons. I had hoped, initially, that Penelope and I would be fabulous friends; I had recently dyed my hair a fake red, too, though a decidedly different shade. My hair was the loud, cheerful color of the clown on my old tin of clown white. Which I had stopped using, having discovered a ghostly shade of foundation available at the downtown beauty supply store. The beauty supply store also sold a line of hair dye called Crazy Color, which offered a variety of vivid hues—fuchsia, cyclamen, ruby red. I chose ruby. Eventually I chose them all, but first I chose ruby. The color of a can of Coca-Cola. Penelope flinched in the face of it, as if the color radiated its own light and hurt her eyes, or her feelings. She scowled at me, whispered to the manager, then ran out the doors, up onto Boylston Street. The manager came over glumly. "You have to dye your hair," she said.

"But it looks great," I protested. It did, especially with a bright red lipstick. It looked excellent. "Penelope doesn't get it," I explained to the manager. By sitting behind the reception desk with my fabulous hairdo I would be drawing people into the salon. My hair was like a carnival barker luring marks with its loud, braying color. The manager chewed her lip and said she would speak to Penelope on my behalf. When the owner next visited the salon there was no mistaking the evil in her eyes when she looked at me. She conferred with the manager and dashed out of the place, leaving a powerful perfumed wind in her wake.

"You have to wear a scarf," the manager said. She felt a victory had been scored—she had saved my job. My hair just had to be covered at all times, with style. "No baseball hats," the manager warned.

I gasped. "Do I look like I wear baseball hats?" I demanded. I wrapped a long pink scarf, shot through with golden threads, around my head, turban-style. Customers looked at me with a new suspicion: Had someone at the salon ruined my hair? What was hiding under the strange, bulbous wrap of fabric? Penelope seemed unsatisfied with the compromise; she stared at me blatantly. Mine was not the face of Penelope's Place.

Saturday night and I was wasted off a half-pint of hundred-proof Smirnoff vodka, mixed into a jar of Veryfine fruit punch until I was drunk enough to handle it straight. Having polished off my alcohol too swiftly, I bopped around the line of kids camping out for New Order tickets, begging sips off people's cocktails. A mouthful of thick, sweet Manischewitz, a shot of something dark and amber, some rum and Coke, lots of beer. When all my cigarettes were smoked, I bummed those too. I wasn't sleeping out for New Order tickets—I didn't have the money—but the alley that led to the Orpheum Theatre box office was the place to be. It was like a death-rock block party. Vinnie was my perpetual ride home, he lived a city over from me, in East Boston. I had been due home hours ago and could only pray that my mother had gone to sleep. I frequently didn't make my curfews; Vinnie had no curfew of his own and could not take mine seriously. He'd get me home when he felt like it.

Meanwhile, I made out with Joshua. Joshua was pink cheeked and freckled. His hair was bleached the most perfect, barely attainable shade of white and still looked healthy, looked natural. Most people's hair got kinked from such an effort or stalled at a nicotine hue, but Joshua's was perfect. In the night alley it gleamed like the moon. It had never before occurred me to make out with Joshua, who spoke with the strange lilt of a California surfer despite living in Brookline, Massachusetts. Joshua's father owned a chain of photography supply shops, probably he was very wealthy. Unbeknownst to me, most of my new Bostonian death-rock friends were quite well-to-do; many of them would inherit trust funds in a few years. Everyone wore shitty thrift store outfits like I did, and so I assumed everyone had grown up swinging between welfare and marginal employment, borrowing occasional shelter from relatives and living on cans of Chef Boyardee. Joshua and I sort of fell into each other and *boom* his tongue was in my mouth and I was touching the silky pale bangs that flopped over his eyes. Joshua was a violent kisser, and I interpreted the force of his mouth on mine as a confession of a deep and long-smoldering desire. I pulled back from his face and gazed at him. There were three of him, three Joshuas. I waited, mooning at him, until the triad shimmered back into a single boy. "What?" he asked. Instantly I was in love with Joshua.

"I don't know, what?" I asked back.

"What?" he insisted. This went on for a moment. "You're just looking at me with those big eyes," he finally said. "You're staring." He didn't sound unkind. It was hard to sound harsh with that accent.

"Joshua," I said grabbing his shoulders. Joshua favored an old man sort of look—faintly plaid pants, wing tips, cardigans. Most all the boys did. A little newsboy cap on his head, those albino bangs hanging out. He rode a skateboard and smoked cloves. "Joshua, what does this mean?" I asked of him. "Are we going out now? Does this mean we're going out?"

Joshua stammered. He seemed a bit slow but I don't think he was; he was too well put together, and could stay on his skateboard. I think it was his affected speech, and the general bewilderment of being fifteen. "I don't know, I don't think so . . ." He looked around as if there were someone standing by, an adult perhaps, who could answer this for us. We drifted away. I had liked being kissed violently like that.

At home, hours later, everyone was asleep. Four little girls, ages two through eight, were sleeping in soft lumps across my living room floor. I had forgotten my little cousins were spending the night. I drunkenly wound my way around them, careful not to kick a small head or fall onto them in the dark. I climbed into my bed and slept for two hours, setting my alarm for my morning shift at Penelope's. When I woke, I wanted to die. I had been poisoned, something was happening to me. I seemed in the throes of an alien birth, my body was trying expel something. I was dizzy, the walls of my bedroom bent and curved, the floor bobbed like something at sea. And the sweat, the sweat was bad. I was coated in it, a fine mist of venom. I leaned against the wall in my closet and tried to select an outfit from the rack of swaying black. There was my scarf, I wound it around my hair, which seemed extra crusty, particularly the ends. I tried to remember if I had thrown up. The thought made my stomach convulse. I stumbled through the kaleidoscope of my house, starting at the sight of so many little girls strewn across the living room carpet, cocooned in their sleeping bags. I made it to the bathroom. Into the toilet I vomited. It tasted like rum. Mostly rum. I puked, but the vertigo remained, the nausea remained. It wasn't like when I was a kid and got a stomach flu, upchucked, and felt better. This was different, this was sinister. I imagined, with dread, feeling this way forever. The force of my sickness seemed powerful enough to never leave, to live out its lifetime in my body if it chose.

"Ma!" I gurgled weakly. To shout pulled too much on my body. I rested my forehead, my sweaty, flushed forehead, on the toilet seat. It was one of those puffy toilet seats that warmed slightly when you set your rear onto it. The feeling of it warming beneath my sweating, poisoned head filled me with new nausea. "Ma!" I shouted, this time with a bit more gusto. My voice shot down into the toilet and bounced around acoustically. Outside in the living room the little girls stirred; like an army of elves they pattered into my mother's bedroom and brought her to me.

"What did you drink?" she asked.

My tongue flailed around the dry, disgusting cave of my mouth, searching for a dominant flavor. Yes, rum. "Rum," I said.

"Rum!" my mother was horrified. "Don't drink rum! I never drink rum!" It was true I had never seen my mother drink rum. I had only ever seen her drink Kahlua poured into milk, and this only rarely, like when she graduated from nursing school. "Michelle," she said sternly, "if you're drinking every weekend, that's a problem. And you should nip it in the bud."

Her warning would become an oft-repeated catchphrase among me and my friends, akin to Faye Dunaway's "Tina, bring me the ax!" or any number of lines from *Rocky Horror*. "Oh Mary," my gay friend Bobbie sighed. "The bud has bloomed."

I knew when I called out sick to Penelope's Place that there would be no second chance. The receptionist does not call out sick on a Sunday. Better the manager, better three of the hairdressers—called *designers* at Penelope's—than the receptionist. And I had been on such thin ice, with my hair and my turban. I was fired.

My next job, at Chuck's Ice Cream at Faneuil Hall, lasted
almost the rest of the summer. Chuck's was another regional
chain. Their big thing was mix-ins: a customer selected a
flavor of ice cream and then requested, oh, crumbled Oreo
cookies and mashed-up Heath candy bars to go into it. I
would scoop out a mound of ice cream and slap it down on
a slab of countertop. With metal spatulas, I would pound
and smash and beat the shit out of the ice cream until it was
softer and flat. I would pour a scoop of cookie and a scoop
of candy into the dairy glob and moosh it all together, using
the spatulas to fold and chop. Finally, I would scrape it from
the counter into a gigantic, chocolate-coated, sprinkle-
encrusted waffle cone, as was popular at the time.

Faneuil Hall was a great tourist emporium. People
flocked from all over the world to eat oysters at the Salty
Dog, to have a beer at Cheers, to look at expensive robotic
appliances at the Sharper Image. The Banana Republic
seemed, back in the day, to actually sell weird safari-ish
clothes, and a fake jeep was fake crashed through the store's
exterior. If you looked, as I did, like a freak, you could frequently catch a tourist taking your picture and intimidate a
dollar from them. There was a gang of postcard punks who
hung around specifically for this purpose; clustered by the
street performers, they would menace and smoke, scanning
for cameras aimed at their mohawks.

Chuck's was very popular, even during my shift, which
began at eight in the morning, when nobody should be
eating ice cream. Right next door to us was a Finagle A
Bagel, across the way was a Coffee Connection, and both
had barely a customer all morning long while we had los-
ers lingering outside our stall before we even opened. The
freezers, shut tight all night, had frozen the ice cream bins

into impossible blocks; my wrists were sprained within a week. But it wasn't a bad place to work. The manager was a thin, angry man with little eyes and little hair, but he wasn't there very often. Mostly I worked with an Irish girl, Heather, whose hair was lush, long, and glossy red, tipped in ringlets like a princess from a myth. She seemed to like me especially, she was interested in my fashion, the music I listened to, where I would go after work. I liked Heather's voice, a brogue. We worked closely, smeared in cream. We took turns wearing stickers that read "It's My Birthday!" in magic marker, designed to squeeze more tips from the customers. We would make up disgusting ice cream combinations and write them on the chalkboard. Squid Crunch with dehydrated banana mix-in. Roast Beef swirl with tripe nugget mix-in. The days Heather didn't work were lousy days. My wrists ached and my hangovers were more stubborn. I would mix lemon sorbet with pineapple juice in the frappé machine, and still dehydration kept my temples throbbing throughout my eight-hour shift. I would prepare my most favorite treat—a cup of crushed walnuts doused in hot fudge and chased with milk so cold a scrim of ice had formed across the surface. It got to be my phony birthday all day long and the tips accumulated in my jar, but still. Work was better with Heather.

One day my friend Katrina stopped by for my break. I cleared my tips for fries and a Coke from the Great American French Fry Co. and together we sat outside, smoking and snacking and staring at the tourists staring at us. Near to the street magicians and jugglers and mimes on unicycles, I let the tourists snap their cameras. I had a real job. Katrina lived in Brookline and didn't have to work. She got money from her parents. She also got booze from them.

While they were out Katrina would take a mason jar and fill it up with a bit of everything in the liquor cabinet. The best was a combination that included Triple Sec and tasted exactly like Froot Loops. Katrina opened her army bag and showed me the jar, full of amber liquid. The plan was, she would pick me up after work and we would sit in the Boston Common, beneath a willow tree by the pond, and drink till we were plastered. Then we would walk up Newbury Street, to the library at Copley Square where all the goths and punks and skaters hung out. "See you later," I said. I returned to Chuck's, stuck my time card into the time clock where it was bit with a crunch.

Heather turned to me. "Who was that?" she asked, sort of breathless. I looked around Faneuil Hall. Who was who? Had a celebrity stopped by? Faneuil Hall was stupid, but once I'd seen the singer from Missing Persons strolling around in leopard stilettos and a matching raincoat. "Your friend," said Heather. "That girl. Who was she? She was beautiful."

"You mean Katrina?" I asked, shocked. I hadn't known Katrina was beautiful. Katrina was just—she was Katrina, she was regular. I thought her hair was kind of weird, actually. Her bleach job was mediocre, and one half of it was a short bob, with bangs, and the other half was completely shaved, with just a skimpy yellow rattail snaking down her neck. Katrina was beautiful? I felt a punch of emotion. "No she's not," I wanted to say. I didn't know why it bothered me to hear Heather call Katrina beautiful. I smacked and I smacked the ice cream, splattering my apron with chocolate, getting bits of Reese's Pieces in my clumpy red hair.

Katrina came with her jar at four, and we walked quietly to our place in the park. I studied her. Her nose turned up. I pondered it. I had read in books about noses shaped like ski slopes, had gathered that this was seen as a positive thing, the pretty way to have a nose. I guessed Katrina had a popular nose. I guessed Katrina was beautiful. I liked hanging out with Katrina—her parents went away frequently, giving us a place to congregate. She liked to get drunk, as did I. She was a regular target of skinheads, so she had a sort of tragic danger about her. The skinheads didn't like her hair, called her a poodle, threatened to kill her all the time. Personally, I had a feeling that Katrina was not as invested in being goth as I was, but I kept my suspicions to myself. Katrina's family had a lot of money, their house was really nice, and Katrina herself spent Sunday afternoons baking cakes from scratch with her mother. I thought there was probably a really great, really normal life available to Katrina if she wanted it and inevitably she would. Beautiful Katrina. I almost told her what Heather had said, but I couldn't.

Toward the end of the summer I bleached my hair. There was a day, the first day, when it was so flat, so straight and pale on my head it looked almost like Joshua's. I looked, I thought, like David Bowie. I couldn't recall him having my exact shade or my exact choppy haircut, it was more of an overall David Bowie feel. I wore my new color to work, to show Heather. Was it beautiful? Swiftly the color turned, became that tarnished yellow. Nobody wanted that color, everyone wanted white, a white so silver it flashed lavender under certain lights. Gay Bobbie, who was in beauty school, told me I had to get a special toner and then a special shampoo, but I had spent all my money on the plastic bottle of developer, the forty-volume peroxide, and the envelopes of Super Blue. I had no more cash for hair dyeing, not if I wanted to drink vodka and smoke cigarettes. I was stuck with yellow hair. And it was falling out. It fell into mounds of ice cream, customers complained. One man bellowed, "Forget it! I just saw your hair fall right into my ice cream!" The manager was around for that one. He made everyone start wearing hairnets. I had ruined it for the staff. My hair looked terrible, squished down, dry and frizzing beneath the black web. Katrina sometimes tucked her asymmetrical hairdo into a little crocheted sack pinned to the back of her hair and it looked good, very elegant, very French, very goth. I tried to do something creative with my hairnet but it was impossible, the thread was thin and flimsy. Even Heather looked bad, her long, magnificent hair snagged. It looked like a shot and bagged fox on her shoulders. "You bleached your hair!" she exclaimed when I came in with it freshly blonded. That was it. "You look beautiful," I'd wanted her to say. "Your hair is beautiful. That shade is beautiful. You did a beautiful job." I just wanted to hear that word, *beautiful*, coming out of Heather's mouth, directed at me.

We went to see the Ramones—me, Vinnie, Gay Bobbie, Joshua, Beautiful Katrina, and a new boy named Jessie who called himself Zebediah. We drove down to Providence to see them at an all-ages club. Zebediah was a runaway from Los Angeles who wanted to be my boyfriend. He worked at the Store 24 in Harvard Square and slept on a mattress in a Cambridge lot. Zebediah had a story. He had run away from a mother who repeatedly told him she wished she'd had an abortion. He did too much of something called crystal meth and set her couch on fire. Then he ran away. Zebediah was sweet; he drank a lot, as did everyone, but he didn't do drugs called crystal meth, and it was hard to imagine him setting his mother's couch on fire. He wore eyeliner and long black prairie skirts, painted his nails black, and was totally straight. Zebediah spoke in a truly authentic California surfer accent. He didn't seem very bright, but I wondered if such accents made people sound dumb. Perhaps I was prejudiced against Californian voices. Because I feared Zebediah was not smart, I resisted his advances, unless we were both drinking vodka—which was any time after sundown—when I would make out with him forever and later pretend it never happened. "Why won't you go out with me?" Zebediah pleaded, and I'd make up some intense reason why I couldn't go out with anyone at all. Something having to do with the deep, dark state of my soul, my impenetrable loneliness, my unfathomable inner pain.

I drank too much at the Ramones. We drank in the parking lot and then stumbled inside. Vinnie and Zebediah went to the men's room to barf. I was okay as long as I leaned against the wall at the back of the room. I leaned and waited for the show to start. A man walked up to me. He was luminous, so pale he glowed, and his hair was long, dragging down his rat-like face, a pair of glasses stuck to his nose. It was Joey Ramone. "Do you have an aspirin?" he asked me. I stared at him. I shook my head. "No, I don't," I said weakly. The shaking of my head had made everything spin, and I had only just gotten it all to stay still. He wandered off, and was swallowed by his crowd. Vinnie and Zebediah returned. "Joey Ramone just asked me for an aspirin," I said. It was a magical night. We almost died on the way home, Bobbie was so drunk. The car veered violently to the side of the road. Everyone screamed, then laughed and laughed.

It was late by the time we got to Katrina's. Her parents

were away, so we all stayed over. Most of my new friends had parents who went out of town. They went on vacations. It was wild. My parents never went anywhere.

At Katrina's we drank an improvised punch siphoned from the liquor cabinet. I had sobered up from the show and could start drinking again. "We saw the Ramones!" we all cheered, though I at least had only seen a hallucinogenic mass of throbbing people moving as one, bouncing up and down, the blob. Occasionally light would glare off Joey Ramone's glasses, like an SOS sent out to me across the ocean of moshers. Even the music was a loud, sonic blur. I had spent the night staving off vomit and Zebediah. Now at Katrina's I could start anew. Where was Zebediah? I walked around Katrina's roomy house, mystery cocktail swishing in a crystal goblet.

I found Zebediah in a bedroom. His shirt was off and he was slicing his chest with a razor. His big, black hairdo flopped down over most of his face, all that showed was his mouth, the curl of his lips. His body was lean and etched with light scars. White and pink, they rose up from his brown skin. I thought of the marks skate blades left on a rink of ice or of stone shot through with marble. Blood beaded up along the freshest cut and slowly slid down his body. It was incredibly sexy. I ran over to where he sat upon a chair and jumped onto his lap. He looked up at me. I took the razor from his hand. "Don't," I said dramatically, and touched his scars. No one was going to be locking Zebediah up. Unlike the others, these kids from Brookline with big houses and vacationing parents, Zebediah was free to slice himself to ribbons. We made out for a while, until he started trying to get me to suck his dick, ruining everything. "Forget it," I said. He looked at me with mournful eyes. I didn't mind touching it but fuck if I was going to put it in my mouth. He put his hands on my shoulders, weighing me down toward his dick. Subtle. I got up and went back to my goblet of alcohol. "Just put it away," I said, motioning to his crotch.

"If you were my girlfriend I'd treat you like a princess," he said, zipping up his tight black jeans. Huh. Princess Blowjob, I figured. I went back into the house, looking for Katrina and the others, leaving Zebediah alone with his skin and his razor.

I woke up the next day around noon. Katrina had prepared some sort of fishy lunch for herself and, having grown bored with it, placed it in front of the fan, to blow the vile smell across the living room where I had passed out on a couch. I crept out in the bright, bright sun, onto the porch where Katrina and Joshua smoked cigarettes.

"I was supposed to be at work," I said. "At eight."

"Oh no!" Katrina gasped.

I thought about what I should do. I had the next day off, so that gave me an additional twenty-four hours to strategize. It seemed like the simplest thing to do would be to pretend I had forgotten. I'd been confused about my schedule. Could happen to anyone. I spent the day longing for Zebediah (who had walked out into the Brookline night after I declined to blow him) to return to Katrina's. I did love making out with him. I loved the way he walked in his combat boots, especially with a skirt kicking out around his legs. Perhaps if I stuck to making out with him in public I wouldn't have to deal with his dick. But if I was making out with him in public all the time wouldn't that make him my boyfriend? My head buzzed with nicotine and hangover. Eventually Vinnie and Bobbie woke and we all walked through Brookline pretending to be droogs from *A Clockwork Orange*, kicking over trash cans. We walked to the movie theater and saw *Wings of Desire*, and then I took the long train ride, the long bus ride, back to Chelsea.

Two mornings later I walked into Chuck's with my normal smile on my face, my hairnet scrunched in my hand like an extra-large dust bunny. The manager stepped into my path, blocking me like I'd come to rob the place. "Hey," I said. I said his name, whatever it was.

"Sorry," he said. "This area is employees only."

I laughed. "I work here," I said. "I'm Michelle."

"You do not work here. You did not show up for work, so you do not work here." The tourists waiting for their mix-ins were getting a show.

I stayed in character. "I had yesterday off!" I cried. "And the day before!"

"You did not. Two days ago you did not show up."

I gasped and feigned outrage, feigned indignation. I snatched at the schedule and looked at the hours written on my slot. "Oh my god!" I feigned shock, feigned apology. "You're going to fire me? It's a mistake!" I tried to move past him. "I have things back there!" I feigned entitlement. Heather stared at me, sadness in her face. She wasn't wearing the "It's My Birthday!" sticker, the manager wouldn't allow it. In fact, he'd been threatening to take away the tip jars altogether.

"I have your things," he said, and thrust the book I'd left behind at me. *The Basketball Diaries*. "Leave," he said, "or I'll call security."

Outside I sat on the broad, stone steps, a few feet away from a clown pulling rolls of rainbow ribbon from his mouth. Tourists lined up to throw money at him, his upturned felt hat glittered with coins. I wondered how much money he made. Wondered if I had any skills that could be performed publicly for change. In a few hours Katrina would come by to share my break with me and I would not be there, but Heather would. Maybe they'd take her break together. I dug out my cigarettes from my army bag and pulled out the last one, my lucky cigarette, upturned in the pack. I lit it with a match and wished for a new job. I smoked it slowly, meditating on my wish. A flash went off and as the glare cleared my eye I saw a tourist smiling at me. "Uh-uh!" I hollered at him, melting the smile from his sunburned face. "That's a dollar!" I yelled, stood up, and started toward him. He reached into his pocket.

Originally published in *Columbia Journal* in 2011.

TELLING YOUR FRIENDS
YOU'RE SOBER

By the time my decades-long chemical spree ended, I had published a memoir about my exploits that a sober friend called a "drunkalogue"—a reference to AA shares that painstakingly detail every gutter puked in, stranger punched, and bedsheet peed upon throughout a person's drinking career. I'd written a sex column for a lesbian magazine that the publisher was concerned had too many drugs in it. Strangers phoned me wondering if I could sell them ecstasy. I wasn't what my mother called a "quiet drinker"—one of those sad sacks who drank alone in their rooms, hiding their inebriation. No way! I had hitched my inebriation to both my queer liberation (It's party time!) and my feminism (If men can get wasted, so can I!) and put on quite a show of it.

To be fair, I put on quite a show of it in general. I'm a fairly open person. I'm honest with my friends and, as I tend to mistake vague acquaintances for actual friends, that means I'm forthright with pretty much everyone. Even still, telling people I'd gotten sober was terrifying.

When you first get sober, you are a mess. Pure and simple. Anyone who finds that they need to quit alcohol has not had a swell run of it lately. You don't give up the booze because of an errant drunk text or a nip of the cocktail flu.

You stop because you're frightening yourself. You've noticed how the alcohol's effects on your body, mind, and spirit have become increasingly harsh. You don't recognize yourself when you're drunk. You feel like shit. You're humiliated. You've ruined relationships. You're losing self-respect. You quit because it's just not fun anymore, and it hasn't been for a while. You quit because you're afraid you can't. You quit because, as bad as it's been lately, you know it could get worse, and you wonder how awful you'll let it get before you're willing to make a change.

But when you're first sober, all this wisdom, a basic understanding of your condition, is elusive. You're fucked in the head. Why are you quitting? "I thought you loved drinking!" friends exclaim. Well, yeah—I sure did. "Isn't it hard?" others ask, making you want to punch them in the neck. Hard? I was quite sure no one had lived through anything as grueling. "But you're so fun drunk!" pout those who miss your conviviality at the bar but have never observed what you look like long after last call, sobbing in your bedroom, puking in the water closet, fighting nonsensically with your date. Doing a line in the bathroom at work the next day to make it through your shift.

When people come at you with their questions, you are likely to wonder, *Yeah, why did I stop drinking?* Because sometimes it will seem like the stupidest thing you've ever done. You've lost your best friend, your primary coping skill, and your identity in one fell swoop. Other times it will seem like there is no way they could understand what you're going through. Either way, it's likely to be a frustrating exchange.

The general public does not understand alcoholism. They don't understand drinking problems, and they don't understand sobriety. People think you can just cut down. They don't get why you can't at least have a glass of wine at dinner—as if you've ever done that! They're baffled as to why you can't smoke pot or pop a recreational Xanax. At first their lack of insight may be painful. But as you become more familiar with your situation, you won't need their understanding as much. The only important thing is that you understand that you can't drink. It is nice to be around folks who get it, of course, which is one reason people turn to twelve-step meetings. Occasionally, I really need to be able to sit in a room and vent about how, though our culture sometimes seems to revolve around alcohol, understanding of alcoholism is scant. It's great to watch people bobbing their heads in agreement, rather than tilting them in a puppy-dog *huh?*

Am I painting a bleak picture of telling your friends about the new you? Maybe it's because I'm remembering that time I tried to quit for just a week, and a friend responded by slamming a whiskey soda down in front of me and demanding I drink it. Of course, I did. That was the first time I tried to quit. The more serious I became about wanting to stop, the more protective I became over who I let in on my fragile new reality.

Part of the problem is, you probably weren't drinking alone. And if you were drinking alcoholically, chances are so were some of your friends. If you need to stop what does that say about them? It's too much for most people to look at. Your sobriety can feel like a judgment on them, and what's even worse, it may be. One of the most annoying things about getting sober is having to pretend you can't spot a fellow alcoholic across the room. It's poor form to "take another's inventory" or decide that someone has a problem. That's for them to decide. And it is really good practice to keep in mind that it's none of your business how much anyone else drinks. But really—no one can read a drunk like another drunk. And if your friends aren't ready to take a look at their partying they're not going to appreciate your newly clear eyes upon them.

Truthfully, you'll probably lose some friends when you get sober. What's remarkable is that you get to see, very drastically, who is a true friend and who, in spite of how much they like you, just doesn't have your best interests at heart. When I got sober there was a deep division between the people around me who embraced it and the people around me who didn't get it. The friends who knew right away that my getting sober was only an awesome thing are to this day my very best friends, almost a decade later. Maybe they were also the ones close enough to really see the shit I was doing: my ex, who saw how insane alcohol made me; my sister, whose bedroom I once destroyed during a drunken visit; one friend who drank with me until she got sober; and another who was hurt by the ways I'd prioritize getting wasted over spending quality time with her. They were 100 percent down with me swearing off the booze.

Other friends, not so much. "I thought you were just going to quit drinking but not go to those meetings," said a friend who caught me on my way to an alcoholic support group. It was enough for her to get her head around not sharing coke with me in the bathroom, but now I was doing something secret and cultish. It was too much.

Real friends are going to support whatever you have to do to stay sober, whether that is staying away from the bar, not allowing drinking in your house, or going to weird gatherings where you hold hands with strangers and say prayers. It's probably going to take you a while to not feel like a major nerd for requiring that your rendezvous be at the tea house and not the ale house, but after your sobriety sinks in, you'll be confident enough to ask for what you need. The only people who think a bar is the only acceptable place to meet up tend to be alcoholics. If your friends aren't capable of hanging out before midnight, they probably don't care that much about your friendship. Take note.

Eventually, you might be fine meeting up at bars. I love the dive bar ambience, and have also found that fancier places generally know how to mix an awe-inspiring mocktail ("Can you make me something amazing and non-alcoholic?" is what I ask). I do serve alcohol when I entertain, and I cook with it too. People's ignorance about alcoholism doesn't make me quite so crazy (usually); I have a sense of humor about it. This might not be your path—I have friends who have been sober longer than I who hate being around drunk people, whereas I sort of love it. Only time will tell. But for sure you'll be able to stand behind what you need to be sober and sane, and happy.

My social calendar is as full now as it was when I drank, the main difference is that I actually choose to stay in some of the time, because I'm no longer chasing the good-time dragon. A revelation that comes with sobriety is that you're not really missing anything. The friends who were phased out don't leave a chasm in your life, because the people who support you take up more of your time, and you're also meeting new people. And every now and then, one of those friends from back in the day will find themselves needing a sober friend to have a confusing conversation with, and you'll get an opportunity to connect on a much more profound level than the drunken bar bonding that didn't really make it outside of the bar.

First published in the *Bold Italic* in 2013.

SISTER SPIT FEMINISM

There is something about the sort of feminism I dig, the sort that tends to be embodied by most of all my closest and most-admired lady writer friends. You know how earlier eras of feminism sort of forgot that there were poor women? Or, the lavender menace of queer women butting in with their own experiences, messing up the hetero sisters' stab at media acceptance? I think that the people who made up Sister Spit, the all-girl performance tour that tore up the United States at the end of the last century, were the living, breathing, writing responses to those particular overlooked patches of feminist experience. We were the lavender menace and the broke-ass menace, we were the never-been-to-college menace and the drunken menace, we were the shove-your-dogma menace and the my-poetry-can-beat-up-your-theory menace. This was not a conscious thing, this acting out. We were grinding our axes when we arrived, the combination of cynicism and idealism pumping through us, through our very nature, unnoticeable. We were all feminists who knew exactly how and where feminism had failed us with its assumptions or its ignorance. We knew the best revenge would be to wrap our stinky, drug-addled, badly behaved selves in feminism, which also, we knew, saved our lives. We would kick out some space for others like ourselves: slightly feral, inappropriate, hungry to connect—with each other, with ourselves, with strangers—wild, reckless, and feminist.

I'm probably speaking on behalf of a bunch of people who don't agree with me. I don't mean to say that everyone who ever toured with Sister Spit was a poverty-stricken alcoholic with little formal education and a penchant for starting bar fights. There were middle-class girls in the van. Clean and sober recovering alcoholics and addicts somehow managed—how?! How did they do it?!—to tour with us, and there were others who miraculously just weren't big drinkers. There were college graduates. There were girls who weren't even queer, despite their best efforts. Some even had had relatively happy childhoods. There were performers who hated the bar fights instigated by others, correctly naming them dangerous and juvenile.

Somehow we managed to get along with each other, mostly. Somehow everyone's candida diet or vegan needs were met, mostly. Incredibly, the money we made, a single wad of cash, never got lost, though it was found lying around unattended in at least three places—a Nevada gas-station parking lot, blatant in the van window in New Orleans's French Quarter, and sitting lonely at a table in New York City. That wad was not enough to pay us, but it got us from city to city.

When our van—bought for $1,500, the fruits of a full year of benefit shows, from an indie rocker whose own band had just upgraded—set off from San Francisco, we had no reason to believe that fate wouldn't have us turning around and driving back home in, like, two days. Why would anyone come to our shows? We were two vanfuls of nobodies, with a couple of underground sensations we were hoping would pull in enough of a crowd to fill the gas tank. Why did we think we could pass through America unmolested? We all had friends who were fearful for us, going out into our hateful country, leaving the bosom of our cities. So many people commented on how we were bound to all hate each other that I made a plan in my head about how to handle anyone who got too bitchy: drive their ass to the nearest Greyhound bus station, and leave them there. Nobody's fears came true. We took right to the road, hanging our feet out the window, chain-smoking, buying real scorpion paperweights at truck stops, watching the sun set to classic-rock stations, scrawling new poems in our notebooks. No one got dumped anywhere (except that time we inadvertently left one person behind at a Mexican restaurant in Albuquerque). And, most amazingly, though none of us necessarily believed that the world cared about us or our poetry, people came to our shows. Sometimes quite a lot of people. We were astonished. Entering a coffeehouse in Athens, Georgia, I felt nervous at what would happen when the large crowd drinking coffee was confronted with a bunch of queer, feminist, debaucherous storytelling. I was shocked to realize they were actually there to listen to us! A crowd that had gathered to hear us in the basement of a sushi restaurant in the South clapped wildly for us before we even said anything, they were just that proud we had even made it to their town. And they were right to applaud, it was a huge accomplishment. With no money backing us, no cell phones, no credit cards in case of emergency, no laptops, no technology to navigate us to the next town, and often no actual plan of where we would all sleep that night; we made it to our shows, rarely, if ever, late. And we always had a place to sleep at night.

Sometimes the shittiest, most oppressive thing about being a girl is how good you're supposed to be all the time. And sometimes that feeling of an enforced, expected goodness can come from feminism. The thing about being a poet, a writer, an artist, is, you can't be good. You shouldn't have to be good. You should, for the sake of your art, your soul, and your life, go through significant periods of time where you are defying many notions of goodness. As female artists, we required the same opportunities to fuck up and get fucked up as dudes have always had and been forgiven for; we needed access to the same hard road of trial and error our male peers and literary inspirations stumbled down. We needed the right to ruin our lives and crawl out from the wreckage, maybe wiser. We needed the right to start a stupid brawl and emerge victorious or with a black eye. We needed to cheat on our lovers and quit our jobs. We definitely needed to shoplift. We weren't everyone's role models, but if we were yours you'd know it.

In a ton of ways, the tour itself was an act of defiance. We were, largely, a group of people who had heard the word *no* a lot. No to being queer, to wanting to be artists, and to thinking anyone would want to listen to our attitudinal manifestos. To think we could do what people in bands did, tour the country delighting audiences and racking up adventures, was a more than a little gutsy. It was possibly delusional. It was amazing that we did not get seriously hurt, or arrested. That we were two vans, thirteen people total, helped a lot. If a creepy cop pulled one of us over, he inadvertently pulled *both* of us over. That's a lot of bother if he was just looking to fuck with some freaks. And we were freaks. Our hair was blue or it was pink. It was short to the scalp or looked like it had never been combed. We had tattoos, many of them not too well executed. We had scars, many of them deliberate. Our clothes were mostly secondhand, if not third or fourth. Many of us were butch, not recognizable as girl or a boy but as some new human the gas-station denizens had never seen before. Soon into each tour—there were three major cross-country ones, a bunch of shorter, regional trips—we would have to figure out who was the most normal looking. That person would be called upon to deal with the authorities, be they cops, auto mechanics, or hotel workers.

We lost our first van due to an oil leak that blew a rod in the engine. This happened on the Mississippi-Alabama border, around midnight on a weekend night. The tow truck driver was drunk and scary. Some of the performers were towed away in the van. I can't remember why we thought that would be a good idea. We stayed overnight in a hotel room, one room for all thirteen of us, I believe. We snuck in through a side door. In the morning everyone had to dump some of their luggage in order for us to keep going. Someone had brought a skateboard; someone else, a tennis racket. A health-food store back in San Francisco had donated tons of healthy food to us. We still had a lot of it, and all of it was dumped in that hotel parking lot. One of our more financially stable performers had an honest-to-goddess credit card, and was able to rent us a van. A cargo van. With no seats in the back. The one menopausal writer claimed the only actual seat in the air-conditioned cab; the rest tumbled around the back. It felt, perhaps, like going over the falls in a barrel.

It is illegal to have passengers in the back of the cargo van. Of course, it is also illegal to drink in the van or do drugs. Or buy drugs, though many times we were simply given the stuff. Once, a yellowed page torn from a paper-back and soaked in LSD was donated by some guys sell-ing tie-dyed thong underwear outside an adult bookstore in Reno, Nevada. Stealing is illegal. So is assault. I think these were all of our transgressions, and mercifully, amaz-ingly, we never got arrested. A Cambridge police officer let me go in spite of my belligerence, screaming in the streets, drunk, in velvet pants and a rainbow-spangled tube top. We always had style. And smarts. When a southwestern cop wanted to search the van, because the devil stickers in our windows lead him to believe there were drugs in there, the performers knew their rights and didn't let him in. There may not have been drugs in the van that time, but that par-ticular van—our second—was so shabby that if you shut it off it wouldn't necessarily turn back on. Allowing the cop to come on board could have cost us that night's show.

There were truly frightening moments. The man at the sandwich shop in Mississippi who said if he had his gun he'd blow our heads off. This was unprovoked—we were just ordering po'boys. A gang of security guards was called to wrestle one of our "men" out of the women's room in Niagara Falls. A Catholic townie from Boston took great offense to our antics at a bar there, prompting a brawl replete with flying glass jars of mustard. We had befriended a group of circus performers, straight dudes, and they fought alongside us for the right to whip out your dildo in a public establishment.

Our friends and supporters were not always who we expected them to be, nor were our foes. An East Coast dyke promoter was majorly offended by our onstage drinking and public revelations of shoplifting PowerBars across America. Bar dykes in Buffalo, New York, tried to kick our ass, ostensibly for flicking cigarette ash on the floor of their dive bar, but really I just think they thought we were freaky nerds, with our weird hair and our poetry. At a bar in Ohio, other lesbians tried to prevent us from performing, then heckled us throughout our show. They couldn't wait till we were done so they could turn the k.d. lang back on and slow dance on the light-up dance floor. Seriously. The tragedy is, these ladies should have been our comrades. A great many assumptions about who we were stoked a resentment to our presence in their neighborhood bars—their second homes—but truly, I felt we had a lot in common (working-class backgrounds, scant college, alcoholism) and that our differences (mullets, acid-washed jeans, dream-catcher earrings) were largely cosmetic.

But for all the asshole guys and aggro dykes we encountered, the scary rednecks and the coppish cops, there were more folks who embraced us. We charmed the Carhartts off a bar full of punkabilly and assorted frat-like dudes in Las Vegas; one performer even sucked a hickey on the neck of a jock who had, inspired by our performance, penned his own poem, a sappy-sweet ode to everybody being friends with everyone else. We heard him on the pay phone after the show explaining to his girlfriend that a lesbian had given him a hickey. Some Christians stuck around for our performance in Atlanta, much more open to us than we were to them. A bunch of older dykes let us camp on their lesbian-separatist land and swim in their pond, which was awesome, except for the biting fish. *L Word* prototypes who we judged on sight bought up all of our merchandise in Los Angeles.

All across the US, we wrote and caused trouble, and

wrote about the trouble we caused, and read it all each night to actual *audiences*. It was stunning. To have our improbable ambitions validated. To have the chips on our shoulders polished and praised. To have our zines and chapbooks purchased by brand-new fans who wanted us to *sign* them, like we were real writers! Some of us already had books published before Sister Spit, but the majority did not. To know that there would be strangers in North Carolina and Arizona and upstate New York reading our writing was incredible. We *were* writers. People bought us drinks and took us home to stay in their beds. They cooked us food. Mostly we were grateful for this, but occasionally our generous hosts had ulterior motives: observing our bravado and braggadocious sluttery on stage, they thought they'd get lucky back at home. What they more often got was turned into a can-you-*believe*-it?! story, to be told and retold, often from on stage at our next show: the woman who whipped off her shirt when we got back to her house, all casual; the woman who walked into someone's shower to recommend a bar of soap that smelled like "sweet woman's pussy" (she didn't understand that, after three weeks in the van we were desperately trying to wash *away* the smell of pussy); the girl who left baskets of sex toys around her house and, unexpectedly in a bad way, shoved her tongue down my throat. Of course, people *did* get lucky; mostly in the van, with each other. Performers hooked up in ways both discreet and mind-blowingly *not* discreet. Like, leaving lube-y hand prints on the back windows. Like, getting it on in a room you're sharing with three other people. Like, steering the van with one hand while fisting someone with the other.

That Sister Spit was a success is partly a miracle and partly a testament to how queer and feminist subcultures take care of their own, be it in big cities or small towns. It is partly proof that some sort of deity watches over the drunk and foolish, and definitely proof that if you want something badly you can make it happen through sheer will, ingenuity, and community support.

Our tour across America proved to all of us that our writing was important, at a time in our mostly young lives where, without such tangible proof, we may have been discouraged away from it by the rigors of everyday living in a world that devalues art—especially the first-person narratives of such a band of ruffians. And it gave us a platform to spectacularly misbehave, to feel temporarily invincible, to feel safe in a world that had taught us firsthand to fear it.

First printed in *Word Warriors*, published by Seal Press in 2007.

I HAD A MISCARRIAGE

Not that there is any good time for a miscarriage, but I do think learning that the embryo in your stomach has stopped developing on the day before your wedding is an especially harsh toke. In the doctor's office, with two grandmothers-to-be wringing their nervous, grandmotherly hands, the Doppler ultrasound skated across my belly on a gob of lube, unable to detect a heartbeat. The would-be grandmothers were in town for the wedding, and it was a no-brainer to bring them along to our appointment with our obstetrician; how excited they would be to see what we'd so recently seen—an amorphous, living blob, its heartbeat flickering inside it like a bulb. But now their faces were drawn, anxious. They tended toward the worst-case scenarios; both Scorpios, both in occupations where they see worst-case scenarios play out on the daily, one being a nurse and the other a social worker. But I wasn't concerned. We'd only just gotten an ultrasound at the fertility clinic that had orchestrated the transfer of one of my wife's healthy, thirty-three-year-old eggs into my healthy, forty-two-year-old uterus. We'd seen the heartbeat, strobing like a lighthouse beacon that cut through our fears. After years of trying we were finally pregnant, and our kid-to-be would be present at our wedding, my first-trimester stomach visible beneath the gown I'd chosen especially for its ability to be altered into an empire-waisted, maternity wedding dress.

When the doctor ushered us into a room down the hall for a scan with a better Doppler machine, I still wasn't worried, though she was. My philosophy is: chances are, the worst won't happen. Never mind that life has sometimes proved otherwise; it has mainly proven true. Usually, the worst *doesn't* happen. But that morning, it did.

"I'm sorry," said the woman working the Doppler, her face thin and her hair frizzed.

"It's okay," I said numbly, not wanting my situation to make her feel bad.

"I'll go talk to your mothers," our doctor said, while the woman wiped the Doppler goo from my belly. When we arrived back in the office, their faces were tighter and sadder than ever.

Let me tell you right now that I dislike emotions very much. If I must experience them I prefer to do it in a dark room where nobody can see me. I hated crying there, in the room in front of the doctor, but not only could I not help it, I figured I should let it out while I could. The rest of the day was packed with prewedding mani-pedis and a rehearsal dinner. Weddings are nothing if not elaborate performances, and miscarriage or not, the show must go on.

Leaving the doctor's office but condemned to hang around the hospital waiting for additional ultrasounds, the first thing I did was get a coffee. For months I hadn't drank the stuff, my normal three-to-five-cup-a-day habit abandoned cold turkey. Though the science around it was murky, there was a study linking coffee consumption to miscarriage, so I'd jettisoned the stuff along with all the other delicacies I was forbidden while pregnant—the soft cheeses, the sliced turkey, the sushi, and the oysters. What had it even mattered? Regardless of all the pains I took each day to consume something from the "Best Food for Pregnancy" lists I found on the internet, somewhere around the eighth week of pregnancy, not long after we'd seen that encouraging heartbeat, the embryo had stopped developing. We'd never know why.

With my half-caf warm in my hand, sending jitters through my caffeine-deprived system, I began texting. I sent a text to everyone I had told I was pregnant, of which there were many. I knew the protective tradition of not sharing pregnancy news until you were past the miscarriage minefield of the first trimester, but I didn't think keeping it a secret was an option for me. I was too public about my attempts to get pregnant; all our friends, not to mention acquaintances and outright strangers, knew we were trying to get pregnant. Lots of friends knew that we'd recently had a transfer, which meant we either were or weren't solidly pregnant. It seemed silly to be cagey about it, especially when the IVF hormones had me bloated enough to pass for a lady in her second trimester. And so we had shared the good news, and now I would share the bad.

I understood, as my phone began to ring with calls I wouldn't answer, why women chose not to share their pregnancies till they were out of the woods. It felt excruciatingly vulnerable to be the object of such an outpouring of love and sympathy. There was something so attractive about silently toughing out this loss, alone with my wife, huddled under blankets eating takeout. I'm not saying it's a healthy urge, but it is a real one. Instead, I fielded texts from all the people who loved us, who shared their shock and sadness.

At each expression of sorrow, I felt my own acutely, like a stab. On the phone with my sister, I finally broke down.

"I feel like our wedding will be a sad thing, now," I hiccupped. "Everyone will be feeling bad for us. It's going to feel horrible."

"Everyone loves you," my sister consoled me. "Everyone is so happy for you and Dashiell and wants to love and celebrate you. You'll see."

Astoundingly, the wedding *was* joyful. The dizzying motion of it all—the dinner the night before, our tear-jerking vows, the hordes of friends, the family brunch the following morning—all served to distract us from our loss. For better or worse, there wasn't a lot of time to sit around and cry. After the D and C—an abortion, basically—which removed the stagnant embryo from my body, we were off on our honeymoon. On a Caribbean island staring out at the fuzzy green atolls rising from the turquoise water, all our baby drama—the years of trying, the recent failing—seemed blissfully far away.

It wasn't until it was all over and we were back in foggy, chilly San Francisco that I came back into my body and mourned what I'd been through. I was at a yoga class, of all places. I'm a sporadic yoga dabbler, always meaning to get a better practice going yet never really committing. This means that yoga is always a bit of a challenge because I never quite know what I'm doing, but I manage to pull it off well enough. Not that night. That night my body, with all its extra weight and alien bulk from the months of hormones and weeks of pregnancy, strained and struggled to hold any pose harder than child's pose, where you lie panting with your face planted on the floor. I had zero balance, and even less stamina. After fighting to keep up,

I finally broke down and slumped onto my mat, into the forgiving child's pose, hearing everyone around me swivel and lunge as they followed the asanas effortlessly. I began to cry into my mat. My poor *body*, I thought. It had been through so much! It had been pumped full of chemicals to get prepped for our high-tech conception, and for a couple months it carried life, shifting and morphing, aching my joints and bleeding my gums, keeping me queasy with a horribly supersonic sense of smell. Then there was the D and C, painless yet grisly, both physically and emotionally exhausting. Now here I was, back in my body in this yoga class, unable to keep up. But what I like about yoga is how it allows you to participate wherever you are in your body. And that night, this is where I was. I kept my forehead to the floor, and cried.

The messages and emails from other women who've suffered miscarriages are still coming in, months later. It's shocking how common they are, how many friends had experienced them, too. The culture of secrecy around miscarriage, while understandable, doesn't really serve women in any way. If there were more openness, perhaps women would understand how *truly* common miscarriages are, and the experience would be rendered slightly less shocking and tragic. The statistic that one in four pregnancies ends in miscarriage is as abstract as all statistics are. But to have one out of four moms you know send you an email saying, "Yes, that happened to me," is something else entirely. And not just the information, but the comfort such notes provided wound up being pretty precious, my issues with vulnerability be damned.

The upside of this, if I must wrangle one, is that women are much more likely to have a full-term pregnancy after a miscarriage. Maybe it's because your uterus has essentially been rototilled, providing fresh soil for the next seed. Perhaps it's because you've gotten your one-in-four miscarriage out of the way, so now the stats are on your side. Either way, it's back to the drawing board for me and my wife. And knowing that so many women survived this setback and went on to pop out amazing, healthy kids makes it a lot easier.

First published in the *Bold Italic* in 2014.

BABA

The hospital room where I recovered from my C-section was as cold and ugly as any hospital room anywhere, but because it was high on a hill in San Francisco the view was magnificent. For four days, high on morphine, the shifting sky outside seemed alive, in cahoots with us, saluting our success with its ribbons of clouds and confetti of stars.

Us was me, having lost a lot of blood, still being monitored lest a transfusion become necessary. Nurses would come with pills, would press the place I'd been cut, watching the incision for seepage. It hurt. "Can you tell me before you press it?" I learned to ask. Us was my son, tiny headed, the upside-down baby, lips ruby like a fairy-tale enchantment. My wife had brought him to me as I lay there—arms outstretched, the blue tarp bumping my nose—vomiting down the side of my face. *What thing, what thing from what fairy tale was so ruby*, I wondered in a drugged haze. "Say something to him," my wife urged, because she wanted him to know my voice. But what does one say to a baby? "Hi," I said. "Hi, baby."

Us was also her, my wife, that prince. Eight months pregnant, I told an old woman sitting beside me on the bus that the egg that hatched my baby came from my wife's ovaries. I didn't know how the old woman would take it; one can never know. She was delighted. "That's like a fairy tale!" My wife is younger than me, and her eggs were nicer and more plentiful. Once the fertility doctor learned of her existence, he would have nothing to do with my eggs. Which was fine with me. It was like a fairy tale, having a woman's baby, although my wife is the kind of woman who in a fairy tale would pass as a boy, and would be unmasked as female only after completing some daring feat or by besting a fleet of men. Impregnating another woman, perhaps.

With the raw mystery of birth still so close and all my lost blood and the morphine, I could feel the truth of death with a starkness and surety I'd never before known. Love, too. I'd heard of this mythic love mothers have for their children; I'd been worried I wouldn't feel it. In the hospital room it throttled me, a seizure of love not only for my son but for my wife, too—a new level of love or perhaps a whole new love entirely, something born with my son, that felt almost painful to hold. In our little room, tended to by endless nurses, we were safe from death but would not be safe forever. Our oneness was so total it ruined language, but we would not be one forever. My mind reeled.

My hormones, a tangle of chemicals that kept my moods plummy through pregnancy, sunk. I felt like I was an elevator with cut cables, picking up brutal speed as it plummeted. If you think you have a personality, a soul, if you think there is anything particularly *real* about "you," try having a baby and watching your hormones retreat to pre-pregnancy levels. You are nothing but trembling and dread and tears. On top of this was the trauma of birth, my blood loss and my wife's terror, the sleep deprivation and drugs, and the wonder of our son's little body, our marvel at the instinct that drew him to my nipple and the magic way he commanded the milk to come. It seemed that time had stopped. Even the sky outside the window, changing with the weather and the hours, resembled a kind of screen saver. I wanted to stay inside that ugly little room forever.

We lived in the room for four nights. I slept on a bed I operated with a series of buttons, my wife sleeping beside me on a cracked plastic chair that the hospital called a "bed," as if we would be tricked. It didn't matter. She was close by, and the baby slept in her arms. Never did we lay him in the bassinet, an institutional plastic box; that was only for changing diapers and wheeling him over to the nursery for checkups. Each night bleeding into those strange, hazy days, the baby slept in my wife's arms.

I go by *Mama*, and my wife goes by *Baba*, a name created for a new kind of parent—part mother, part father; part neither, part both—and increasingly adopted by masculine women who can't relate to the binary genders lodged in *Mom* and *Dad*. Watching her become a baba, I keep my love to myself, because if I try to express it I burst into tears. It overwhelms me completely—*and*. *And* the language is a bust. It does not fit inside "I love you," even "I love you SO MUCH," delivered intensely and with serious eye contact, doesn't do it. And anyway, this is a love that's got death on its tail. To speak of it will attract the attention of some vengeful deity that I didn't believe in until right now.

For the three weeks of her allotted parental leave plus one extra week of federal family leave, my wife changed our son's every diaper. She brought me nipple cream and pale pink pads to slip into the cups of awful, industrial nursing bras the color of Band-Aids. She brought me plates of cut fruit and giant glasses of water clacking with ice. She wouldn't put the baby down until he began to bleat with hunger. After he'd fallen asleep with his mouth on me, I would hand him back. Friends watched us, family too. "A well-oiled machine," one said. "A dance." A grandmother grew unexpectedly sad at the sight of us, which brought the sudden revelation of how little help she'd had with her own babies. "It could have been so much easier," she said. My mother tells a family story I've never heard before, and I'm shocked that I haven't yet heard them all: The day I came home from the hospital, my father, angry that his own father seemed not to give a fig that this birth had occurred, violently opened up a box with a knife, stabbing it. My maternal grandmother—the daughter of a violent man, a wife- and child-beater—grew pale at this and quickly left the house. *Poor Nana*, I thought. Also, *My father loved me when I was born. My father was hurt by his father.* But of course he was. Where else do fathers learn to be hurtful? I think of our fatherless son. There exists a very generous drag queen whom we will someday point at and say, "Him, he helped us make you."

"Boys need to get dirty," the man across the street keeps telling my wife when she passes him standing, stoned, by his own son playing in a pile of dirt. *Kids* need to get dirty, I fume. Is he telling her this because we're women, two women with a son? To be different inside a culture is to constantly swat away paranoia. "When he gets older I'll teach him how to throw a ball around," a male acquaintance offers, believing himself helpful. "I know how to throw a ball," my wife says, confused. Well, not confused. We see the culture, and we see it seeing us. I see my wife holding our son in the tub, the pink of their skins; I see her pluck the cradle cap from his scalp, see her sing down into his upturned face, his ruby-red lips. My hormones have leveled, but it can still be too much to see. *What have I done to be this lucky?* I press my eyes closed until my chest loosens. At night the baby kicks his legs up and down, up and down, and we both think of a whale kicking his tail against the water. We bring him into the bed with us, and only then does he settle down, falling asleep with his little feet warm on my thigh, his fingers wrapped around our own.

First published in *Harper's* in 2015.

DIRE STRAITS

My mother calls me at my home in San Francisco as I work on my computer in my kitchen. In San Francisco, I live alone in a spacious one-bedroom. People visit and crane their necks, looking for my roommates. My monthly rent is more than I've ever paid, but only $300 more than what I formerly paid to live with three twentysomethings—a bartender/performance artist, a banker/drag queen, and a student. I decided to move out when I found our fridge filled with sickly, shriveled houseflies. They moved slowly in the cold, among the leftovers. I realized they must have been born there, and that baby flies are maggots. I was thirty-nine years old and feared that if I celebrated my fortieth birthday there I would have a crisis. So I moved.

My mom calls me from the lanai of her own home in Florida. She lives there with her husband. Because my mother is a graveyard-shift nurse and her husband suffers from a disease that makes sleeping difficult, their bedroom goes mostly unused. They take turns sleeping on the puffy, fake-leather couches in the living room. They sleep before the blaring television, always tuned to Fox News though neither is Republican. The television doesn't seem to bother them, nor do the cups of coffee they drink like water throughout the day. Their circadian rhythms are so busted from overnight work shifts and around-the-clock naps that neither coffee nor hysterical blather has any effect.

My mother tells me that they've moved the futon from the spare room into the living room and are trying to sleep together again, there on the floor, between the couches and before the TV. Her husband's disease—a spinal cord pocked with holes and stuffed with cysts—makes it hard for him to get out of a normal bed, but a futon on the floor is manageable. They haven't slept together in a very long time and seem to be excited, though he has already rolled off of the bedding, bruising himself.

I leave my computer when my mother calls and lie down in bed to talk to her. My own bed is a very firm mattress sunk into an antique French headboard carved with an argyle pattern and also flowers and ribbons and birds. My room is filled with light. My mother tells me her husband is probably experiencing the beginning stages of congestive heart failure. They're not sure. He doesn't have health care, and so attempts to understand what is making his feet swell up and his stomach bloat into a hard ball, what is making him short of breath, have not gone well.

"It's just an awful situation with the health care," my mother says. Her voice betrays forty or so years on the North Shore of Boston, where the accents run thick. No r's to speak of, and then certain words, say, *half*, have such a refined pronunciation that the dialect's British roots are revealed. My mother is from New England, specifically the city of Chelsea, a place that made national news when it went into state receivership in the early nineties. The amount of people living below the poverty line is about double the state average.

My mother has health insurance and her husband

doesn't; because of his preexisting condition, she can't add him to her plan. He was turned away from their local free clinic because my mother's income is too high. I don't ask my mother how much money she makes; it seems rude. On occasion my sister and I will send them checks, most recently when my mother broke her knee at work and needed groceries. Through a series of bureaucratic bamboozlements my mother was not given any paid leave for her accident. Her time away uncompensated, she returned to work too soon after the accident, on painkillers and in a wheelchair, to care for a ward full of seniors, some younger than she. She'd hurt herself slipping in a puddle of urine.

My mother's friends suggest she lie and say that she and her husband are separated. He can get a post office box and redirect his mail there. My mother can say that she allows him to stay in the house at night while she is at work, but she kicks him out in the daytime when she returns. This could help him get better health care.

"I can't do all that lying," my mother says. "You shouldn't have to go there."

In San Francisco, where I have lived for almost twenty years, I have had health insurance three times: for one year while working at a housing clinic, facilitating the removal lead from low-income apartments in the Tenderloin; for one year while working at Mills College, teaching fiction; and for the past five months since my partner put me on the insurance she gets through her employer. The majority of my care has been through the city's free clinic system. I could walk into any clinic and wait all day but eventually be seen and with a little paper card my medicine was five dollars. The staff worked to find ways to cover your costs. Though I am a lesbian, for years my annual gynecological checkups were covered through a federal family-planning fund. The free clinic closest to my mother and her husband is only open one day a week, on a first-come, first-served basis.

My mother's husband was just rejected for social security benefits for the third time in a row. She says that having more than a high school education worked against him, as well as how much money he'd made the year before he got sick.

Both my mother and her husband attended the School of Practical Nursing offered by the Soldiers' Home in Chelsea, a vets' hospital. The program is free and you work at the home after graduation. My mother graduated when I was nine, then promptly divorced my father; I often think of the program as a way of giving the city's many uneducated women in bad marriages the tools and the income to get out.

It was while working at the home that my mother met her husband. He was an orderly with homemade tattoos on his fingers and an earring. She was scared of him. They married a year after her divorce, and within another year he too attended the Soldiers' Home School of Practical Nursing and got his LPN.

My mother has continued to work in geriatric nursing, even though she dreamed of being a pediatric nurse. The extra year or two of schooling needed to get her RN, with its attendant pay scale and increased opportunities, has been disregarded; my mother said she doesn't want to be like "those people."

"What people?" I cried. "People who make more money? People who live more comfortably?"

"They think they're better than everyone," my mother said. "And plus, I'm too old to go back to school."

My mother tried and failed to get a part-time job at the Big Lots! near her home. The management feared she would be bored with such work. She dreams of working at a bookshop or as a Walmart greeter.

Before he became sick, my mother's husband was promoted to manager at the assisted-living facility he worked at. He had to report to work in a tie, which disturbed him. He was asked to overcharge the patients from wealthier families to make up for the economic drag of the poorer residents. He also was expected to discipline the staff, his fellow nurses and aides. He quit. My family is not cut out for positions of authority; having spent too much of their lives resenting those in charge, the transition into such a role is psychologically impossible. For years I'd thought that my own raging against the upper classes, my resistance to bettering my standing, was a punk-Marxist stance born of my own moral spirit. It wasn't until I was in my thirties that I realized I was parroting everything I'd heard in my home my whole life.

After leaving the management position, my mother's husband found work as a home care nurse. He would drive to different housebound patients, administering medicines and routine care. Apparently, he was a favorite. Both he and my mother are proud of what good nurses they are. My mother has told me the very first thing she does when she gets to work is wash her patients' eyeglasses with warm water and soap, an image I can dwell too heavily upon when feeling especially sorry for her. The tenderness and the duty of it strikes my heart.

Both my mother and her husband talk to their charges like normal people, like equals. They treat them with compassion and respect. They possess a certain snobbery about having received their training in New England, in

"Boston," my mother will stress. Not in Florida or any of the other podunk regions where her coworkers were certified. My mother did internships at Brigham and Women's Hospital, at Beth Israel. A New England health-care education is world-class.

My mother's husband began to chafe against his job. He did love the freedom, no one breathing down his neck, alone in his truck listening to Aerosmith on his way to his next patient, goofing and palling around while administering care, but management wasn't reimbursing his mileage, and gas is expensive. Plus, the wear and tear on his truck. Though they sometimes wouldn't have work for him, he was forbidden to sign up with other agencies. Then he became sick, and employment was no longer an option.

A combination of shames keeps my mother from sharing her and her husband's problems. She doesn't want to be a burden on her children. Parents are supposed to give their children money, support, help, not the reverse. She doesn't want me to worry. I've had a strained relationship with her husband, and perhaps she doesn't want to give me more reason to wish they weren't together. Her husband, too, can be secretive. Sometimes I think they're both shady. It can seem like they're hiding things, not telling the full story. Maybe they're not.

At the beginning of the end of the mortgage bubble, when my sister and I sent them checks in hopes they could hang onto their home, I was confused. My mother put her husband on the phone to thank me for the money. He sounded ashamed. I spoke despite the fist of guilt and pity in my stomach. "Why aren't you working? Why aren't you helping Ma?" It would be a little while till I got the whole story. By then, their house was gone.

The last time my mother's husband left Florida was Christmas 2007, when they came to San Francisco for the holiday. My sister came as well, and her husband and his family. My sister and I put my mother and her husband up at a hotel in Union Square, in the middle of the hustle-bustle, where the cable cars clang all day. We hadn't expected him to be so sickly. The three blocks down Powell to grab a hamburger in the mall food court killed him. He seemed to be in tremendous pain as he walked, the kind of pain that evicts you from your body. He seemed to be both intensely focused on moving forward and also totally checked out, ignoring his body's command to *stop*. He was present and not present.

"What's wrong with him?" my sister asked in the hotel lobby. "He's going to need a wheelchair."

"Oh, he'll shoot himself before he ends up in a wheelchair," my mother said, fearful and defensive. "Or winds up in a home, god forbid. He'll kill himself."

Suicide as a sane response to a more draggy ending is something my family has always championed. "A bottle of Seconal and a six-pack," my grandmother would say about her time, should it come preceded by cancer or dementia. And it did, by lung cancer at the age of fifty-four, and there were no barbiturates or alcohol, just a painful, drawn-out death at Massachusetts General, where she lay in a bed convulsing, bald from chemotherapy, her body shrunk and whittled into something resembling a Chinatown chicken.

My mother shared her depressive death wishes with me until I ordered her to stop, and still she lives. My grandfather requested not a burial but to be "thrown in a Hefty bag and tossed into the Bay," but a burial he got, replete with handsome young Navy officers sounding taps in his honor.

No one dies well, but it is true that the poor die worse, with less care, more terrible care, no care at all, and then burial costs their families can't afford. It took my mother a year to come up with the money for my grandfather's memorial—the stone, the cremation. A burial was not an option. It makes sense they'd try to control the eventuality with gallows humor and a DIY attitude.

In San Francisco my mother took her husband to a traveler's doctor downtown. He saw them after-hours, late in the night, and prescribed painkillers that could only be filled at the twenty-four-hour pharmacy in the Castro. She took a cab there and back to fill it. I learned this the next morning, when it was all done and her husband was floating on a cloud of pills. Actually, he wasn't floating, not in the way narcotics lift you when you don't actually need them. He was just normal. The medicine had absorbed his body's struggle and he could be among us on Christmas Day, smiling, excited to see San Francisco, hanging off the side of the cable car that took us into Nob Hill, to the French bistro where we'd be eating our holiday dinner. He had beef Wellington for the first time and found it pleasing, as did I. We both enjoyed the lobster risotto. We'd agreed on a Secret Santa plan to stop everyone from spending money on everyone else, but my mother cheated and gave me a light-blue sweater from Old Navy. My sister's mother-in-law picked up the bill; on the cable car back downtown she shoved a pocketful of bills into the operator's gloved fist and expressed sympathy for his having to work on Christmas. He dinged the bell at her.

In the hotel lobby I said, "Ma, you should have called me, I could have gone to the Castro for you, I could have come to the doctor's." But my mother didn't want to worry me, she was too busy worrying *about* me: my recent breakup, my new AA sponsee. My mother was happy I wasn't drinking anymore, but she didn't like me hanging out with so many alcoholics. Her husband is an alcoholic as well, though he hasn't taken a drink since the early nineties. He went to AA for a moment, to get his footing, but all the talk about God and the members' dependence on the meetings bugged him.

On the telephone my mother tells me that their car broke down again. She laughs when she tells me, though it isn't funny. My mother has a peculiar tic wherein she laughs broadly while delivering bad news. It used to drive me crazy. "Why are you laughing," I'd asked. "Do you think it's funny that the car broke down/your husband fell while mowing the lawn/was run over, somehow, by his own truck/lost his truck/was declined for Social Security?" The hurt in her response made me feel like a monster. Of course she was laughing because it wasn't funny. I'd grown up in this family. If I didn't understand their ways by now, age forty-one, I was hopeless.

I ask her what happened to the car, and she tells me it was the oil pump. The good news is the oil pump is new, less than a year old, and therefore under warranty. The bad news is she has to fix whatever broke the oil pump. The badder news is that the car has been in the shop going on four days and she's having to take a cab to and from work, a city or so away. "Do you trust your mechanic?" I ask her. Because her car is always breaking down.

My sister has a theory about their car always breaking down. The theory is that my mother's husband is a secret drug addict. No longer with an income of his own, he has rigged up a situation with their car mechanic, who would have to also be a drug dealer in order for this to operate. The theory is nothing is ever really wrong with the car, it's just a cover for my mother's husband to pay the drug dealer for his pills. Before my mother's husband stopped working, when he was a home health-care nurse, always on the road, my sister speculated that he was actually seeing prostitutes. My sister's theories sound far-fetched, but similarly outrageous ideas in the past have proven to be true.

"We're going to a new mechanic," my mother tells me. "That last one, he's a nice guy but he makes too many mistakes." My mother pauses, feeling a bit guilty for judging the mechanic. "But then, you know, the car is twenty years old. It took all the money I'd saved to visit your sister, so she's going to have to feed me while I'm there."

All we want to do is feed our mother when she visits, and buy her things, as if we could somehow save her with tuna sandwiches and hamburgers and tchotchkes from the Disney Store. But she is our mother, and all she wants to do is take care of us, to pay for our lunches and dinners and buy me cast-iron pans and glittered silicone spatulas from the fancy kitchen shop by the water. It is hard to accept things from my mother, but to refuse them robs her of her dignity, her desire to be a mom taking care of her kids. It would take from her the feeling that all is right with us, that our family demonstrates the natural order of things: parents take care of kids. Kids don't take care of the parents—not until they're very old, anyway—and even then, you inherit something, don't you?

My mother and her husband make ridiculous decisions with money. The way that she came into any at all was from throwing her back out at work in the nineties. Her settlement was enough to buy a house where they lived in Massachusetts. Soon after, my sister and I confronted my stepfather about his creepy behavior while we were younger. The family fell apart for a while, which my mother dealt with by maxing out her credit cards on trips to Disney World. Her husband became a certified diver and took trips off the Keys, swimming with whale sharks. Eventually, they decided to live inside their vacation and moved to Florida. She sold her home to her husband's brother at a deep discount, not bothering to try to make any money on the sale, let alone get what they paid for. Her brother-in-law struggled, with a lazy wife who wouldn't work and two teenage boys. Plus, the houses in Florida were cheaper.

About a year after they moved, the brother-in-law sold the house at a profit and joined them in Florida. The house he bought was bigger and had a cage pool.

When a hurricane ripped apart their town, my mother's house was spared, though she was traumatized by the experience. The windows on her floor of the managed-care facility had imploded, spraying glass across her patients. The tornado in the parking lot created an otherworldly atmosphere that popped her ears and sucked the elderly toward the hole in the wall. She found her staff, a group of certified nursing assistants from Trinidad, holed up in a nurses' lounge holding hands and crying out to Jesus, and ordered them back into the ward. When she returned home, her house was so obscured by fallen trees she thought it was gone. She cried with relief to see it wasn't, and she continued to cry for the next month, erratically bursting into tears at the Home Depot, buying a flat of water, or talking to me on the phone from her home, a dark and oily place, powered on generators, the windows boarded, fans replacing air-conditioning, weakly trying to push the Florida swamp out of their home.

When a man came around offering to haul downed trees out of their yard, she paid him up front for three days' work. He was a stranger, but he had a little girl with him and seemed like he needed money, and she felt bad. She gave the little girl lemonade. The man worked for half a day and never returned.

When my sister got married my mother's anxiety about the cost of the wedding consumed her. She decided to sell the lot that came with her house. It didn't matter that the wedding was paid for or that her plane tickets and housing would be taken care of, she wanted to help. She wanted to buy a dress and pay for a lunch the day after the wedding. The possibility of a sale rose and fell, rose and fell.

"Do you know about Joseph in the Ground?" my mother asked me. European Catholic nuns once buried statues of St. Joseph in the ground outside of property they wanted for their convents. Now people buried the statues on their own property when they hoped to sell their homes. She'd purchased a Joseph-in-the-Ground kit from a Catholic Supply Center and dug him into the wild lot beside her home. She signed off on a fast sale, less money than she could have gotten had she waited, but the wedding was coming.

My sister tried to block my mother from spending any of the lot money on the wedding. She wanted her to put it in the bank. "Do you have any savings at all?" My sister demanded. "How are you going to take care of yourself when you retire? We're going to have to take care of you."

My mother bristled. "Retire? I'll work till I die," she snapped. "You're not going to take care of me."

I told my sister that she needed to let our mother pay

for the lunch. "It's important to her," I said. "She needs the dignity to make her own decisions with her money." My sister's therapist said this was true, and so my mother paid for the lunch.

My mother's husband's medicine runs her $400 a month. It is harder and harder for him to get his prescriptions filled, as their region of Florida is plagued by "pill mills," illegitimate pain clinics staffed by doctors who will prescribe morphine and Oxycontin to addicts. Morphine and Oxycontin are his medications. The pain clinics have become tiny police states, with all patients presumed guilty—addicted—by the cops who patrol and raid the places. Squad cars idle in the parking lot; my mother is not allowed to wait there for her husband, waiting in the car is prohibited. Because he is not insured, her husband can get his prescription at the pain clinic, but he can't get it filled there, as they don't take cash. He goes to the pharmacy at Walmart, but they are clean out of narcotics. He finds a private pharmacist that is scared to take on a pain-pill client. My mother's husband talks him into it.

I think about writing about what my mother's husband is going through in order to get his medicine, and ask if I can talk to his pharmacist about it. His response is terrified. "Oh no, no," he says on the phone. "He won't talk to you, and he'd stop filling my prescriptions."

"I don't understand," I say. "Nothing illegal is happening, why is he so scared, why is it so hard to get your meds?"

Why do some people have really, really hard lives while other people's lives are easy? Why don't I have a degenerative spine disease? My mother learned from a friend from Chelsea that three other men of her husband's generation have strange spinal disorders. They all grew up in the same neighborhood, a series of streets that dead-ended into a large waste dump.

"What are you gonna do," my mother says, and it's not a question. "It's just what's going on." She's talking about her husband's body, the swollen feet and belly, his trouble catching a breath. "It is what it is."

But we don't know what it is. Could it be the meds? "I wonder if they're not bothering his liver?" my mother wonders. "Your liver, your heart, your lungs, they all coincide."

My mother and her husband are the least healthy health-care professionals on earth. They have done nothing to supplement the education they received in the 1980s. They chain-smoke, and have resigned themselves to the deaths they'll be rewarded with. My mother reacts with fury against the anti-smoking legislation popping up around the country. When she arrives in California, she's not allowed to smoke outside the airport. In San Francisco, she cannot smoke in parks. "Before you know it, they won't let you smoke in your own house," she rails.

"Mom, you're paranoid." I said. "People just don't want to breathe in cigarette smoke, it's gross."

"I know," she says, slightly ashamed. "It's terrible." Her addiction butting up against her desire to make everyone happy, or not make anyone mad.

Her husband has a high white blood cell count. "What does that mean?" I ask. "How did you find that out?"

"When we went to the free clinic and they told me I made too much money," she scoffs. "They handed him an inhaler and sent him home."

"How is he doing today?"

"He's down in the dumps." Her husband has been depressed about his condition, about his inability to contribute to their life. To compensate he'll mow the lawn or take on a chore beyond his ability, resulting in falls and increased pain. He has burst into tears, afraid that she will leave him. For years my sister and I have wanted her to leave him. Now, if she leaves him, he'll die.

"If his feet swell up bad again, we'll go to the emergency room," she tells me. "He's not in dire straits, like I need to call 911 or anything." *Dire straits* is something my mother will say a lot. They're waiting for him to reach this level to bring him in. But I wonder if they are able to accurately recognize what dire straits looks like. To me, they have been in dire straits for quite some time. What does the bottom look like to them?

"His feet came down some once he put them up on pillows," she explains. "They were so red and shiny."

It is hard for my mother to explain a situation in a straightforward manner. I think she is in a state of perpetual overwhelm. "Why are there fluids in his feet?" I ask her.

"It's a congestive heart failure thing," she says. "The heart's not pumping, and the fluids pool in the feet. I noticed Thursday or Friday, he took a shower and came to sit down. I said, 'You don't look good.' He was huffing and puffing." My mother got one of her nurse tools, an oximeter. "It's a little gizmo you put on your finger and it tells you how much oxygen is in your blood. I said, 'Put it on and go walk into the kitchen.'"

He shuffled into the kitchen, where their untrained Maltese, Kira, pees on newspapers on the floor. He shuffled back.

"Ninety-one," she said. "Not good. We put people on oxygen at ninety-two. But then it went back up again. He's not in dire straits."

Dire straits. Only my mother talks like my mother. Who says dire straits? They're a band. There are all sorts of old, regional phrases that my mother carries on. *Not for nothing*. As in, "Not for nothing, but I should have looked into the situation for nurses before I moved to Florida. There's no union. It's a right-to-work state, meaning you have the 'right' to work, and they have the 'right' to fire you." Or, *Light dawns on Marblehead*. Marblehead is a fancy town by the sea in Massachusetts, but it is also your own thick-headed noggin, slow to understand.

"He's going to talk to his doctor," my mother continues. "He wants to get off some of his medication."

"Wait, I thought he doesn't have a doctor."

"His pain-management doctor, at the pain clinic. She does labs but she's not his primary care. He doesn't have that. I could have him go to Mapatan"—that's her doctor—"but he won't do shit. He'll say, 'Put your feet up and watch your salt.'"

"You don't know that," I said. Is it because my life is so comparatively easy that I'm quick to access hope? Because my life has turned out well, do I presume everyone else's will too? "Why don't you just try Mapatan?"

"Because he doesn't have insurance. No one wants to see you. They literally tell you they don't take uninsured patients."

I begin a rant about the Hippocratic oath. Don't all doctors take a pledge to not let people die? I am ruined from a life in San Francisco, where people like to do good things. I do not understand how the real world works.

"We'll see," my mother says. "Like I said, he's okay right now. I'm a realist, Michelle. I'm just a realist. He's got a disease process in his back. He's a heavy smoker, though he's cut his smoking way down, and people get sick."

I am relieved that my mother is so detached, because I fear her being in emotional pain over her husband dying before her eyes. And I am chilled at her detachment. When they found a cancer in my grandfather's nose, my mother was also a realist. "He's an old man," she repeated. She didn't think surgery was a good idea. But they took care of the cancer and he lived another decade.

"I don't think I'm exaggerating," she says. "I just know what I see. And his belly's gotten huge."

I would never think that my mother exaggerated. My mother and our whole family downplay everything, they do not exaggerate. They are a meek people. For years my mother would play the lottery, elaborating humbly on how she would spend the money. "I'd keep some," she'd say, "but I'd give it to you kids, I'd give it to Papa and Willie"—Papa's girlfriend—"I'd give it to Darlene and the kids, I'd give some to Carlie." It was a prayer of sorts. My mother is truly Catholic, and believes that selfless altruism is rewarded with the granting of more selfish desires. The pagan roots of her Irish Catholicism exist within her without her knowledge, her prayers often resembling spells. Joseph in the ground. Playing our birthdates on the lotto. In her cold acceptance of death she is a Scorpio, in her work she is Hecate, ushering the dying out of life.

Her husband also believes in the value of aiming low. Wanting to transition out of nursing and into his passion, diving, he dreamed of washing the windows for a dive shop. "Wouldn't you want to lead dives?" I asked. "Or work on the boat?"

"Nah, I don't care, I'd be happy just washing the windows." These goals filled me with a heartbreaking rage. I saw in them the history of my own low standards and lost potential. It made me want to kill them both. That was before he got sick, when I spent the visit researching universities that had programs in marine anthropology, registering him for information. He wanted to study shipwrecks. Why would I think someone satisfied with washing windows at a dive shop would have the wherewithal to enroll in college? I hadn't even had such wherewithal, and had not attended a university. This was once their fault, but at this point it's my own.

My mother is explaining her husband's body to me. "It's just that your heart doesn't pump right, so the fluids in your body, instead of moving they stagnate. You got valves in your legs that pump the blood back into your heart."

"What is the fluid?"

"Blood, plasma, lymph fluid. Your blood isn't just blood."

"What does he want to do about his meds?"

"I think he wants to get off all of them and start all over again and see how he does without them. They don't know enough about syringomyelia." That is her husband's disease. When he was diagnosed, my mother called and asked me to look it up on the internet, something she didn't have. I printed out pages of information and sent them off to Florida in an envelope. "Duke, UCLA, and Mass General are just starting to do tests." There is a new medicine available, called Neurontin. "It's for neuropathy pain, from nerves. It's not a narcotic."

"The whole thing is no health insurance," my mother says. "You can't even go in and get it straightened out. We'll see what we can do. It seems to be a chronic thing—it's not like, 'Oh my god, I've got to call 911, he can't breathe.' But the shortness of breath is new."

Her husband doesn't want to go to the hospital, anyway. "'Oh yeah, and there's another bill for you,'" she mimics him. "'And I can't contribute.' But I don't care about that.

You think I care if I get a $2,000 bill from the ER? Seri-ously, I'm sixty-two, what are you gonna do about it? I'll give you ten dollars a month. As long as you give them something, what are they gonna do?"

There's no debtor's prison, my mother is fond of saying, and good thing. She went bankrupt traveling to Disney, moving to Florida, installing a hot tub on the lanai of the house they eventually lost.

"I'm reading a lot about that generation," she says, refer-ring to her husband, a decade or so younger than she. "The sixties and seventies. People did a lot of shit and it took a toll on them, their livers and hearts, and it's showing up now."

I wonder if he could have hepatitis C, like a lot of people who once shot drugs.

"They were wild childs," my mother says, and shifts from vaguely cavalier yet agitated, to somber, and guilty. "Part of me feels bad for talking to you about it. I haven't even talked to you in a week and now I just dump all this on you."

The doorbell rings and Kira the Maltese begins to bark wildly. "Hold on, it's my pizza," she says. I wait on the phone while she pays the delivery guy. My mother doesn't have many people to talk with. Maybe some casual friends at work. A couple of old flames from childhood she's recon-nected with on Facebook, both with sickly wives. They commiserate. Her parents are dead and her only brother is a mentally ill drug addict so far gone that, at this point, it is impossible to tell when he is high and when he is having an episode. She comes back on the line.

"I think you need to talk about it," I say to her, and she says, "I guess I do."

We have confusing boundaries, my mother and I. I have

forbidden her from sharing so much of her pain with me, because I didn't want to hear how she wanted to die. When I wouldn't speak to her husband, I didn't want to hear about how hard it was for her.

"Maybe it's hard for me to not have a family?" I'd lash out. "To have had a Peeping Tom stepfather?" Now, she shares this new trauma in a stop-and-go fashion, bursting with it, then sheepishly backtracking. But I think it's okay for her to talk me.

My mother's pizza is getting cold. She has to go and eat it.

"I love you," I tell her, and she counters with, "I love you more." It's what she always says. "Kisses and hugs," she singsongs and makes a bunch of squishy kissing noises into the phone, and hangs up.

First published in *n+1* in 2014.

AGAINST MEMOIR

My twenty-month-old son sleeps in a twin bed on the floor of his bedroom, wedged into a corner so he doesn't tumble out, the corner stuffed with pillows so that he doesn't bonk his head during bouts of violent toddler sleep. I think there is something wrong with the corner; bad feng shui, or perhaps a terrible energy, has snagged there. In the haunted punk rock flophouse I spent my twenties in, my bandmate Cheryl once told me that black balls of energy were roosting in the corners of my kitchen "like bats." Cheryl was clean and sober and Native American and a mystic; when she got in fights with people she prayed for them, which baffled and infuriated her enemies. I believe there were bad-energy bats flapping through that house because of the nightmares I'd had, the prickly sensations, the creaking floorboards, and the shadows moving room to room. Classic haunted-house bullshit. The transient roommate population tended toward the alcoholic and the pill addled, smokers of crystal meth and injectors of ecstasy. People with badly compromised psychic immune systems. None of us would have felt the sting of the bad-energy bats as they sank their fangs into our auras and sucked out all the pretty colors.

Lying in my son's bed, as I do nearly every night, I wonder if the bad-energy bats are with us, tucked into the spiderwebby corner of his pale-blue bedroom. He's been sleeping worse than usual, tossing and turning, crying tears through dreaming eyes. What do babies dream? Lying beside him one night, I too began to cry. At forty-five I seemed to have just realized I would never again be sixteen years old. I would never again feel what it feels like to be high on that particular mixture of youth and hormones, my still pillowy brain not yet hardened to risk, everything possible, probable, permissible. When I think of being sixteen I think of wearing a very short black velvet dress, the torn hem dangling thread. My hair was home bobbed, choppy and chunky, a harsh burnt-orange color, the result of a failed effort to bleach my hair from a chemical black. I'm drunk, of course. Did I land on sixteen because drinking never felt as good as it did that summer, drunk in the Boston Common, making out with boys, riding in the trunk of my best friend's car all the way to Worcester to see the Cure? The ghost of this girl hovered just above my son's bed, flapping her black wings, and I wept. Later I texted my sister: "I'm sobbing because I'll never be sixteen again." She texted back: "I'm sorry you will never be sixteen again. That's a hard truth. And I'm sorry you have PMS."

It was not bad-energy bats, of course. Later I lay on the couch and tearfully live-tweeted my period: "Amidst feelings of intense greasy zit bloat absurd horniness gross."

But then weeks later I lie in the same spot, and on the verge of falling asleep, I have the startling revelation that *there is no god*. I get that feeling, like stumbling from a curb; I jolt awake and quickly there are tears. My son, exhausted from kicking me repeatedly in the abdomen, sleeps through my jerk and sob. The despair is intense, the disappointment. *This is all there is*, a sprawling dark flash cracked like lightning the length of my universe. *What will I pray to?* I think dumbly. *Oh, no more prayer.* I realize that I actually love praying. Something I began skeptically on recommendation became a more habitual way to harness my mind, became something that brings me real joy. I love sending love out to the world with my son each night as he falls asleep, even though he actually refuses love to most everyone.

"We send love from our hearts to Uncle Bear?"

"No."

"We send love from our hearts to cousin Chloe and cousin Jude?"

"No."

"Yes, we do," I insist, annoyed.

And he responds, "No, no, no, no, no." Even a child can tell you there are no webs of magical energy strung between the hearts of those who love each other. I'm a fool. Everything fun about life seems gone. I cry myself to sleep.

The next day I take a smoldering bundle of sage and walk it around the house, spending extra time in the corners above my son's bed. I tell my wife we've got to move it to a different part of the room, it's got bad feng shui. I tell her about my crying jags. "What the fuck do I care about never being sixteen again?" I rant. "I hate nostalgia." Same for god or no god. I pray regardless, because it makes me feel good and even science has acknowledged it changes your brain. Changing my brain is my favorite high. I pop three Celexa a day with the intention of sinking new grooves into that busted record. "Have you been taking your meds?" she asks. "Yup." This has to be a magical problem.

It's hard to know where to put my son's bed. The room is small and cluttered with toys, with dressers and shelves.

I lie down with him again, stretched out beneath the flap of the bad-energy bats. Drowsy, I think about how in my last book I called an ex-boyfriend "Cruise Dude." Because he took me on a cruise, a bad cruise, the most miserable two weeks of my life, as is the point of the story. Cruise Dude. I cringe. *Why did I call him that?* I feel utterly humiliated. We will never, ever be friends again; how could such a moniker ever be forgiven? *Dude*, a shade less grotesque than *bro*. Named after a two-week getaway, no identity outside of the bad feelings he gave me, barely a mention of the decades of friendship that preceded our doomed affair. I vaguely remembered a *fuck it* feeling as I wrestled with what to call him. Cruise Dude was a place-holder that stuck; mostly I didn't want to care too much about it. There is a certain stance you must take to write a memoir, a spell you cast upon yourself at the keyboard. You must not remember that your characters are actual *people*, people you once loved or maybe still do. Cruise Dude was brought into my memoir to illuminate a point, that I had dated people I shouldn't have, and thusly have learned hard romantic lessons. Still, why didn't I call him, like, *Charles*, or something? Shutting the laptop on that passage, I had smirked internally. Look, he didn't even warrant a *name* in the book of my life. That's what you get, Cruise Dude! If you don't like it—goes the memoir-ist's familiar refrain—you shoulda acted right! It felt good enough at the time. Now, in bed beneath the bad-energy bats, a low-level shame pervaded my body. How petty. I always told students not to write for revenge, just tell the story, but when your story is "I've been done wrong," how can you help but steal a morsel of pleasure from the inherent vengeance of tattling? How can you, the wounded author, be trusted?

"If I understood the desire to confess, it would have saved me a great deal of unhappiness." That is neurologist Alice Weaver Flaherty in her book *The Midnight Disease: The Drive to Write, Writer's Block, and the Creative Brain.* "Neurologists have found that changes in a specific area of the brain can produce hypergrafia—the medical term for an overpowering desire to write." Flaherty herself became hypergrafic in the storm of a postpartum depression that followed the late-term miscarriage of twins. She had always been wordy, but now her pen flew off the margins. Her brain had been changed. When she became happily pregnant a second time, her brain was changed again and the writing mania came back. "Mental illness is not completely separable from sanity," she writes. "There is a sense in which mental illness is awfully like sanity—only much, much more so."

I have always written. In second grade I started a class newspaper, the *Schoolyard Gazette*, of which I was the editor, publisher, and sole staff writer. "Chicken Pox Is Sweeping the Second Grade" rang my first, sensationalist headline. I did the comics page, inking a crude heart coming at another heart with an ax. "Don't go breaking my heart!" the caption quipped. When I too fell victim to chicken pox I decided to use the time to pen my first novel. Using a paperback as a model, I removed the scratch-proof socks I had on my hands and got to it. Beginning at the beginning, I drew my cover. With a glance at the back, I wrote some blurbs boasting of the story's special genius. Then I had to write the actual book. I was stumped. I returned to an earlier project, a humorous rewriting of the dictionary, where *abundance*, for example, was a social mixer for pastries.

In fourth grade I took inspiration from the headlines of the garish *Boston Herald American*, the lowbrow alternative to the *Globe* and what my grandfather read at the dinner table. When a young girl was finally killed by a mother who had long abused her, I wrote a fictionalized version and dedicated it to her memory. After scanning a piece about the unfair treatment endured by developmentally disabled individuals I penned a short story called *The Retard's Sister*. In it, a girl makes a wish that her sister die so that the horrible kids at her school will stop teasing her. And her sister does die, and the guilt is such that she will never again have a happy day for the rest of her punishingly long life. In fifth grade I wrote scripts for *The Facts of Life*, in particular one wherein Jo inveigles the Go-Go's to perform at a dance at Eastland Prep. In sixth grade I tried to adapt Judy Blume's *Blubber* into a play. In seventh grade I mainly wrote and rewrote Billy Idol lyrics in Lisa Frank notebooks.

Then, when I was twenty-one, powerful things happened. I realized I could have sex with girls, and my life exploded. I realized all of society and culture was a misogynist conspiracy to oppress women, and that this web of oppression tangled with other oppressions, racism, say, or how people liked to beat up homeless people, or go fag bashing; it linked up with anti-Semitism, fascism. The connection between a police officer in Provincetown who would not allow me to sunbathe topless on the beach and the obliteration of generations at Buchenwald was so clear to me it stung my brain. When I called that cop a Nazi, I meant it. The way agriculture is produced, with chemicals, harvested by brown people sleeping in tents and pissing in the hot sun, was linked directly to slaughterhouses which were linked directly to American slavery. I stopped eating. My stepfather admitted he had been spying on me and my sister, for many years, through holes he'd carved into our walls. This was no different than my mother phoning our old landlord, a friend she had had a falling out with, to warn them that a Haitian family was coming to view the apartment. None of this was any different than the dumping of nuclear waste into third-world dumps. My brain was thoroughly changed.

I moved to San Francisco, and began writing. In earnest. I remember being inside a nightclub, sitting up on top of a jukebox, scribbling in my notebook by the light that escaped it. All around me the darkness writhed with throngs of females, their bodies striped and pierced, as shaved and ornamented as any tribe anywhere, clad in animal skins, hurling themselves into one another with love. What feeling it filled me with. An alcoholic, an addict, I know what it is to crave, and the need to take this story into my body was consuming. For years I sat alone at tables, drunk, writing the story of everything I had ever known or seen. Hypergrafia manifests primarily as personal narratives, memoir. My brain did this to me.

In workshops I always tell students to read *The Midnight Disease* so that they can understand their affliction. We are not unlike alcoholics, and it does seem like so many writers are alcoholics, doesn't it? *Writing is a mental illness*, I tell them. Sometimes it helps me understand *everything*; through this lens I make a perfect sense to myself, much the way accepting my alcoholism contextualized so much of my temperament, my actions. Or how a thorough astrological reading can relieve you of guilt you hadn't known you were carrying. I was *born this way*. But I am sober, now. I know it's not my "fault" I inherited my particular genetic hash; so many alcoholics, Polish and Irish, I never had a chance. I did what alcoholics do, betray and lie and play the victim, be grandiose, grandly delusional, humiliate myself, shit my pants, and so on. It is so very blameless, an animal being its specific type of animal, but people get sober and they stop. If I truly see memoir as a compulsion on par with alcoholism—and so similar does it feel, an ecstasy of communion with yourself that facilitates the transcendence of your self; typing this, right now, I'm hardly even here—if I am powerless over this desire, and if, on occasion, it has rendered my life unmanageable, am I not required to abstain? What would it mean to get sober from writing memoir? What would a memoir bottom be? Lying in my son's bed thinking, *Cruise Dude, ugh, what a loser I am.* Or, my mother nervously making dinner as I stammer my intention to write a book about how her husband hurt me, how she stood by his side. "But why do you have to publish it?" Is part of hypergrafia the need to have these writings witnessed by the world? I am sure I would never write if it were never to be seen by another.

The first time I shared my writing it was a poem about an ex-girlfriend who had *done me wrong.* I was at an open mic in a dive bar in San Francisco. I knew it was possible my poem was bad, but I reasoned that people all around me enjoyed things I found atrocious. There was, I believed, an audience for everything. If only one person on earth would like my poem, then I would read it for her. But, even as I knew it was possible that my poem was bad, I knew also it possibly was good. I had felt an exhilaration while writing it, and now, anticipating my reading, I felt similarly exhilarated. Probably this was a sort of mania. "While my hypergrafia felt like a disease," writes Flaherty, "it also felt like one of the best things that has ever happened to me. It still does."

Personal narrative is a mental illness, but you don't want to be well. This is not unusual. Many mentally ill people don't want to take their meds. Every so often I fantasize about the gorgeous mania that could fill me up if I just stopped eating my three Celexa. The one time I abstained, a cartoon cloud, gunmetal gray, drifted into my house and settled itself over my head. Oh, that. Of course I only remember the euphoric highs, not the daily gloom. I gobbled my pills. When I was an alcoholic I didn't want to get sober. I couldn't imagine who I would be without alcohol. I realize how sad that sounds, like, literally pathetic. But it is true. Alcohol gave me everything. It was 100 percent the fuel that fired me. It made me move, made me write, fuck, fight, love, motivate.

I don't want to get sober from writing. I can't imagine who I would be without writing. This I can embrace, it does not feel pathetic. Even though the list of people who have been hurt by it grows. You can't really make amends when you're still drunk. I can't really do anything while I'm still writing. I can't email my ex and say, "Sorry I called you Cruise Dude. I feel bad about it." Plus, I already betrayed him in a totally different piece I'd written for *Nerve* about fifteen years ago, in the wake of our first dumb affair, and I had already apologized for *that*, and of course this feels bad. I'm a repeat offender. Another ex furiously pleaded with me not to write about him, and so I wrote a book about not writing about him. But before that book came a different book where I also wrote about him. For two weeks he would not speak to me. "You used me as your foil," he accused. But he was my foil. I said I was sorry. I was sorry that I made fun of him for watching *The Real World*. My television habits have worsened since our breakup and now I too watch all kinds of terrible television, things far worse than *The Real World.* I could apologize for that, but that is all. "I thought we were family," he said, as if he hadn't watched me betray my family in writing a thousand times. "We are," I said. "But if I can't be honest about what our relationship was like for me, then it's just not going to work." I think we are friends. He keeps a certain distance. I do not think we are family anymore.

When I was in pain from my breakup with this person, I doubled down on Buddhism. I had always wanted to study it more deeply, and now I was lonely and hurting with tons of free time, what could be better. In fact, most white people come to Buddhism after a trauma. The temple I attended was full of divorcees and bulimics, alcoholics, people dealing with deaths, their imminent own or someone else's. It had a somber vibe. But everything I ever heard struck me as the truth. I bought a lot of Pema Chödrön books. My nightstand was Pema Chödrön, Al-Anon literature, and a Hitachi Magic Wand. A particular still life.

It soon became apparent that writing memoir is the least Buddhist thing you can do, worse even than physical violence, as there is a tradition within Buddhism of whacking acolytes with a stick if they seem to need it. Chödrön's whole message is *drop the story line*:

The story line is associated with certainty and comfort. It bolsters your very limited, static sense of self and holds out the promise of safety and happiness. But the promise is a false one; any happiness it brings is only temporary. The more you practice not escaping into the fantasy world of your thoughts and instead contacting the felt sense of groundlessness, the more accustomed you'll become to experiencing emotions as simply sensation—free of concept, free of story line, free of fixed ideas of bad and good.

Memoir *is* the story line. Again and again I repeat to myself what has happened to me and what it has meant. This begins in my head and becomes material on the page and I repeat it forever as I read aloud from my work, perpetuating an idea about myself when, as Buddhism insists, there is no "self." This understanding provokes despair. Will I be compelled to give this up too? By "too" I mean in addition to drugs and alcohol, compulsive sex benders, gossip, and sugar. In one of my tarot decks, the card for the Tower is illustrated as an eye opening in the heavens, the tower crumbling beneath it. It's about the irrevocability of revelation. When you see so clearly that something is wrong, you are required to change. Or are you? I saw once, so clearly, that eating animals is wrong, and still I believe it probably is and still I eat animals. Does turning against your highest knowledge do something bad to some very good part of you? I refuse to drop my story line.

Though something did happen in the temple, during a class I was taking. It was a basic Buddhism class that went deep into early texts and mythologies, and it got me feeling mystical. There was much talk about there being no self. Or, a self behind the self, a hidden self somehow more real, your Buddha nature maybe, I don't want to act like I grasped it because I didn't, but something happened and I realized I was not Michelle Tea. I was some other thing that was wearing Michelle Tea like a robe. I was riding Michelle Tea's life like a ride at Six Flags. It gave me a good feeling. It still does. I think, quite often, *I am not*

Michelle Tea. Or, *I am not Michelle Lippman*, my married name. *I am not Michelle Swankowski*, my birth name. *I am not Michelle Tomasik*, my legal maiden name. Who is this girl, why did she have so many names? She was a memoirist. Michelle Tea was a memoirist. I think of it like this, and it satisfies me.

But still. Says Maggie Nelson, our stories "trap us, bring us spectacular pain. In their scramble to make sense of nonsensical things they distort, codify, blame, aggrandize, restrict, omit, betray, mythologize, you name it." Once I was reading at Edinburgh Castle in San Francisco's Tenderloin, upstairs in a low-ceilinged, black room that felt like a firetrap. The event was part of a series, Seven Deadly Sins. I was assigned envy. I didn't want to write anything new. My book *Valencia* is filled with envy, I read from that, no matter that it was many years old, the time documented is older still. This is from my book *Valencia*. It's about this bitch who stole my girlfriend. I had been introducing that chapter as such for a very long time. The "girlfriend" hadn't been my girlfriend for over a decade. Currently I had a boyfriend, had had one for years. It was a serious commitment; we'd even gotten fake married by a witch who had charged us nineteen dollars and ninety-nine cents for her services and provided a Safeway carrot cake as a wedding cake. We wore wedding rings bought for cheap at a joyería on Mission Street. But I opened the piece like it had all just happened, my girlfriend, *stolen*, some bitch out there with my heart in her claws.

After the reading an acquaintance came up to shake my hand. He liked the piece. He was laughing at the outlandishness of it. "I can't believe that was Sara," he said, knowing the real name of the homewrecker bitch I called

Emma. "And I was sitting right there with her!" I paled. Sara was *here*? "Yeah, we were sitting right behind you." A flood of shame hit me. I flashed on my performance, truly a *performance*, acting out this old, tired outrage, a hurt I hadn't actually felt in years. Someone had *done me wrong* and I'd etched it in stone and become its keeper, its caretaker. Times change and people change, perspectives shift and new information comes to light, and forever in the pages of that book Sara is the destroyer of my young lesbian romance. I am forever *done wrong*.

I went downstairs and found her sprawled morosely in a booth. "Hello," she said. Years ago, when she was with my ex and the two of them would show up at readings, I would scan the crowd to make sure she wasn't there before reading something terrible about her. Then this one time I didn't care. I was reading with Eileen Myles and I wanted to perform the piece I liked most and the piece I liked most right then was very "you did me wrong" and predicted that our mutual girlfriend would eventually leave Sara/Emma the same way she had left me. I read it. And Sara/Emma was there. And the ex had left her earlier that day. Sara/Emma walked out of the reading and kicked the glass of a Muni bus stop. She broke her foot, and walked around with a crutch for a while.

"I am so sorry," I said to Sara at the Edinburgh Castle. The bar has a red feel to it, a subterranean feel, and it smells like every beer ever downed beneath its roof. "It's okay," she said wearily. She'd been dealing with this for so long. And plus, she was a poet.

If I were to write *Valencia* right now it would be a totally different book. Because everything is totally different. Doesn't wine retain the flavor of the weather the grapes were grown in? The particularities of the soil, the storms that came or didn't? Memoir is like that. It picks up the essence of the moment you wrote it, where you were sitting, the quality of the sun, amount of car exhaust or freshness in the air, the quality of your heart, it being open or not, how close its most recent breakage, how you are regarding your family of origin, is it a "they did the best they could" week or a "your best was not fucking good enough" week? All of this will color your story. What you have or haven't eaten, how hungover or not you may be, your various levels—emotional or physical—perhaps you have a toothache, perhaps you took a lovely walk, or else your shoulder is pained from hunching over a deeply nonergonomic flea-market desk. You just read some-thing inspiring or have the theme to a children's song calliopeing through your head. You fear your best friend hates you. You just made up with your partner and are swelled with love and gratitude for them. You will never be in this precise state ever again. Its marks lie all over the version of your story you are telling today.

I guess it's enough to just know this. I guess it's enough to simply be aware because I don't want to get better, sober, or whatever. Wrote Eileen Myles, "I would like to tell everything once, just my part, because this is my life, not yours."

First published in the *Normal School* in 2017.

ACKNOWLEDGMENTS

These pieces span much time and are the product of much individual generosity, whether from editors inviting me to write for their publication or those who found themselves, often unwi(ll)ttingly part of my story. Some people I would like to thank for this include Jennifer Baumgardner, for taking such chances on me at the Feminist Press; Kathleen Black, for her unending support and emotional generosity; Lynnee Breedlove, Nancy Jean Burkholder, Jody Caravaglia, Carina, Sadie Crabtree, Anu Cze, my beloved agent Lindsay Edgecombe. Lauren Rosemary Hook, for her vision; Alyea Canada, for her thoughtfulness; and others at the Feminist Press including Jamia Wilson, Jisu Kim, and Suki Boynton. Dave Eggers, Geyl Forcewind, Jack Gallant, Richard Hanson, Jeff Jones, Rocco Kayiatos, Kelly Kegger, Jennifer Maerz. Eileen Myles, for their existence; Peter Pizzi, Leo Plass, Johnny Ray, Itzy Rothstein, Julia Serano, Sister Spit, Becky Slane, Marya Taylor, Tracie Thomas, Tobi Vail, Ren Volpe, Sean Uyehara, and Sarah Fran Wisby. CEC Artslink, the Creative Work Fund, Ali Liebegott, Emily McCombs, Maggie Nelson, Beth Pickens, and Tin House. And to Dashiell Lippman, who makes everything possible with her most elegant love.

The Feminist Press is a nonprofit educational organization founded to amplify feminist voices. FP publishes classic and new writing from around the world, creates cutting-edge programs, and elevates silenced and marginalized voices in order to support personal transformation and social justice for all people.

See our complete list of books at
feministpress.org